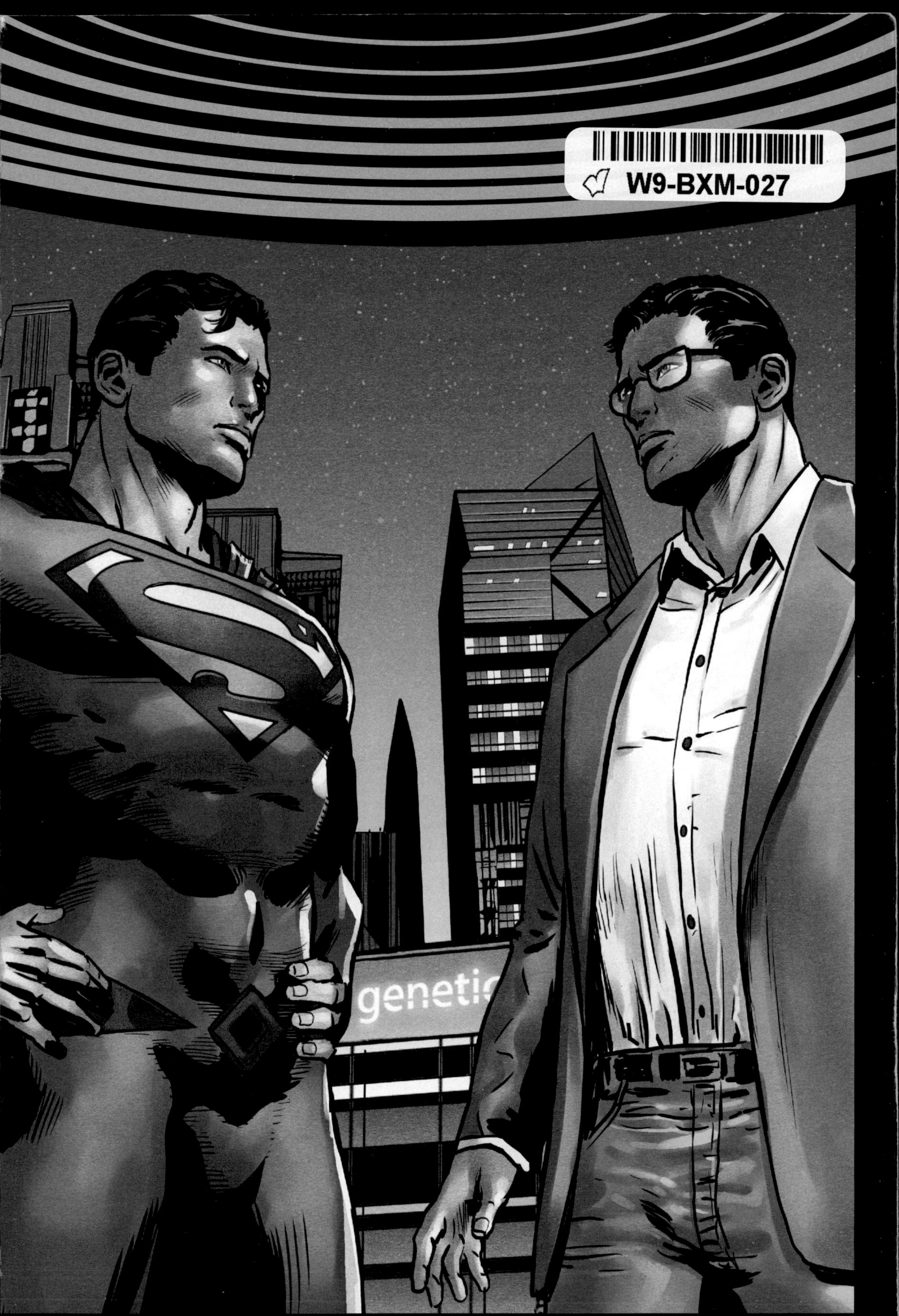

SUPERMAN ACTION COMICS

VOL.2 WELCOME TO THE PLANET

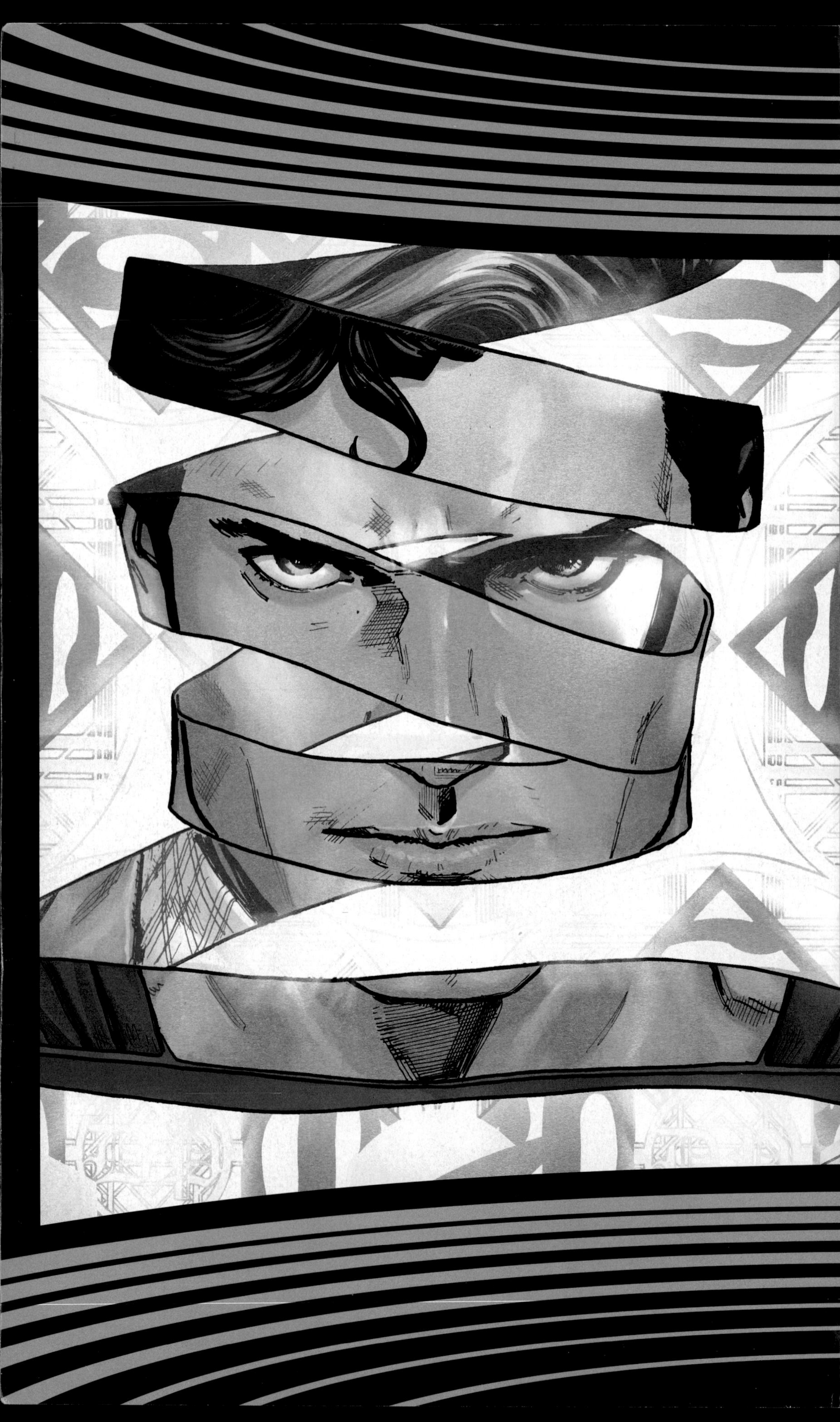

SUPERMAN ACTION COMICS
VOL.2 WELCOME TO THE PLANET

DAN JURGENS
writer

PATCH ZIRCHER * **STEPHEN SEGOVIA** * **TOM GRUMMETT**
ART THIBERT * **DANNY MIKI** * **MARK MORALES**
SCOTT HANNA
artists

ARIF PRIANTO * **ULISES ARREOLA** * **GABE ELTAEB**
colorists

ROB LEIGH * **CARLOS M. MANGUAL** * **DAVE SHARPE**
letterers

CLAY MANN and TOMEU MOREY with DAN JURGENS
collection cover artists

CLAY MANN and TOMEU MOREY with DAN JURGENS
PAUL PELLETIER, TONY KORDOS and ADRIANO LUCAS
original series cover artists

SUPERMAN created by **JERRY SIEGEL** and **JOE SHUSTER**
By special arrangement with the Jerry Siegel family

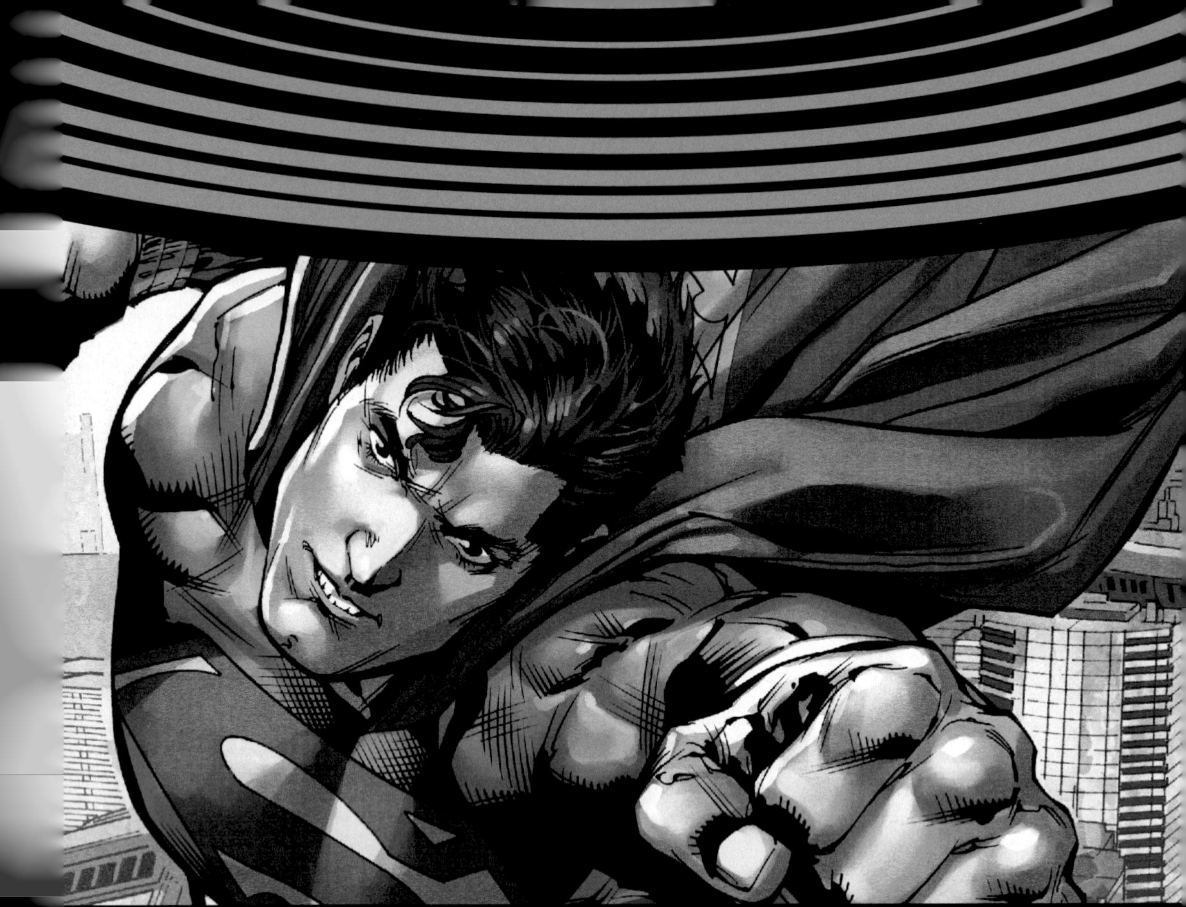

MIKE COTTON BRIAN CUNNINGHAM Editors - Original Series
PAUL KAMINSKI Associate Editor- Original Series * **AMEDEO TURTURRO** Assistant Editor - Original Series
JEB WOODARD Group Editor - Collected Editions * **SCOTT NYBAKKEN** Editor - Collected Edition
STEVE COOK Design Director - Books * **MONIQUE GRUSPE** Publication Design

BOB HARRAS Senior VP - Editor-in-Chief, DC Comics

DIANE NELSON President * **DAN DiDIO** Publisher * **JIM LEE** Publisher * **GEOFF JOHNS** President & Chief Creative Officer
AMIT DESAI Executive VP - Business & Marketing Strategy, Direct to Consumer & Global Franchise Management * **SAM ADES** Senior VP - Direct to Consumer
BOBBIE CHASE VP - Talent Development * **MARK CHIARELLO** Senior VP - Art, Design & Collected Editions
JOHN CUNNINGHAM Senior VP - Sales & Trade Marketing * **ANNE DePIES** Senior VP - Business Strategy, Finance & Administration
DON FALLETTI VP - Manufacturing Operations * **LAWRENCE GANEM** VP - Editorial Administration & Talent Relations
ALISON GILL Senior VP - Manufacturing & Operations * **HANK KANALZ** Senior VP - Editorial Strategy & Administration
JAY KOGAN VP - Legal Affairs * **THOMAS LOFTUS** VP - Business Affairs
JACK MAHAN VP - Business Affairs * **NICK J. NAPOLITANO** VP - Manufacturing Administration
EDDIE SCANNELL VP - Consumer Marketing * **COURTNEY SIMMONS** Senior VP - Publicity & Communications
JIM (SKI) SOKOLOWSKI VP - Comic Book Specialty Sales & Trade Marketing * **NANCY SPEARS** VP - Mass, Book, Digital Sales & Trade Marketing

SUPERMAN: ACTION COMICS VOL. 2 – WELCOME TO THE PLANET

DC Comics, 2900 West Alameda Ave., Burbank, CA 91505. Printed by LSC Communications, Salem, VA, USA. 3/17/17.
First Printing. ISBN: 978-1-4012-6911-1

Library of Congress Cataloging-in-Publication Data is available.

PEFC Certified
Printed on paper from sustainably managed forests, controlled sources
PEFC
PEFC/29-31-337
www.pefc.org

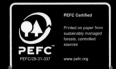

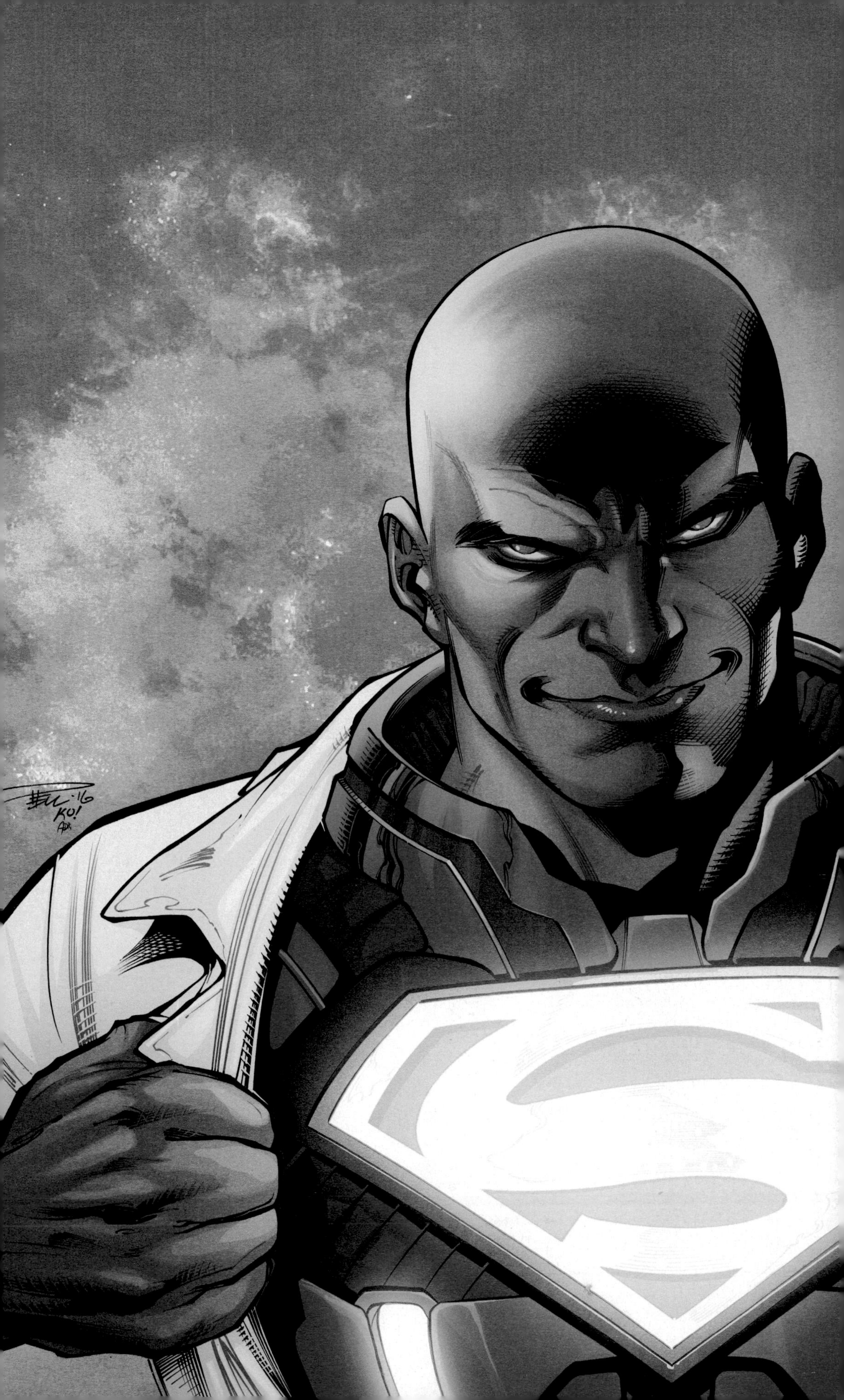

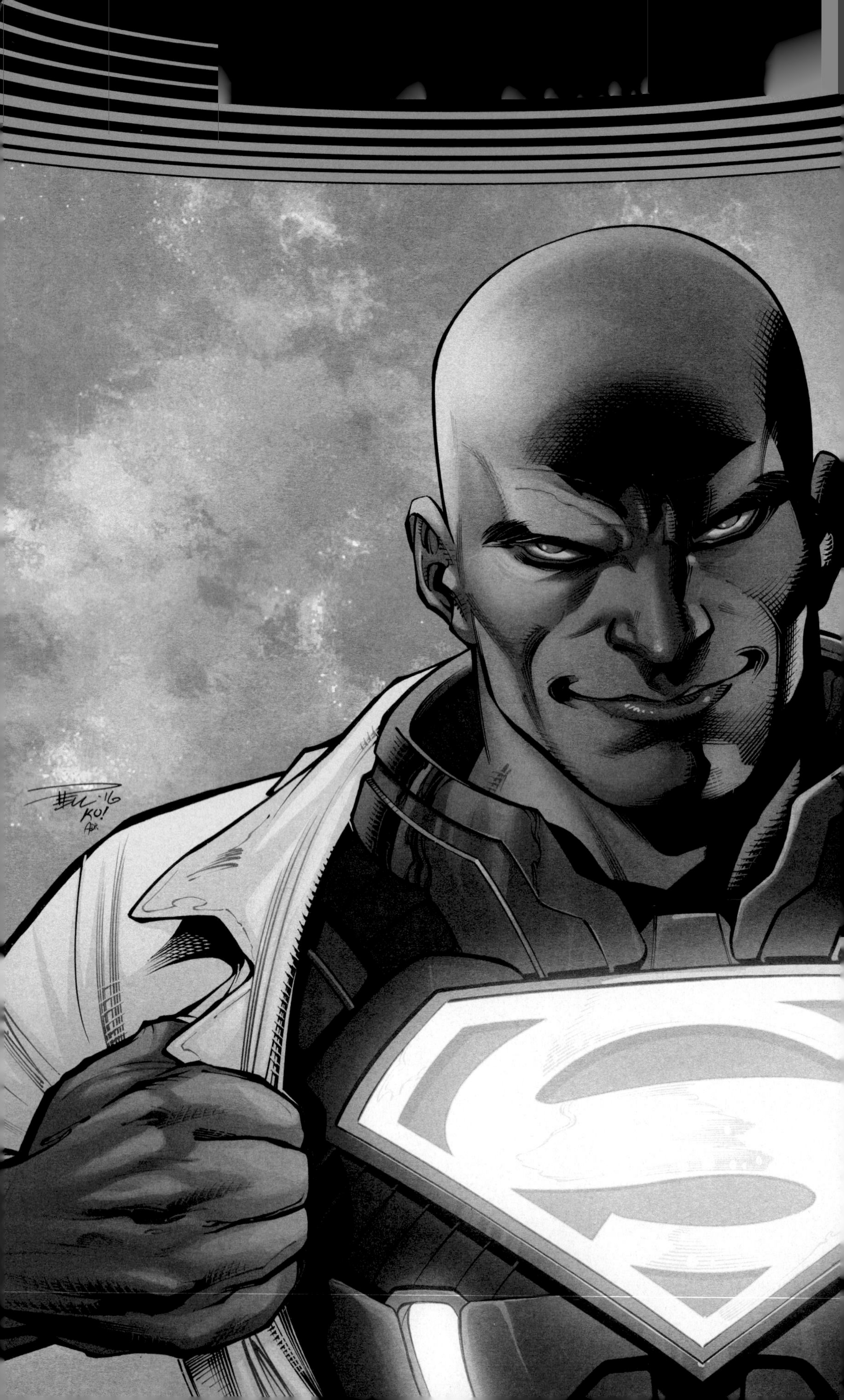

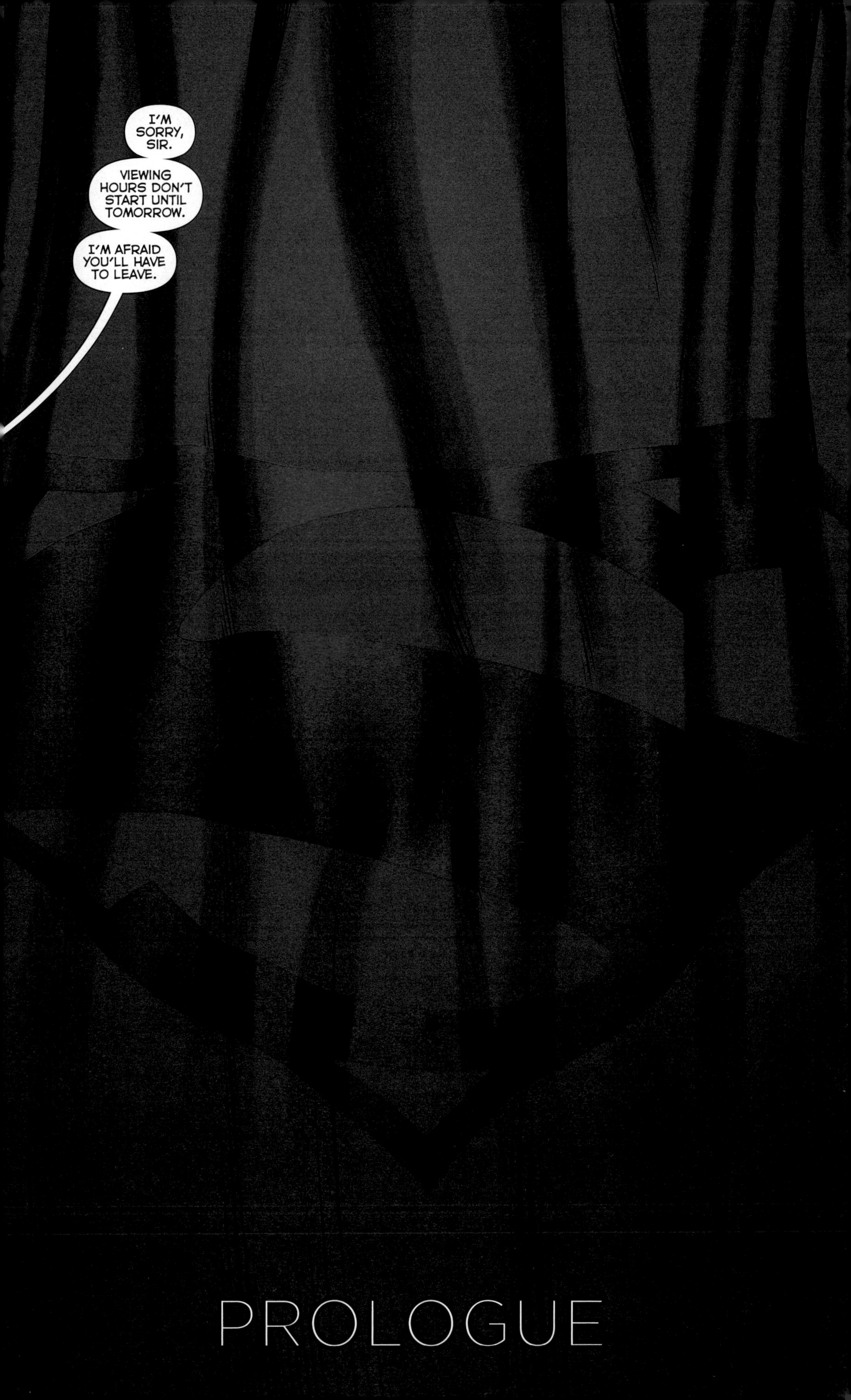
I'M SORRY, SIR.
VIEWING HOURS DON'T START UNTIL TOMORROW.
I'M AFRAID YOU'LL HAVE TO LEAVE.

PROLOGUE

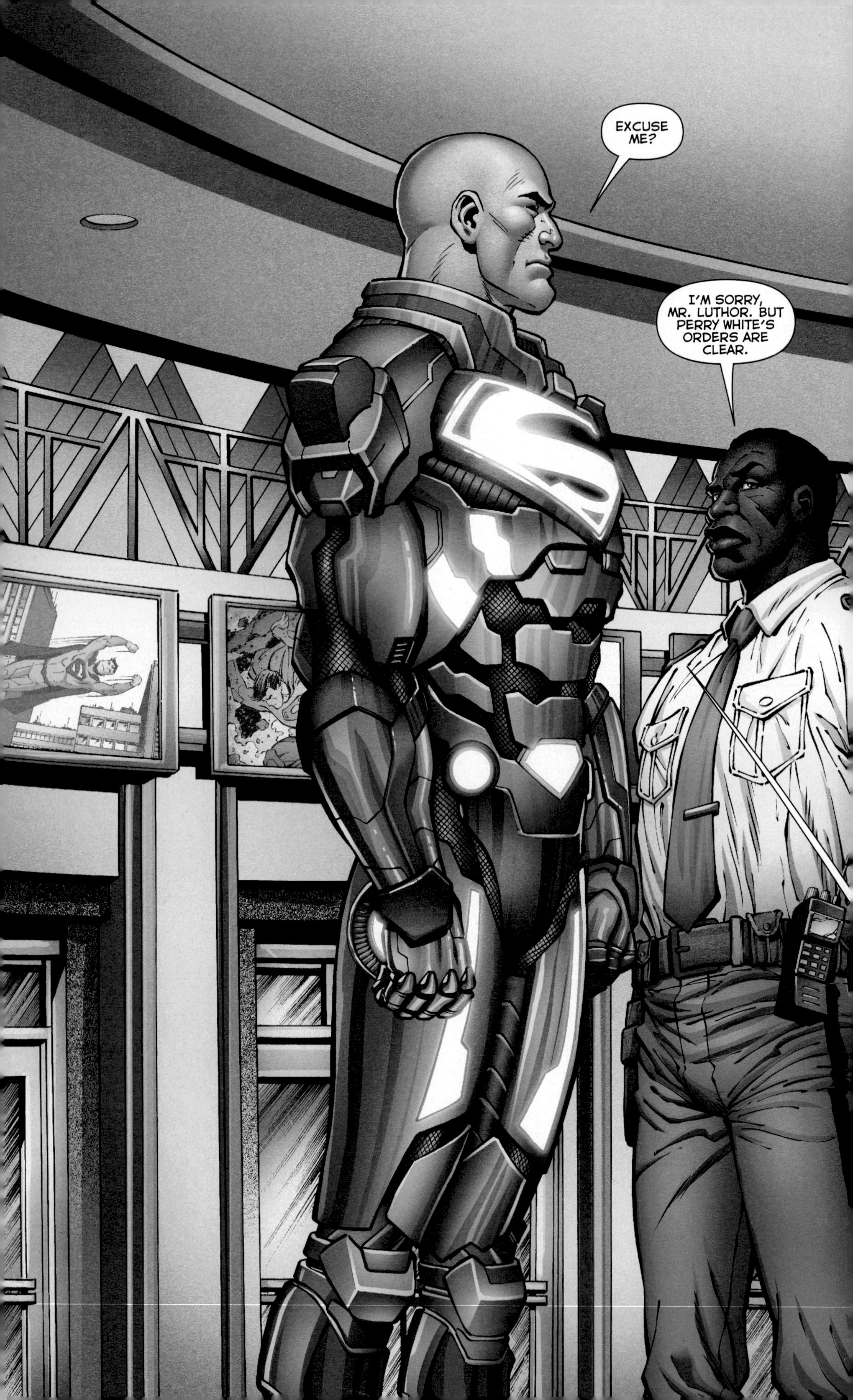
EXCUSE ME?
I'M SORRY, MR. LUTHOR. BUT PERRY WHITE'S ORDERS ARE CLEAR.

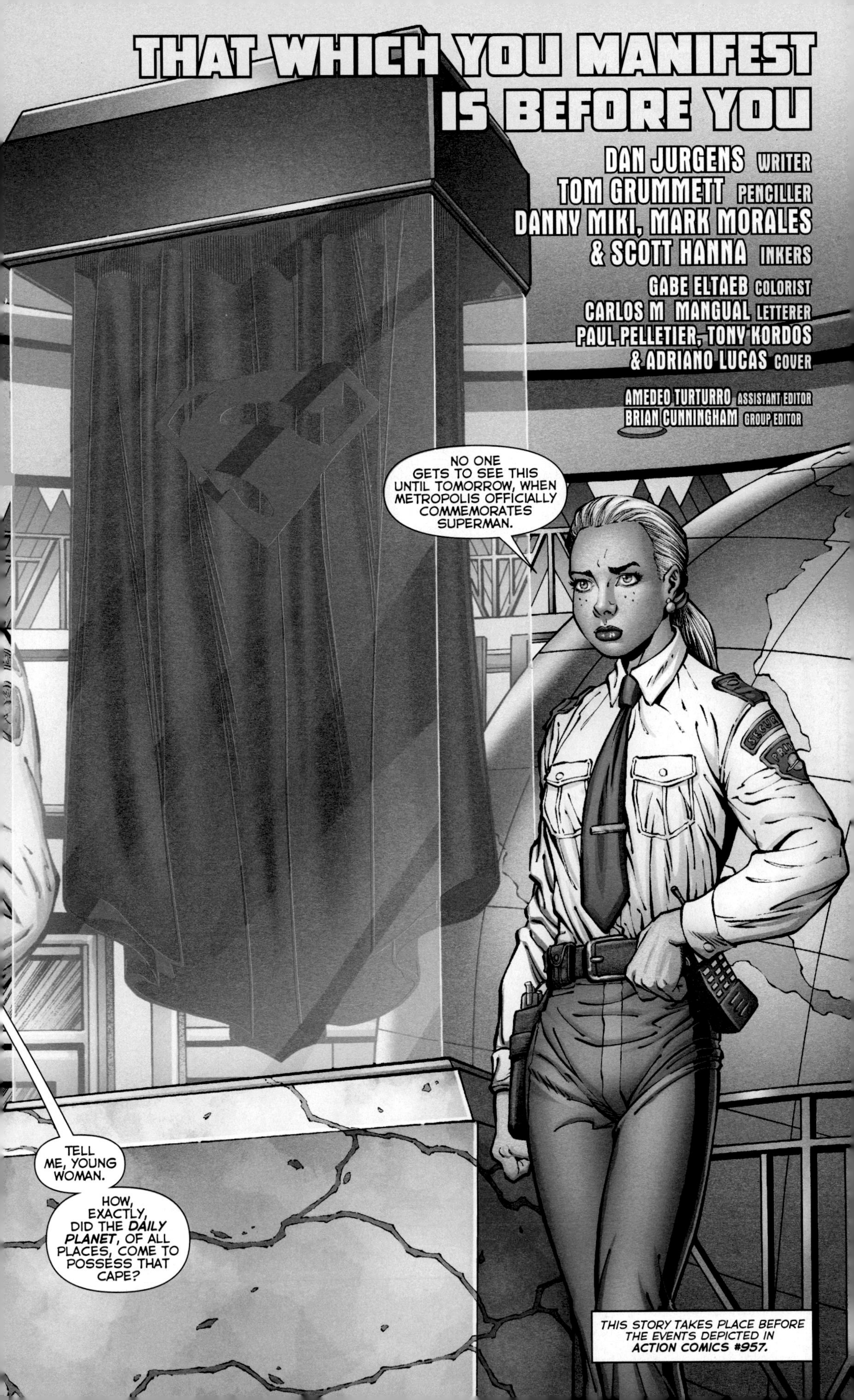
THAT WHICH YOU MANIFEST IS BEFORE YOU
DAN JURGENS WRITER
TOM GRUMMETT PENCILLER
DANNY MIKI, MARK MORALES & SCOTT HANNA INKERS
GABE ELTAEB COLORIST
CARLOS M MANGUAL LETTERER
PAUL PELLETIER, TONY KORDOS & ADRIANO LUCAS COVER
AMEDEO TURTURRO ASSISTANT EDITOR
BRIAN CUNNINGHAM GROUP EDITOR
NO ONE GETS TO SEE THIS UNTIL TOMORROW, WHEN METROPOLIS OFFICIALLY COMMEMORATES SUPERMAN.
TELL ME, YOUNG WOMAN.
HOW, EXACTLY, DID THE *DAILY PLANET*, OF ALL PLACES, COME TO POSSESS THAT CAPE?
THIS STORY TAKES PLACE BEFORE THE EVENTS DEPICTED IN ACTION COMICS #957.

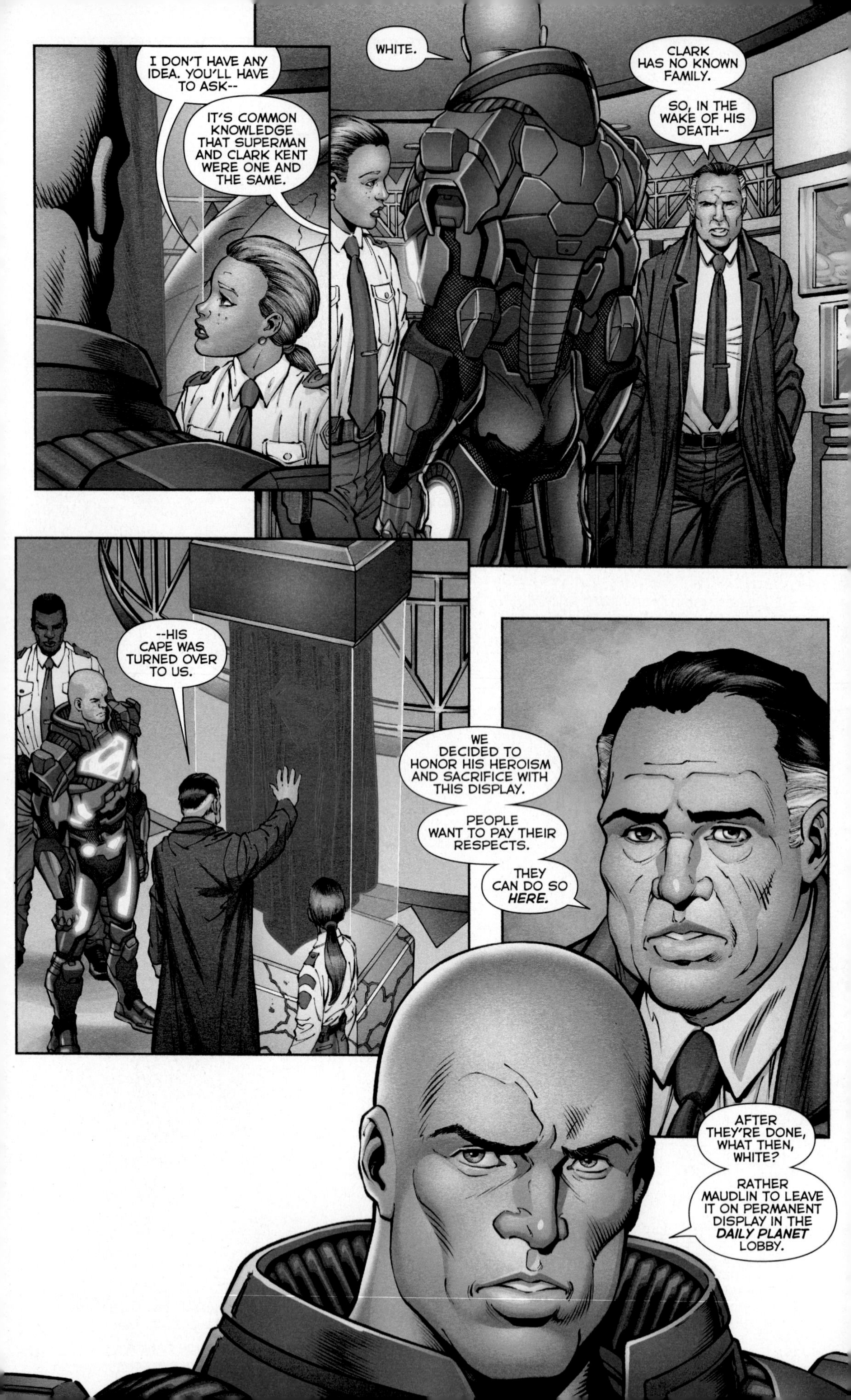

I DON'T HAVE ANY IDEA. YOU'LL HAVE TO ASK--
IT'S COMMON KNOWLEDGE THAT SUPERMAN AND CLARK KENT WERE ONE AND THE SAME.
WHITE.
CLARK HAS NO KNOWN FAMILY.
SO, IN THE WAKE OF HIS DEATH--
--HIS CAPE WAS TURNED OVER TO US.
WE DECIDED TO HONOR HIS HEROISM AND SACRIFICE WITH THIS DISPLAY.
PEOPLE WANT TO PAY THEIR RESPECTS.
THEY CAN DO SO *HERE.*
AFTER THEY'RE DONE, WHAT THEN, WHITE?
RATHER MAUDLIN TO LEAVE IT ON PERMANENT DISPLAY IN THE *DAILY PLANET* LOBBY.

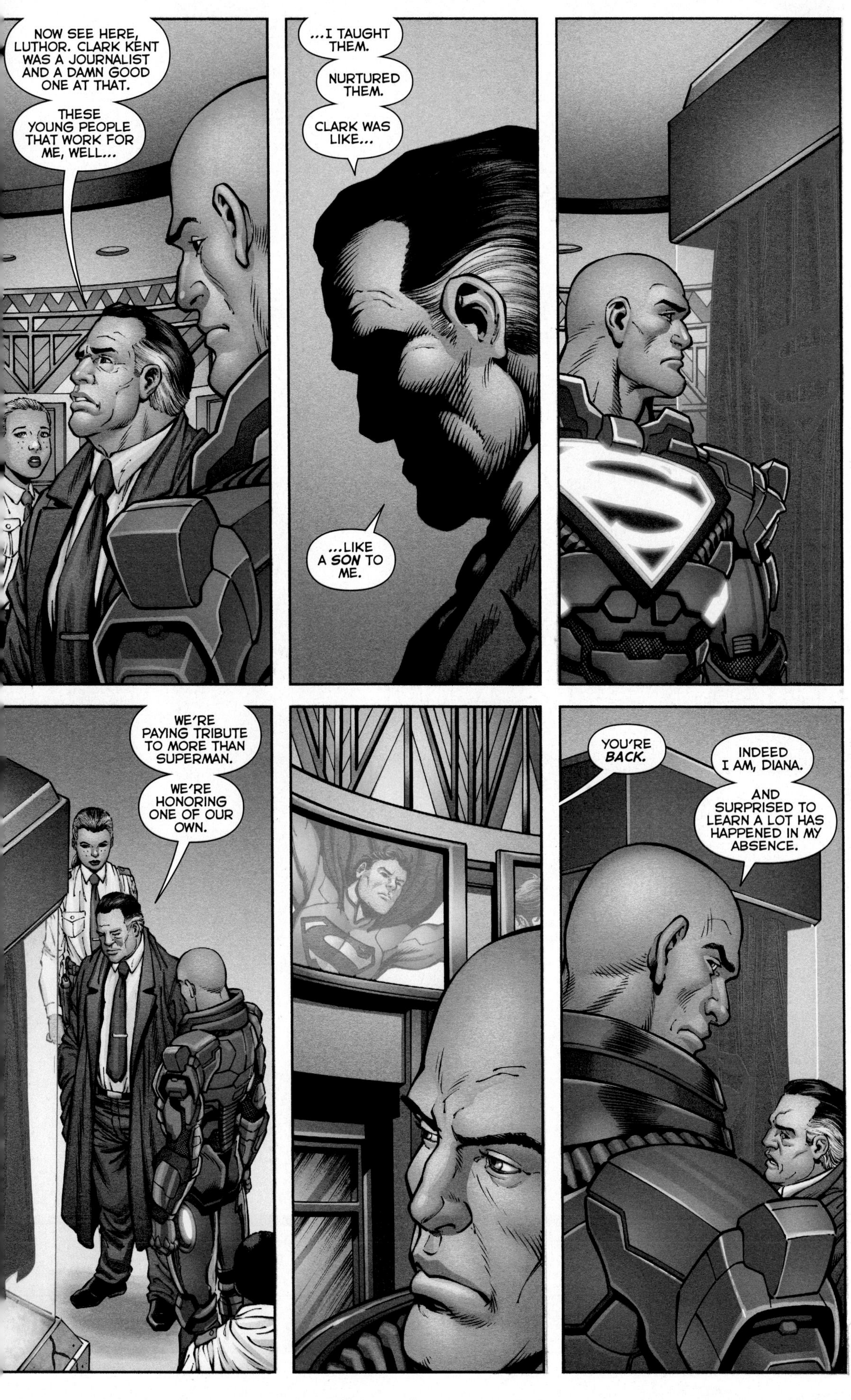
NOW SEE HERE, LUTHOR. CLARK KENT WAS A JOURNALIST AND A DAMN GOOD ONE AT THAT.
THESE YOUNG PEOPLE THAT WORK FOR ME, WELL...
...I TAUGHT THEM.
NURTURED THEM.
CLARK WAS LIKE...
...LIKE A SON TO ME.
WE'RE PAYING TRIBUTE TO MORE THAN SUPERMAN.
WE'RE HONORING ONE OF OUR OWN.
YOU'RE BACK.
INDEED I AM, DIANA.
AND SURPRISED TO LEARN A LOT HAS HAPPENED IN MY ABSENCE.

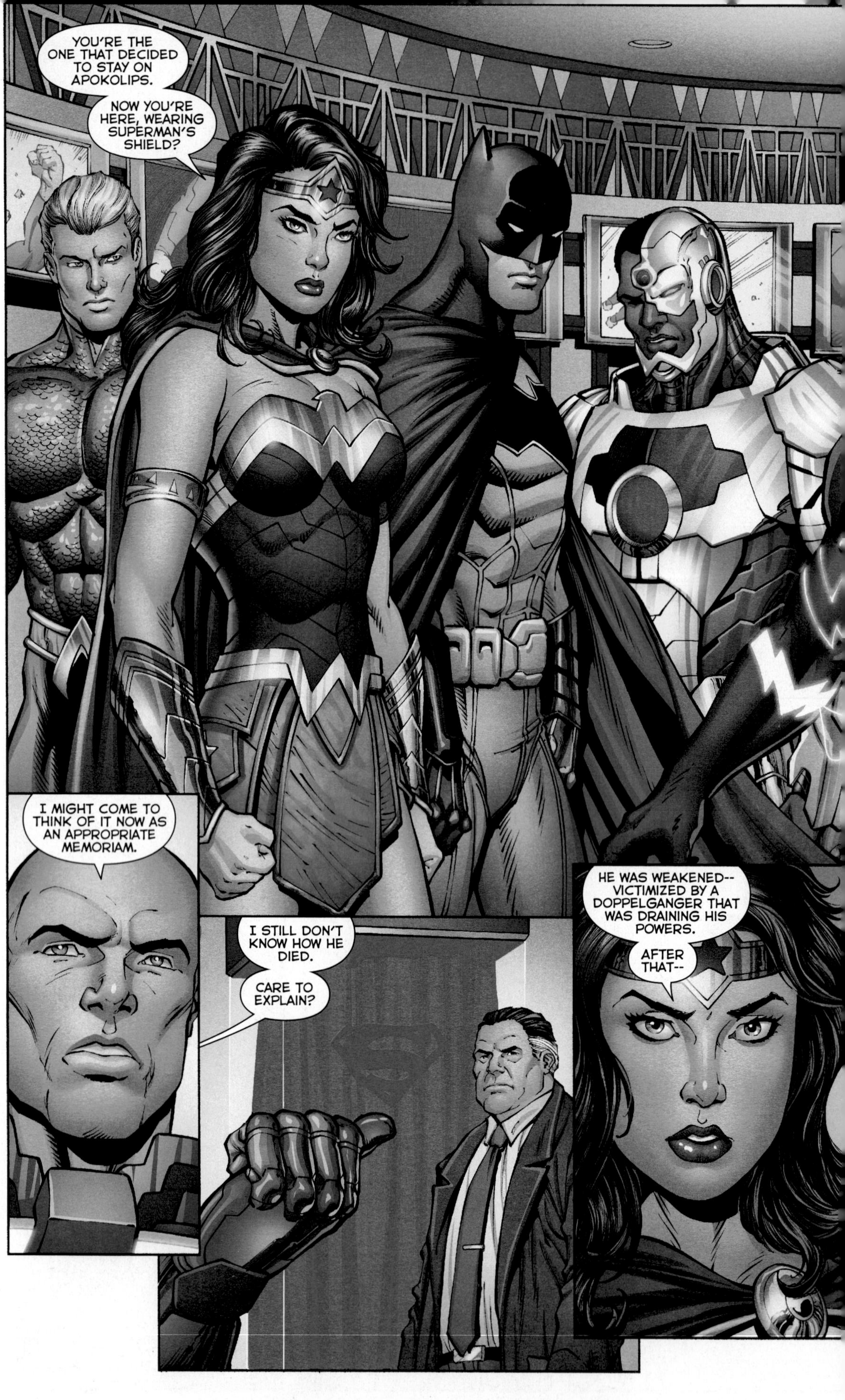
YOU'RE THE ONE THAT DECIDED TO STAY ON APOKOLIPS.
NOW YOU'RE HERE, WEARING SUPERMAN'S SHIELD?
I MIGHT COME TO THINK OF IT NOW AS AN APPROPRIATE MEMORIAM.
I STILL DON'T KNOW HOW HE DIED.
CARE TO EXPLAIN?
HE WAS WEAKENED-- VICTIMIZED BY A DOPPELGANGER THAT WAS DRAINING HIS POWERS.
AFTER THAT--

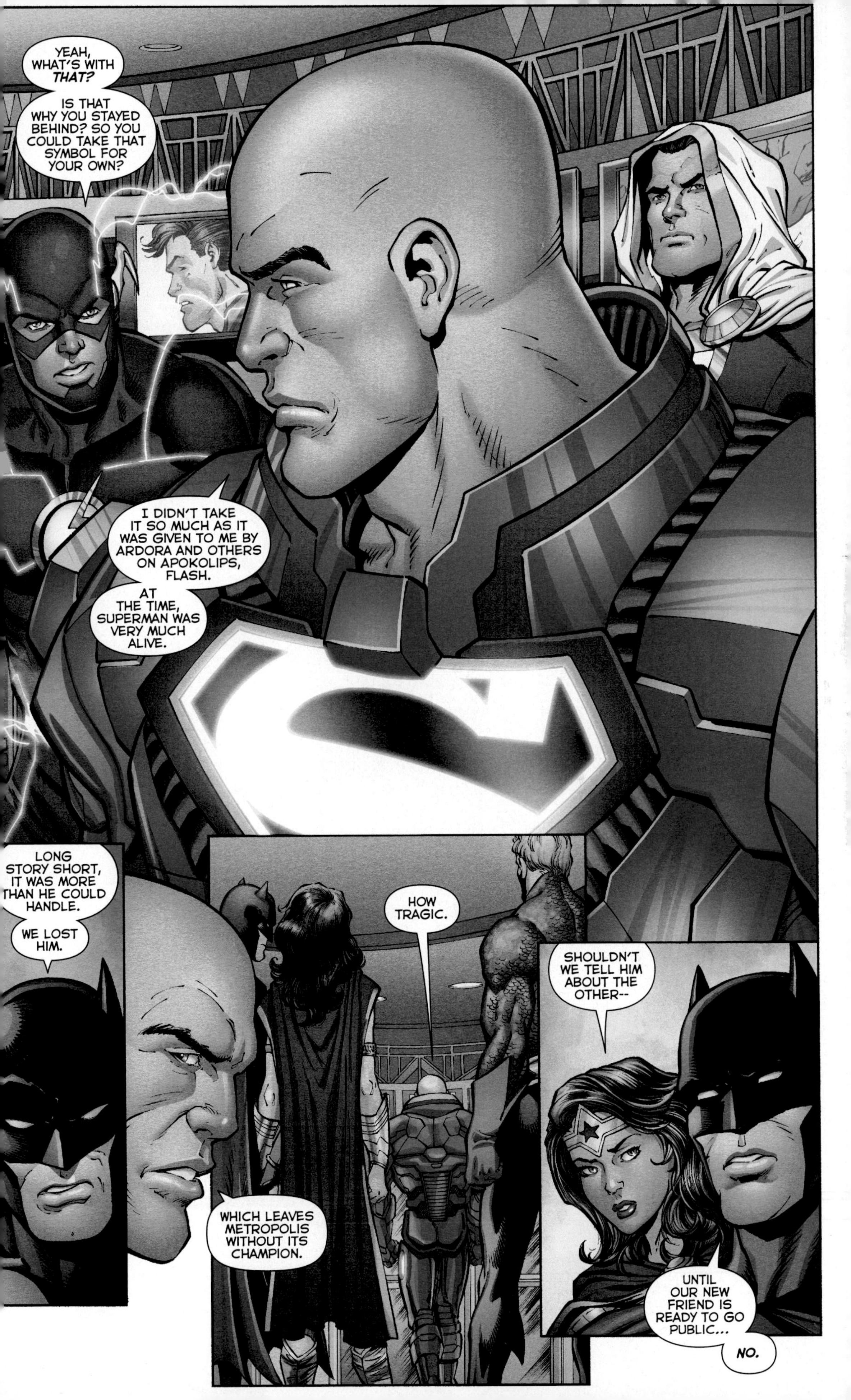
YEAH, WHAT'S WITH *THAT?*
IS THAT WHY YOU STAYED BEHIND? SO YOU COULD TAKE THAT SYMBOL FOR YOUR OWN?
I DIDN'T TAKE IT SO MUCH AS IT WAS GIVEN TO ME BY ARDORA AND OTHERS ON APOKOLIPS, FLASH.
AT THE TIME, SUPERMAN WAS VERY MUCH ALIVE.
LONG STORY SHORT, IT WAS MORE THAN HE COULD HANDLE.
WE LOST HIM.
WHICH LEAVES METROPOLIS WITHOUT ITS CHAMPION.
HOW TRAGIC.
SHOULDN'T WE TELL HIM ABOUT THE OTHER--
UNTIL OUR NEW FRIEND IS READY TO GO PUBLIC...
NO.

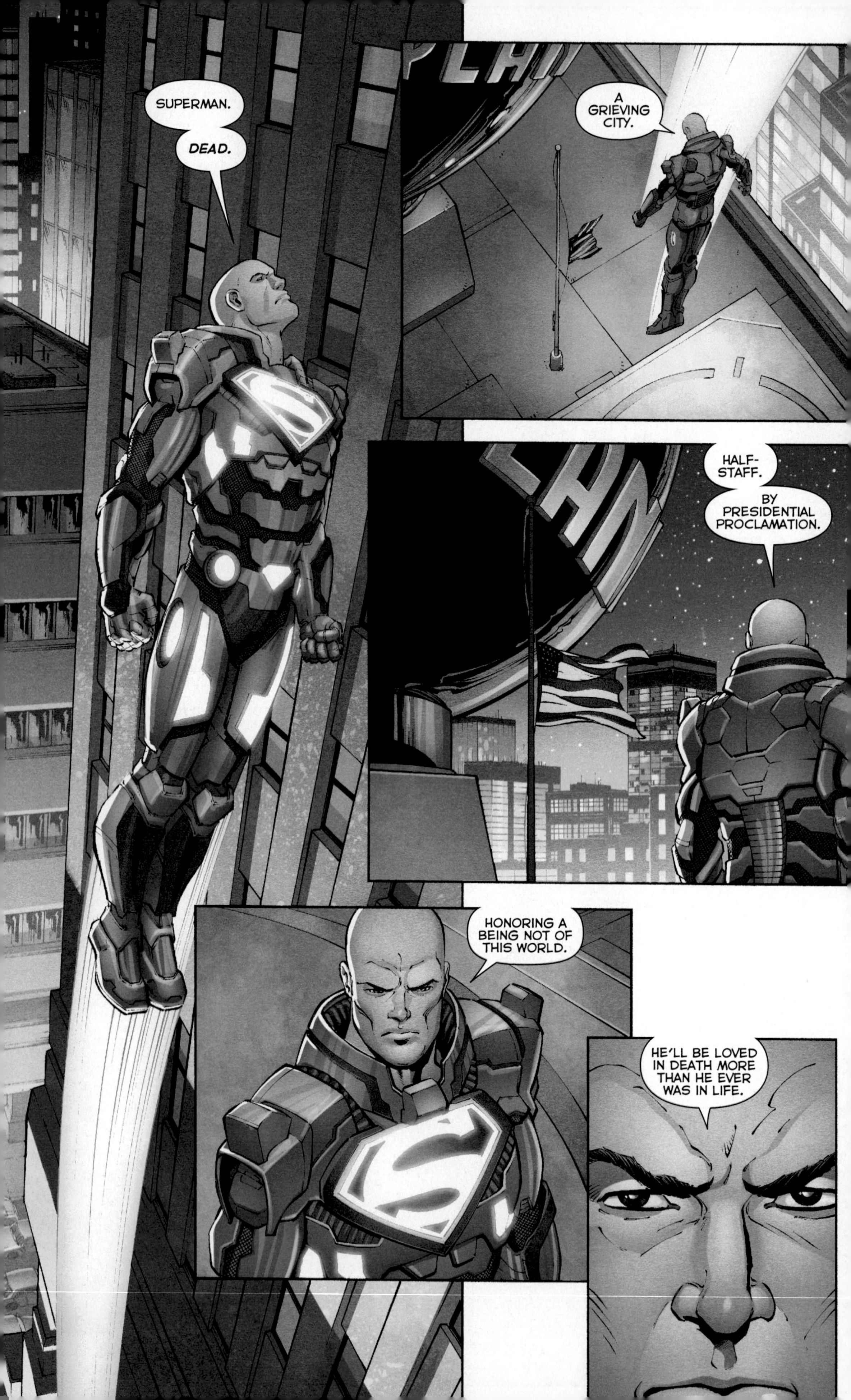
SUPERMAN.
DEAD.
A GRIEVING CITY.
HALF-STAFF.
BY PRESIDENTIAL PROCLAMATION.
HONORING A BEING NOT OF THIS WORLD.
HE'LL BE LOVED IN DEATH MORE THAN HE EVER WAS IN LIFE.

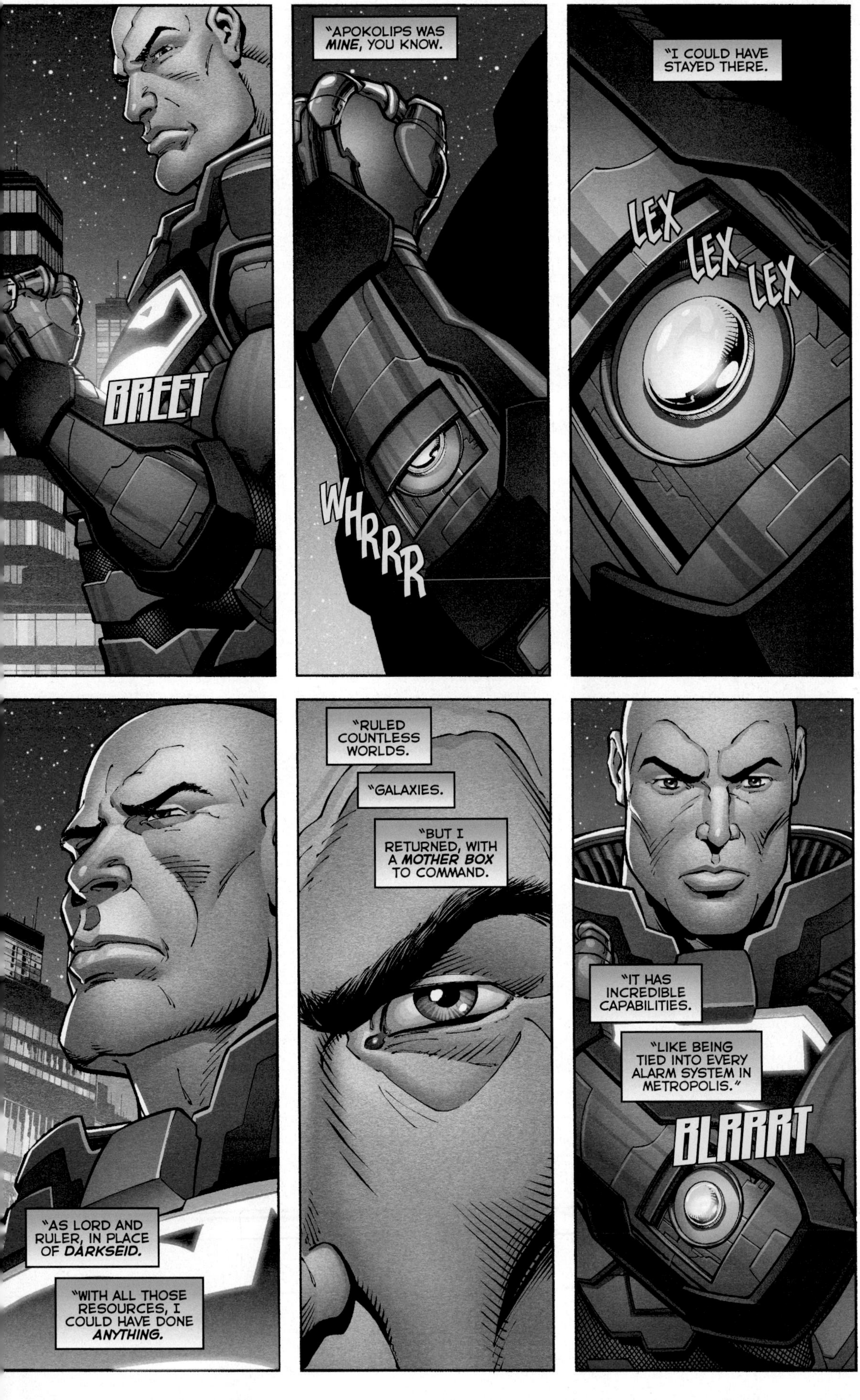
BREET
"APOKOLIPS WAS *MINE*, YOU KNOW.
WHRRRR
"I COULD HAVE STAYED THERE.
LEX
LEX
LEX
"AS LORD AND RULER, IN PLACE OF *DARKSEID*.
"WITH ALL THOSE RESOURCES, I COULD HAVE DONE *ANYTHING*.
"RULED COUNTLESS WORLDS.
"GALAXIES.
"BUT I RETURNED, WITH A *MOTHER BOX* TO COMMAND.
"IT HAS INCREDIBLE CAPABILITIES.
"LIKE BEING TIED INTO EVERY ALARM SYSTEM IN METROPOLIS."
BLRRRT

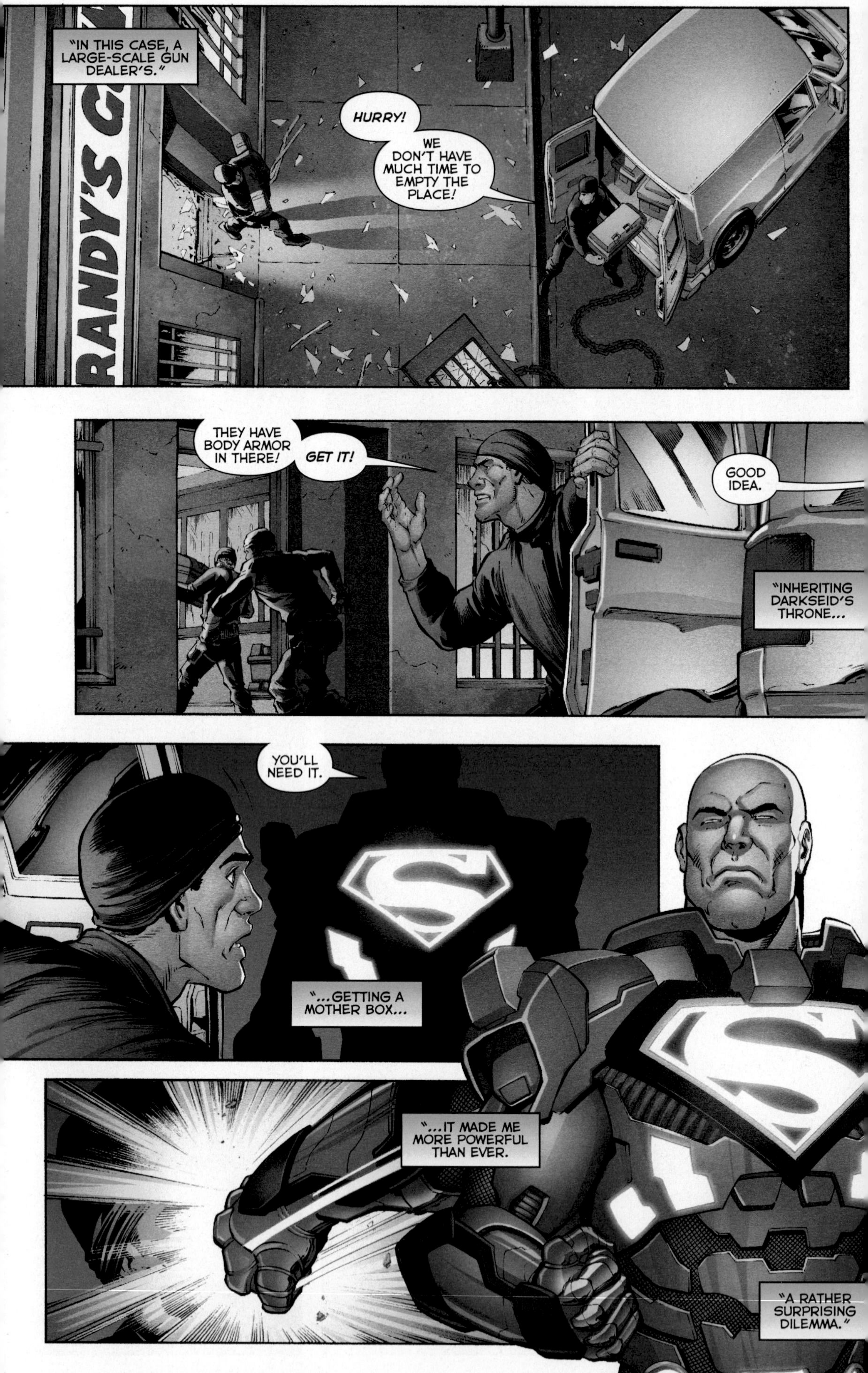

"IN THIS CASE, A LARGE-SCALE GUN DEALER'S."
RANDY'S G
HURRY!
WE DON'T HAVE MUCH TIME TO EMPTY THE PLACE!
THEY HAVE BODY ARMOR IN THERE!
GET IT!
GOOD IDEA.
"INHERITING DARKSEID'S THRONE...
YOU'LL NEED IT.
"...GETTING A MOTHER BOX...
"...IT MADE ME MORE POWERFUL THAN EVER.
"A RATHER SURPRISING DILEMMA."

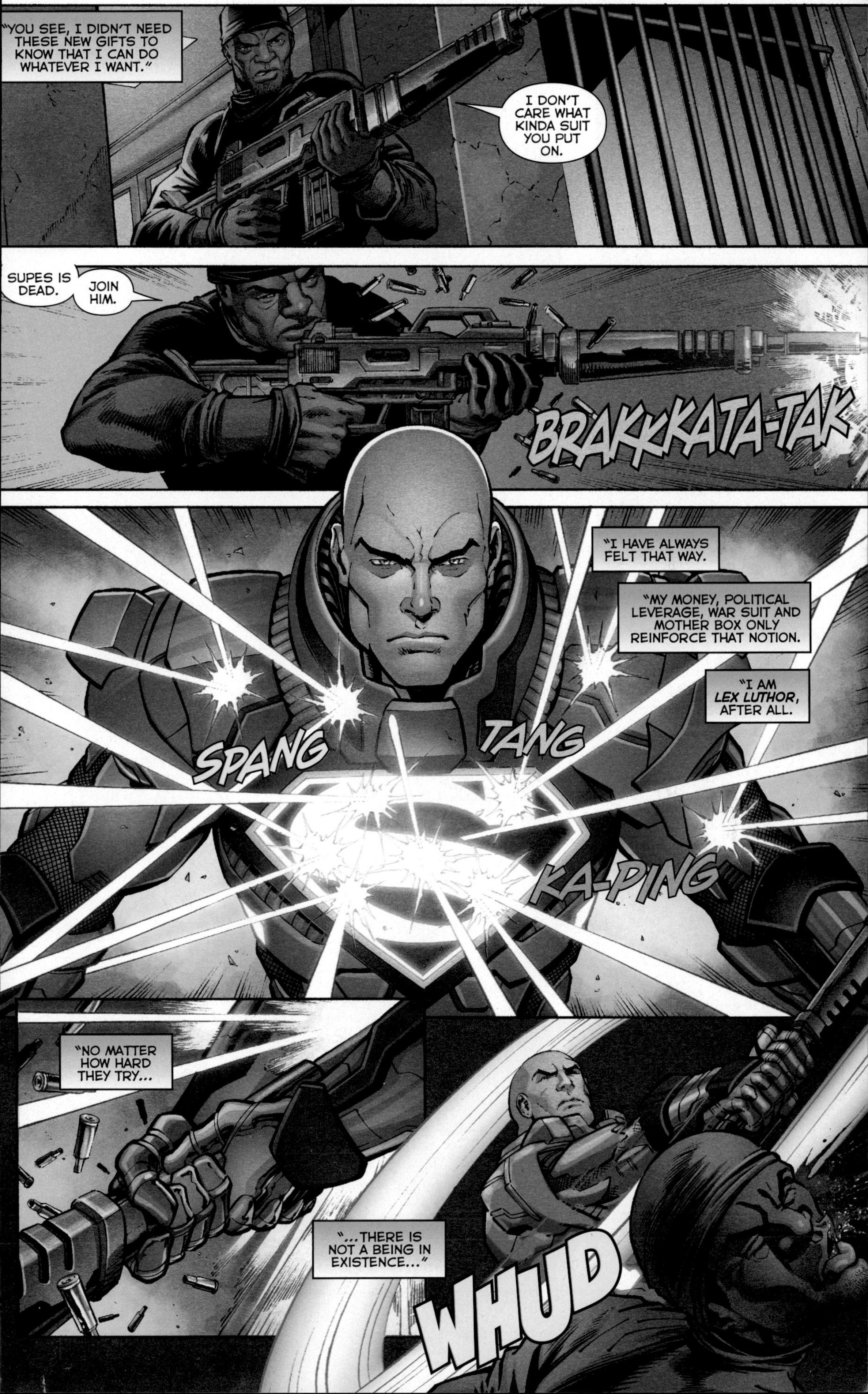
"YOU SEE, I DIDN'T NEED THESE NEW GIFTS TO KNOW THAT I CAN DO WHATEVER I WANT."
I DON'T CARE WHAT KINDA SUIT YOU PUT ON.
SUPES IS DEAD.
JOIN HIM.
BRAKKKATA-TAK
"I HAVE ALWAYS FELT THAT WAY.
"MY MONEY, POLITICAL LEVERAGE, WAR SUIT AND MOTHER BOX ONLY REINFORCE THAT NOTION.
"I AM *LEX LUTHOR*, AFTER ALL.
SPANG
TANG
KA-PING
"NO MATTER HOW HARD THEY TRY...
"...THERE IS NOT A BEING IN EXISTENCE..."
WHUD

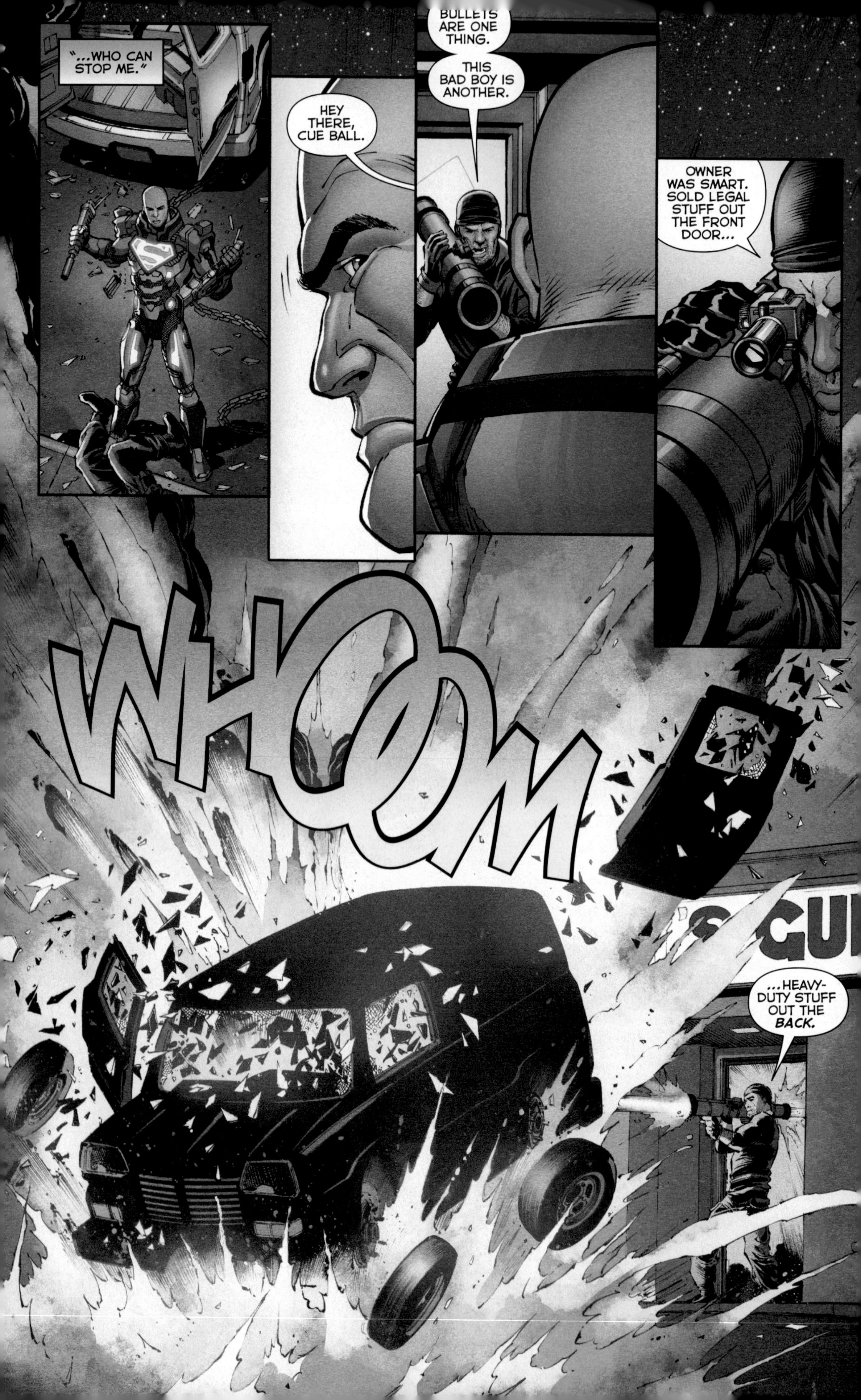
"...WHO CAN STOP ME."
HEY THERE, CUE BALL.
BULLETS ARE ONE THING.
THIS BAD BOY IS ANOTHER.
OWNER WAS SMART. SOLD LEGAL STUFF OUT THE FRONT DOOR...
WHOOM
...HEAVY-DUTY STUFF OUT THE *BACK.*

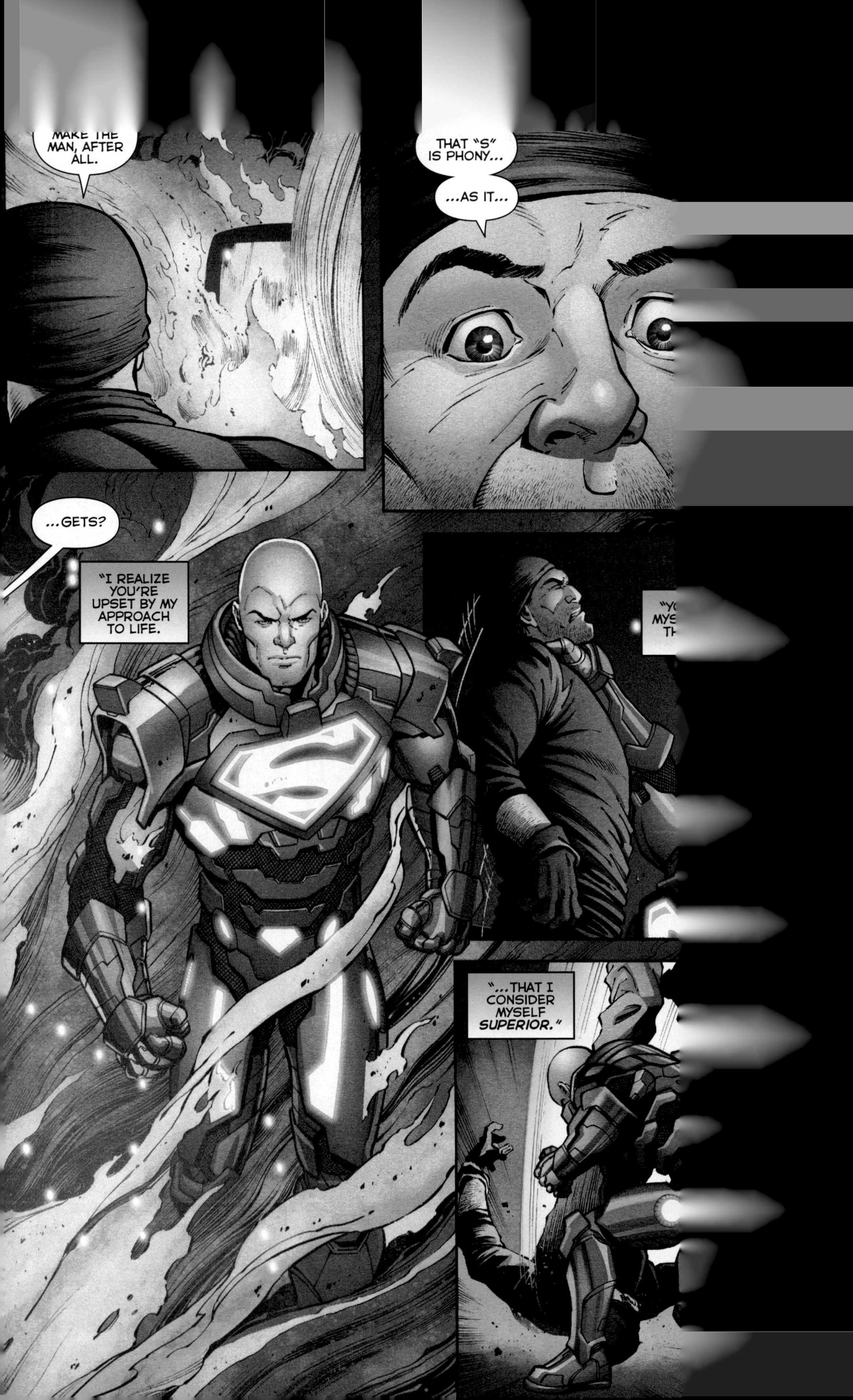

MAKE THE MAN, AFTER ALL.
THAT "S" IS PHONY...
...AS IT...
...GETS?
"I REALIZE YOU'RE UPSET BY MY APPROACH TO LIFE.
"...THAT I CONSIDER MYSELF *SUPERIOR.*"

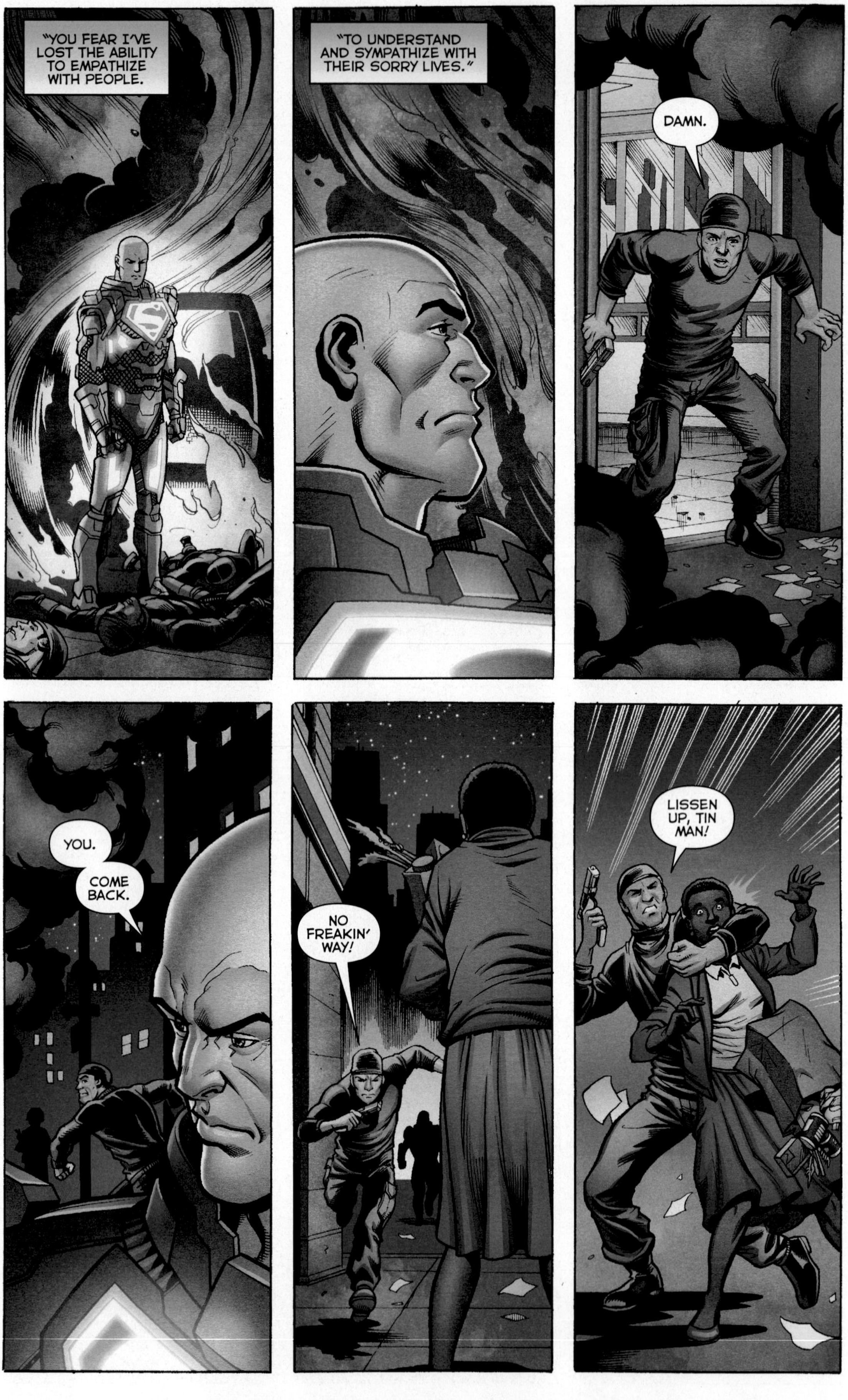
"YOU FEAR I'VE LOST THE ABILITY TO EMPATHIZE WITH PEOPLE.
"TO UNDERSTAND AND SYMPATHIZE WITH THEIR SORRY LIVES."
DAMN.
YOU.
COME BACK.
NO FREAKIN' WAY!
LISSEN UP, TIN MAN!

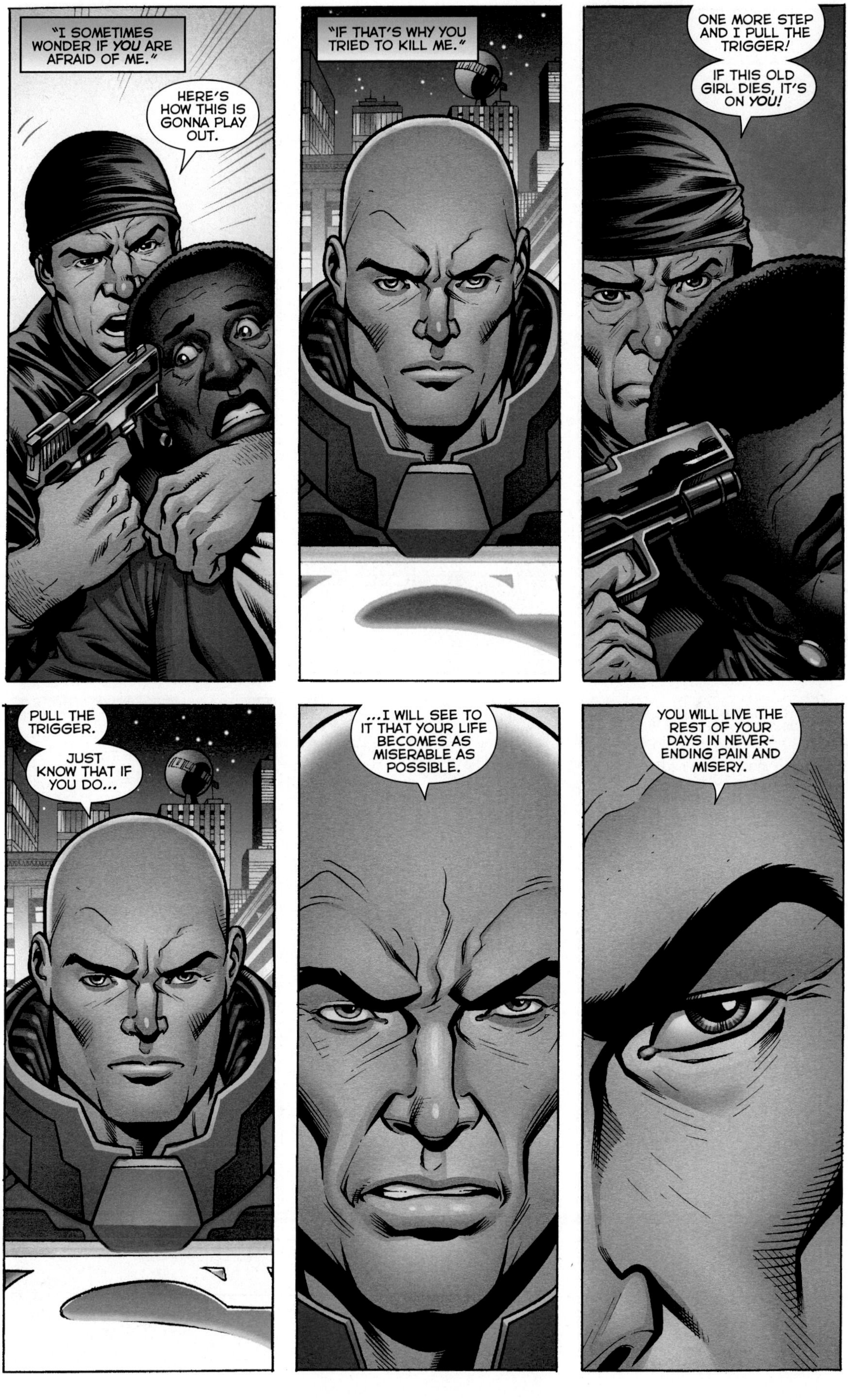

"I SOMETIMES WONDER IF *YOU* ARE AFRAID OF ME."
HERE'S HOW THIS IS GONNA PLAY OUT.
"IF THAT'S WHY YOU TRIED TO KILL ME."
ONE MORE STEP AND I PULL THE TRIGGER!
IF THIS OLD GIRL DIES, IT'S ON *YOU!*
PULL THE TRIGGER.
JUST KNOW THAT IF YOU DO...
...I WILL SEE TO IT THAT YOUR LIFE BECOMES AS MISERABLE AS POSSIBLE.
YOU WILL LIVE THE REST OF YOUR DAYS IN NEVER-ENDING PAIN AND MISERY.

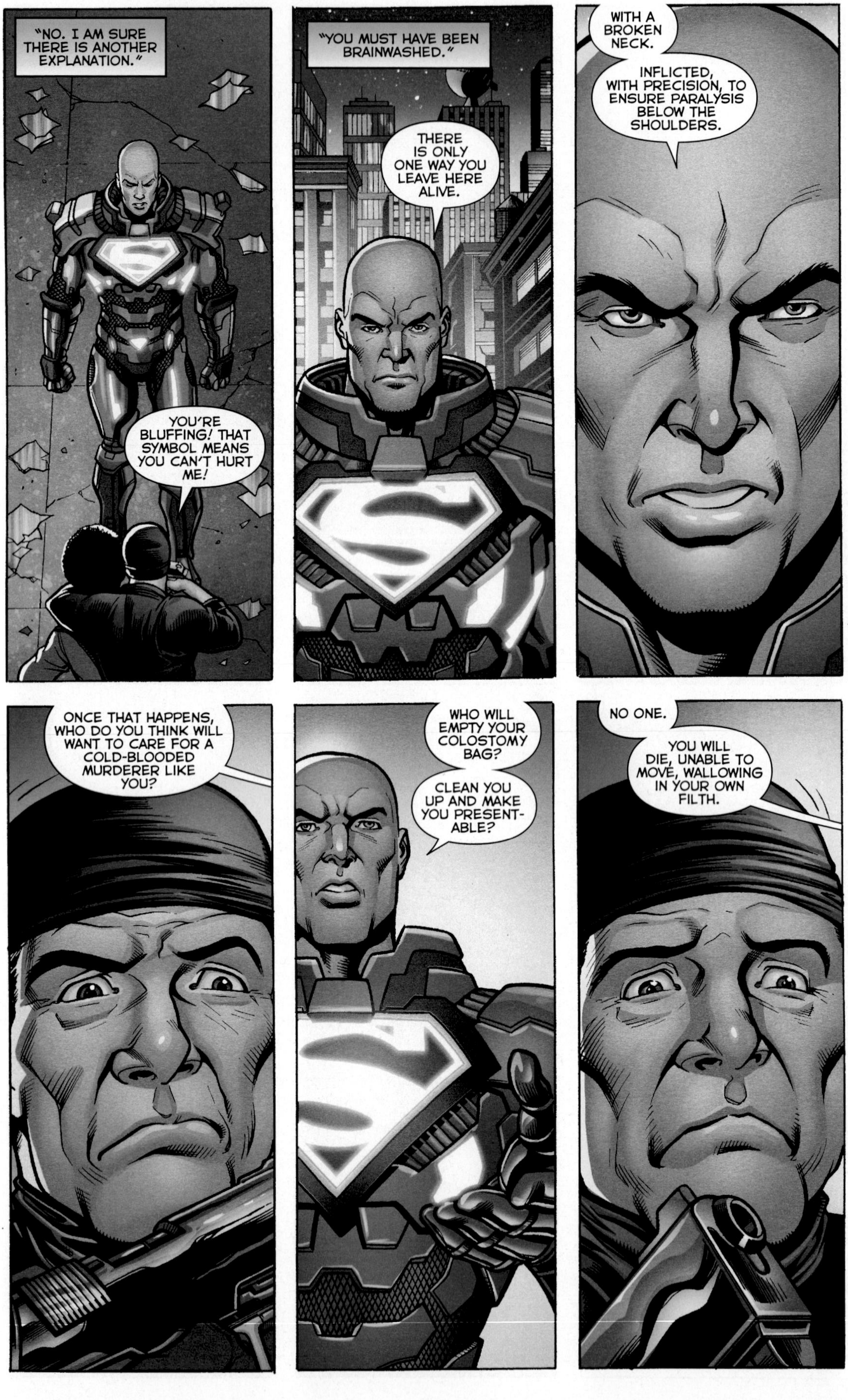
"NO. I AM SURE THERE IS ANOTHER EXPLANATION."
YOU'RE BLUFFING! THAT SYMBOL MEANS YOU CAN'T HURT ME!
"YOU MUST HAVE BEEN BRAINWASHED."
THERE IS ONLY ONE WAY YOU LEAVE HERE ALIVE.
WITH A BROKEN NECK.
INFLICTED, WITH PRECISION, TO ENSURE PARALYSIS BELOW THE SHOULDERS.
ONCE THAT HAPPENS, WHO DO YOU THINK WILL WANT TO CARE FOR A COLD-BLOODED MURDERER LIKE YOU?
WHO WILL EMPTY YOUR COLOSTOMY BAG?
CLEAN YOU UP AND MAKE YOU PRESENT-ABLE?
NO ONE.
YOU WILL DIE, UNABLE TO MOVE, WALLOWING IN YOUR OWN FILTH.

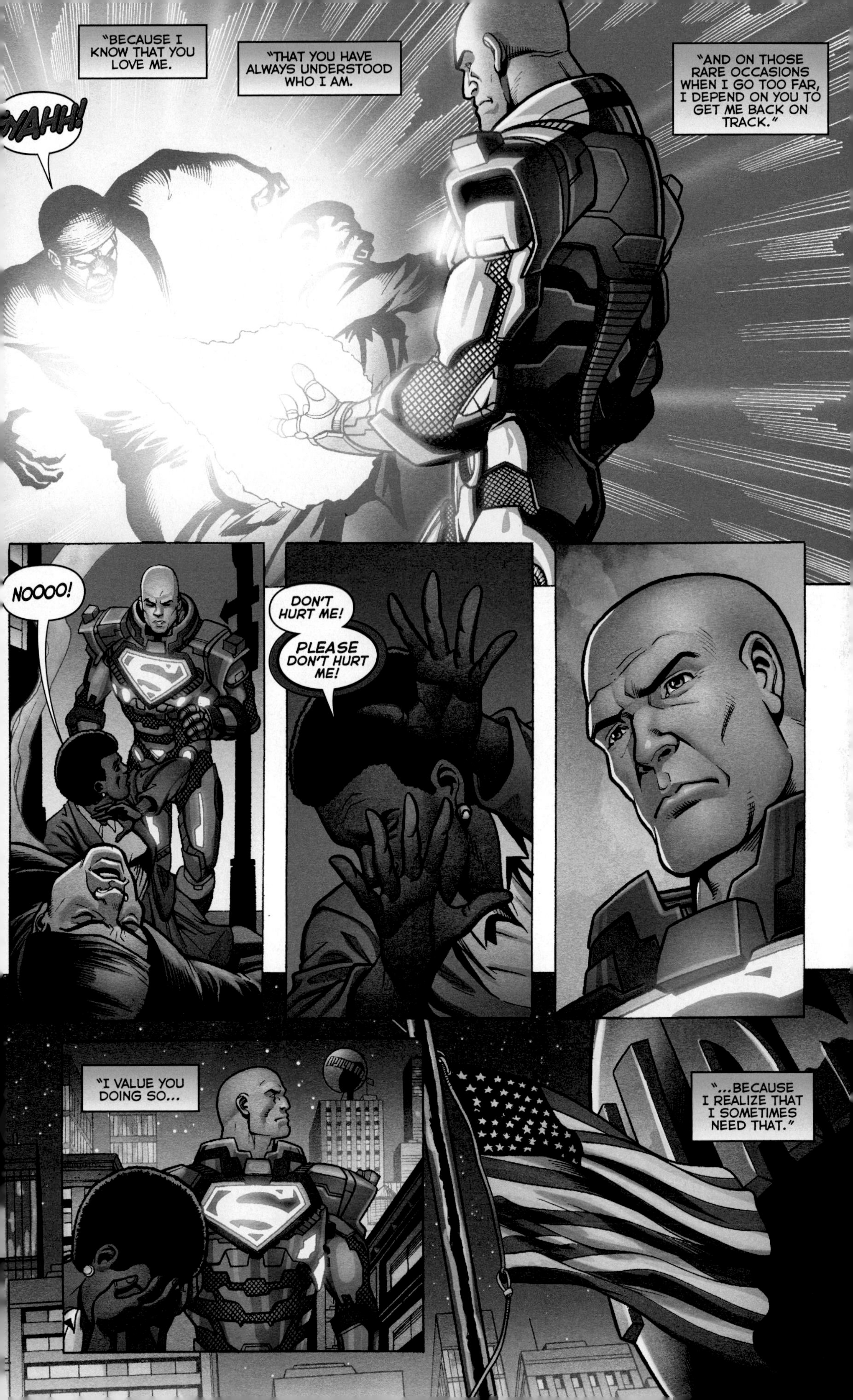
"BECAUSE I KNOW THAT YOU LOVE ME.
"THAT YOU HAVE ALWAYS UNDERSTOOD WHO I AM.
"AND ON THOSE RARE OCCASIONS WHEN I GO TOO FAR, I DEPEND ON YOU TO GET ME BACK ON TRACK."
NOOOO!
DON'T HURT ME!
PLEASE DON'T HURT ME!
"I VALUE YOU DOING SO...
"...BECAUSE I REALIZE THAT I SOMETIMES NEED THAT."

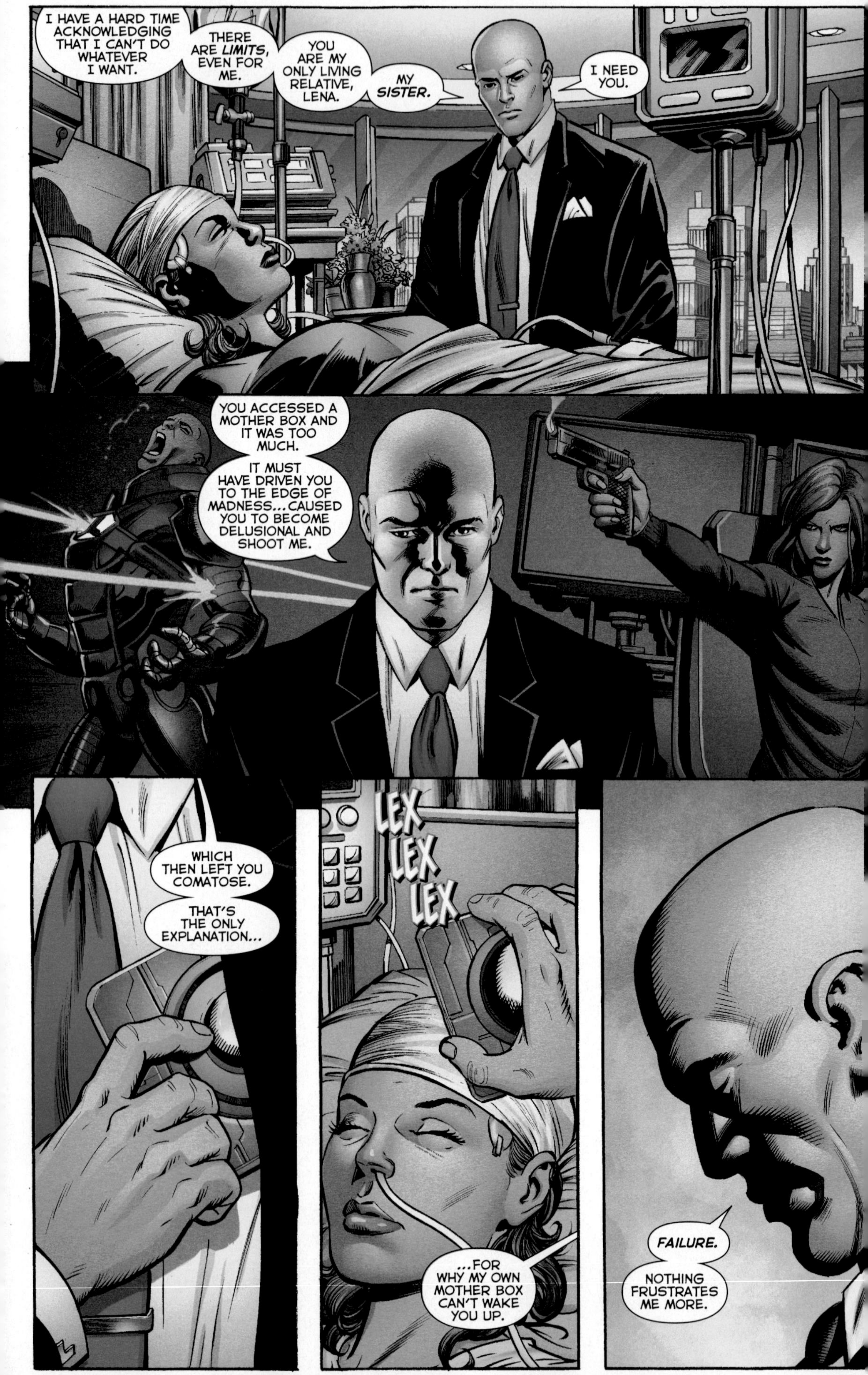
I HAVE A HARD TIME ACKNOWLEDGING THAT I CAN'T DO WHATEVER I WANT.
THERE ARE *LIMITS*, EVEN FOR ME.
YOU ARE MY ONLY LIVING RELATIVE, LENA.
MY *SISTER*.
I NEED YOU.
YOU ACCESSED A MOTHER BOX AND IT WAS TOO MUCH.
IT MUST HAVE DRIVEN YOU TO THE EDGE OF MADNESS...CAUSED YOU TO BECOME DELUSIONAL AND SHOOT ME.
WHICH THEN LEFT YOU COMATOSE.
THAT'S THE ONLY EXPLANATION...
LEX
LEX
LEX
...FOR WHY MY OWN MOTHER BOX CAN'T WAKE YOU UP.
FAILURE.
NOTHING FRUSTRATES ME MORE.

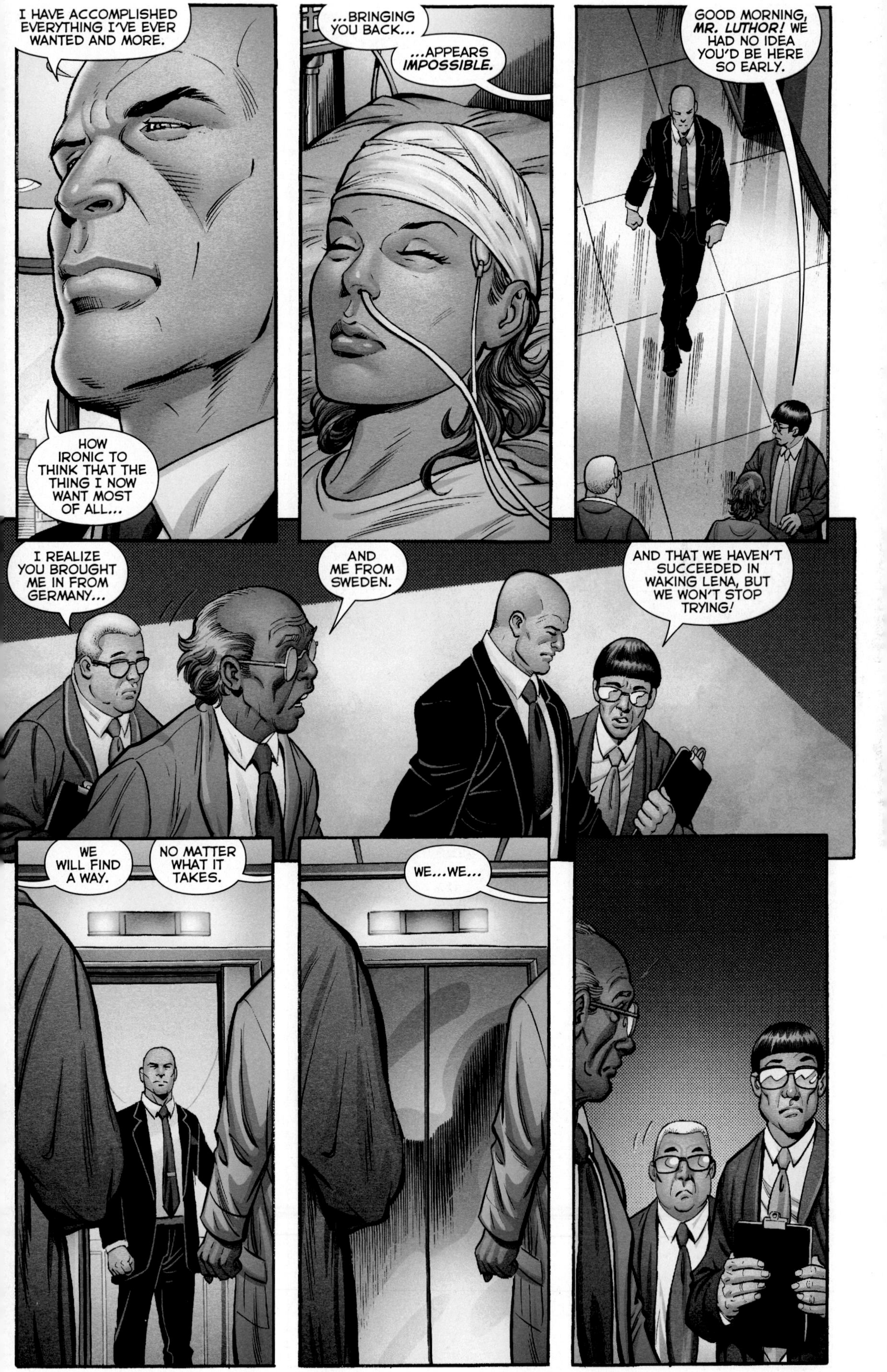

I HAVE ACCOMPLISHED EVERYTHING I'VE EVER WANTED AND MORE.
HOW IRONIC TO THINK THAT THE THING I NOW WANT MOST OF ALL...
...BRINGING YOU BACK...
...APPEARS *IMPOSSIBLE.*
GOOD MORNING, *MR. LUTHOR!* WE HAD NO IDEA YOU'D BE HERE SO EARLY.
I REALIZE YOU BROUGHT ME IN FROM GERMANY...
AND ME FROM SWEDEN.
AND THAT WE HAVEN'T SUCCEEDED IN WAKING LENA, BUT WE WON'T STOP TRYING!
WE WILL FIND A WAY.
NO MATTER WHAT IT TAKES.
WE...WE...

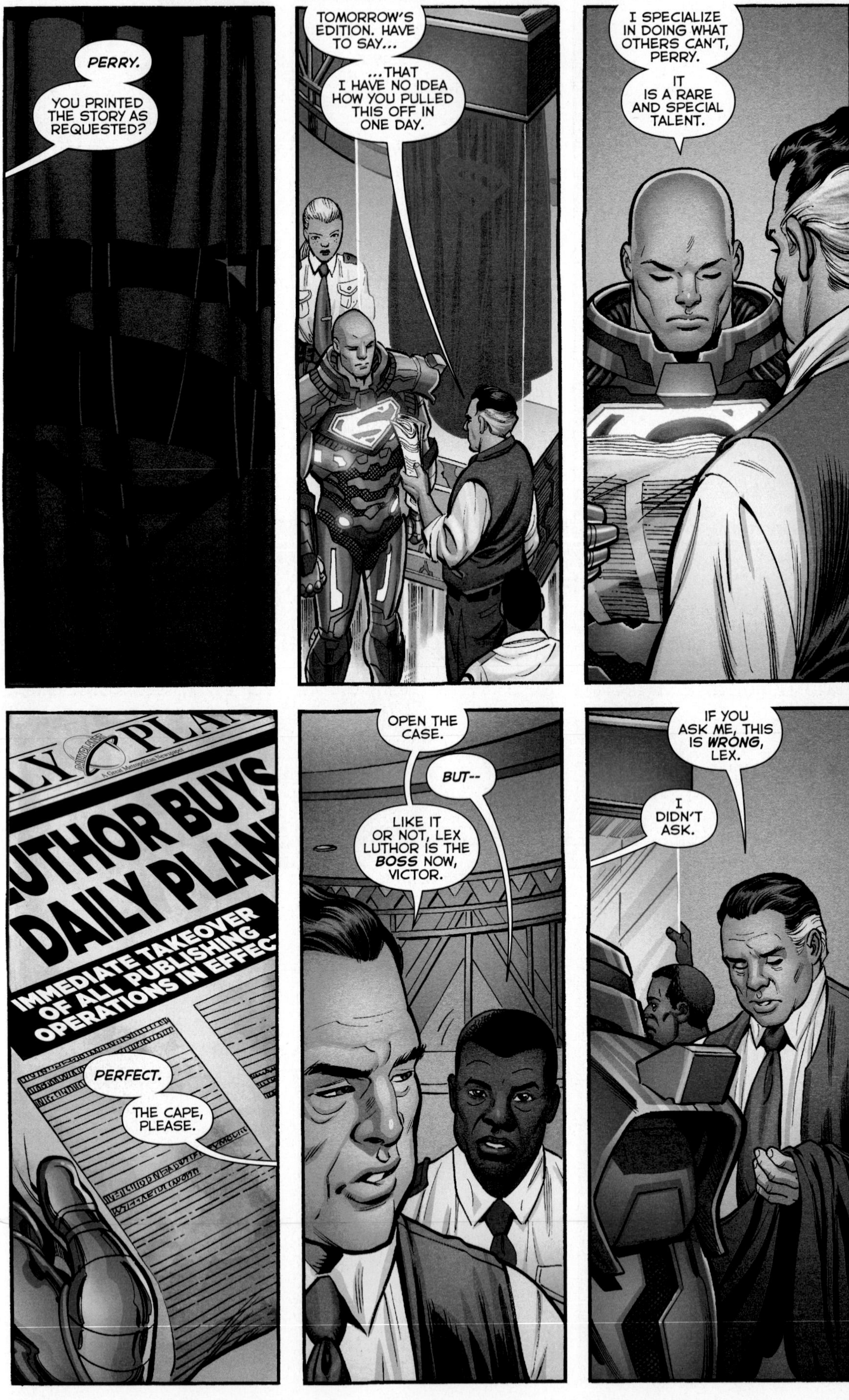
PERRY.
YOU PRINTED THE STORY AS REQUESTED?
TOMORROW'S EDITION. HAVE TO SAY...
...THAT I HAVE NO IDEA HOW YOU PULLED THIS OFF IN ONE DAY.
I SPECIALIZE IN DOING WHAT OTHERS CAN'T, PERRY.
IT IS A RARE AND SPECIAL TALENT.
UTHOR BUYS
DAILY PLAN
IMMEDIATE TAKEOVER OF ALL PUBLISHING OPERATIONS IN EFFEC
PERFECT.
THE CAPE, PLEASE.
OPEN THE CASE.
BUT--
LIKE IT OR NOT, LEX LUTHOR IS THE BOSS NOW, VICTOR.
IF YOU ASK ME, THIS IS WRONG, LEX.
I DIDN'T ASK.

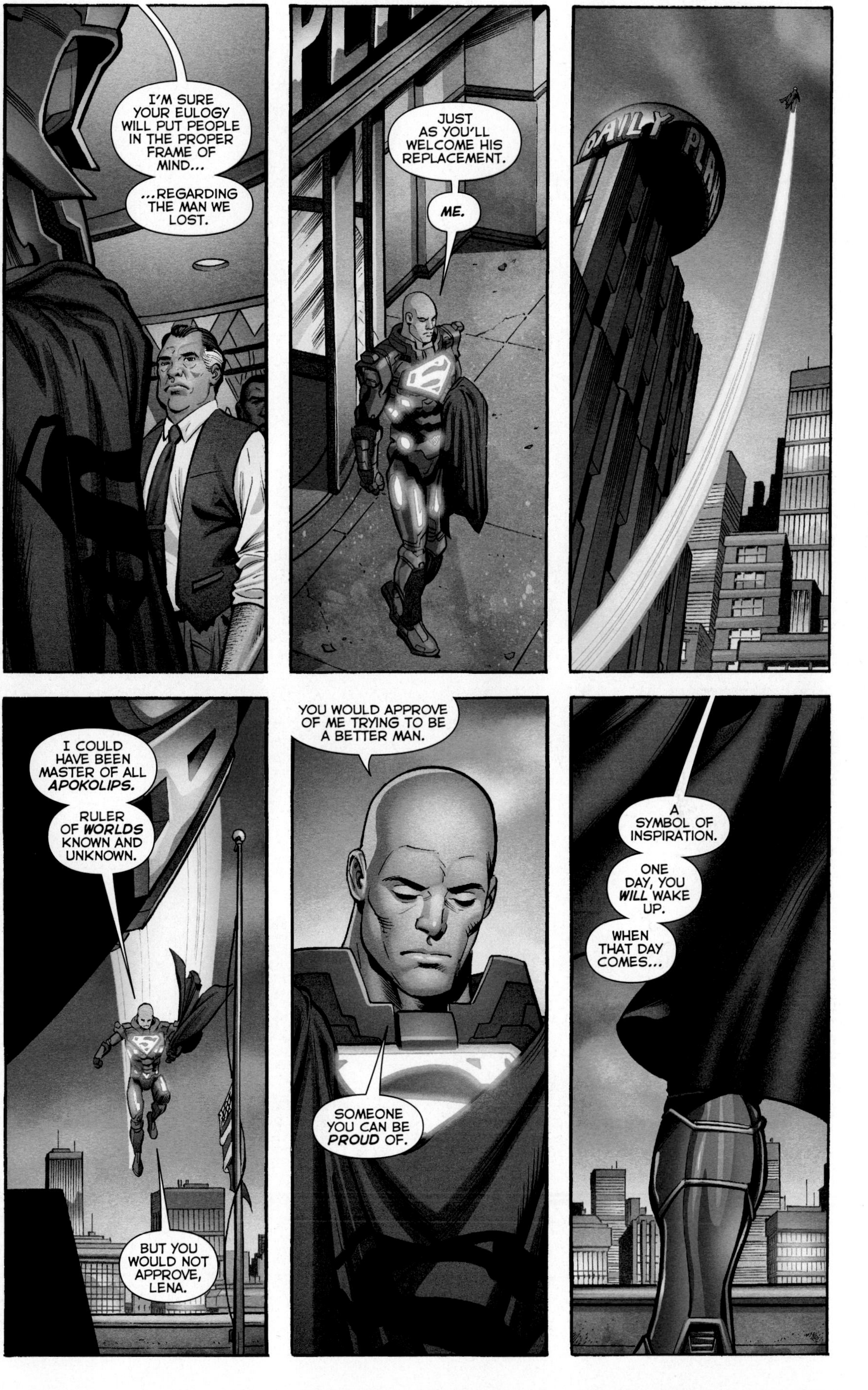

I'M SURE YOUR EULOGY WILL PUT PEOPLE IN THE PROPER FRAME OF MIND...
...REGARDING THE MAN WE LOST.
JUST AS YOU'LL WELCOME HIS REPLACEMENT.
ME.
DAILY PLANET
I COULD HAVE BEEN MASTER OF ALL APOKOLIPS.
RULER OF WORLDS KNOWN AND UNKNOWN.
BUT YOU WOULD NOT APPROVE, LENA.
YOU WOULD APPROVE OF ME TRYING TO BE A BETTER MAN.
SOMEONE YOU CAN BE PROUD OF.
A SYMBOL OF INSPIRATION.
ONE DAY, YOU WILL WAKE UP.
WHEN THAT DAY COMES...

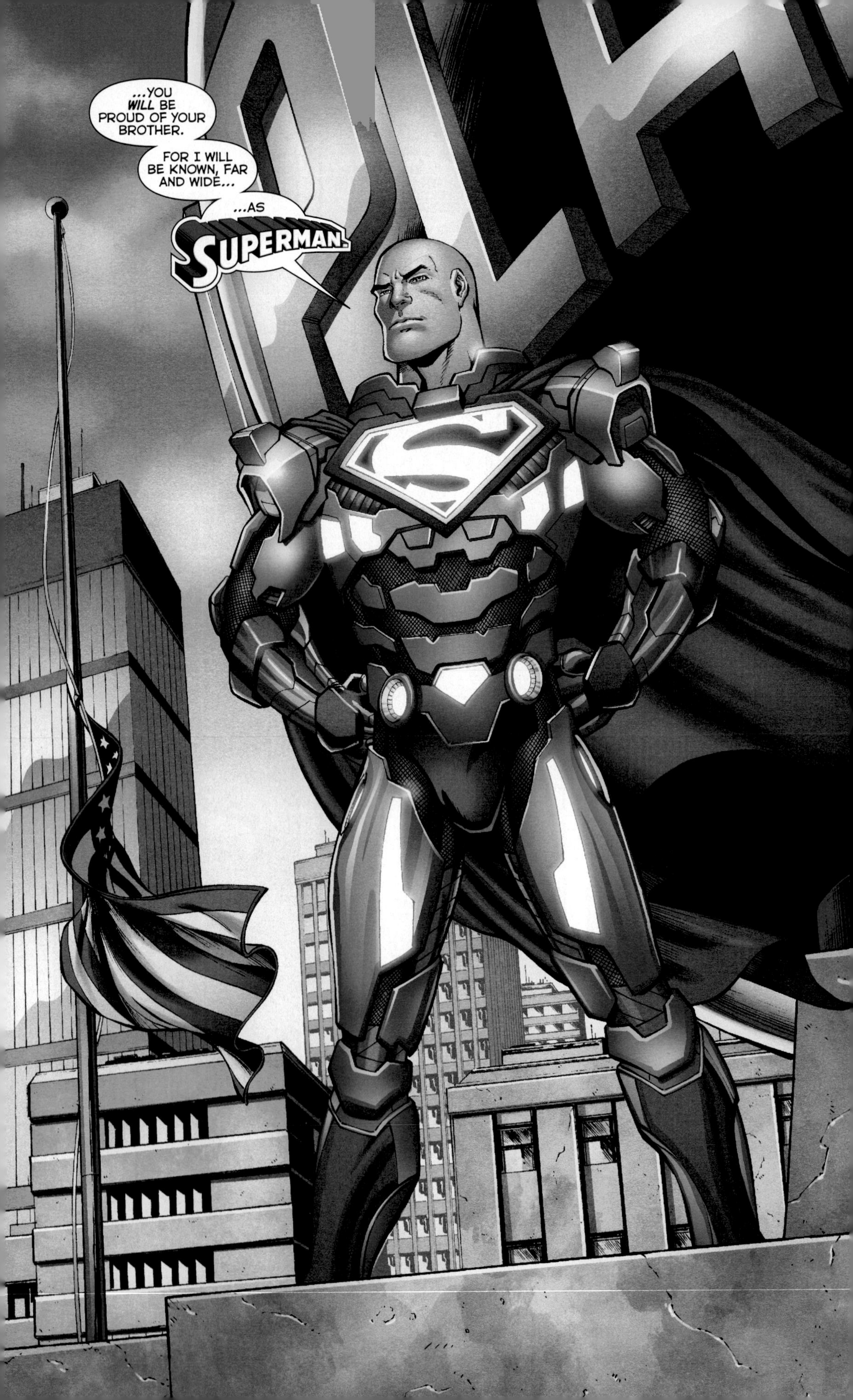
...YOU WILL BE PROUD OF YOUR BROTHER.
FOR I WILL BE KNOWN, FAR AND WIDE...
...AS
SUPERMAN.

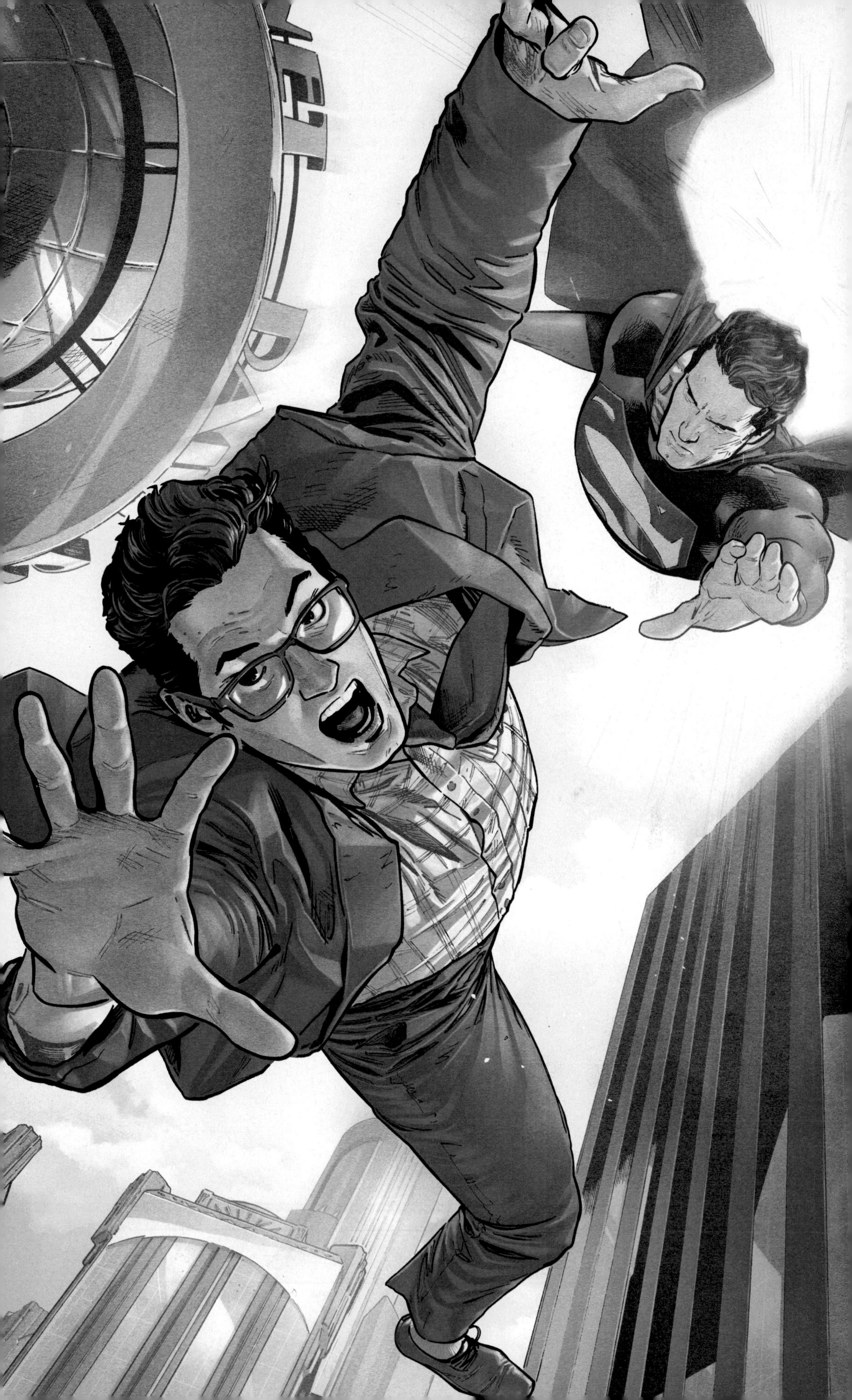

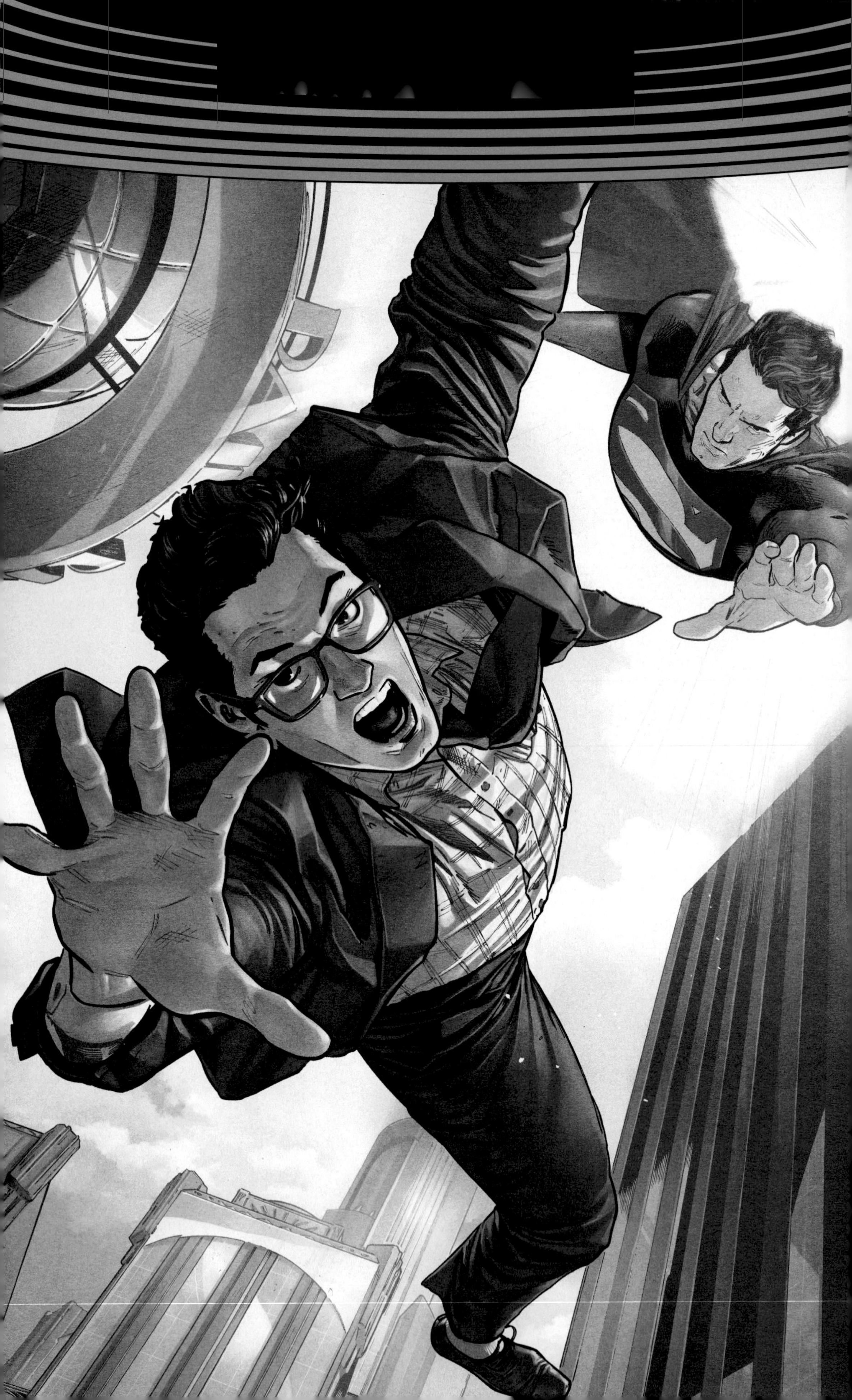

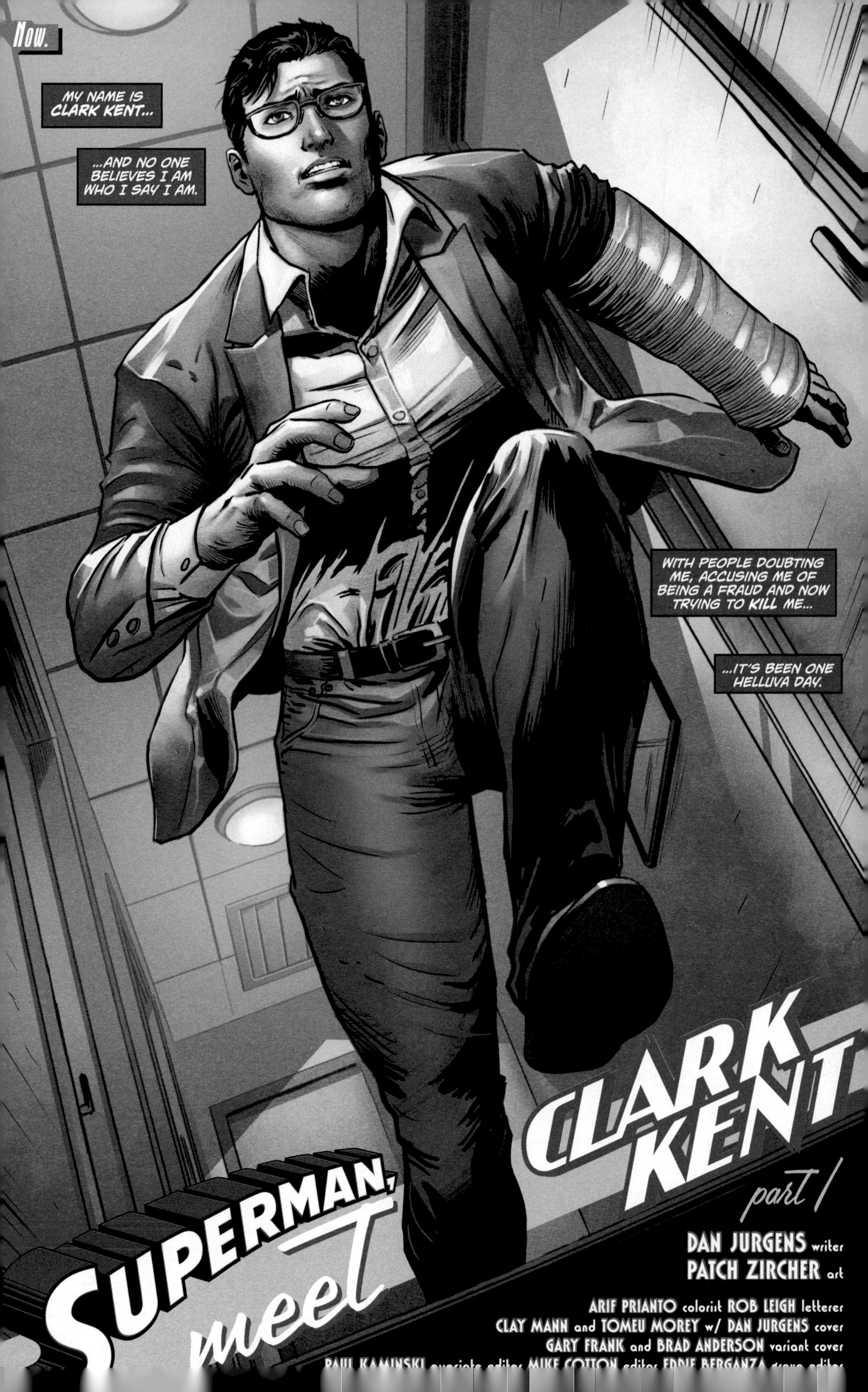

Now.
MY NAME IS CLARK KENT...
...AND NO ONE BELIEVES I AM WHO I SAY I AM.
WITH PEOPLE DOUBTING ME, ACCUSING ME OF BEING A FRAUD AND NOW TRYING TO KILL ME...
...IT'S BEEN ONE HELLUVA DAY.
SUPERMAN, meet CLARK KENT
part 1
DAN JURGENS writer
PATCH ZIRCHER art
ARIF PRIANTO colorist ROB LEIGH letterer
CLAY MANN and TOMEU MOREY w/ DAN JURGENS cover
GARY FRANK and BRAD ANDERSON variant cover

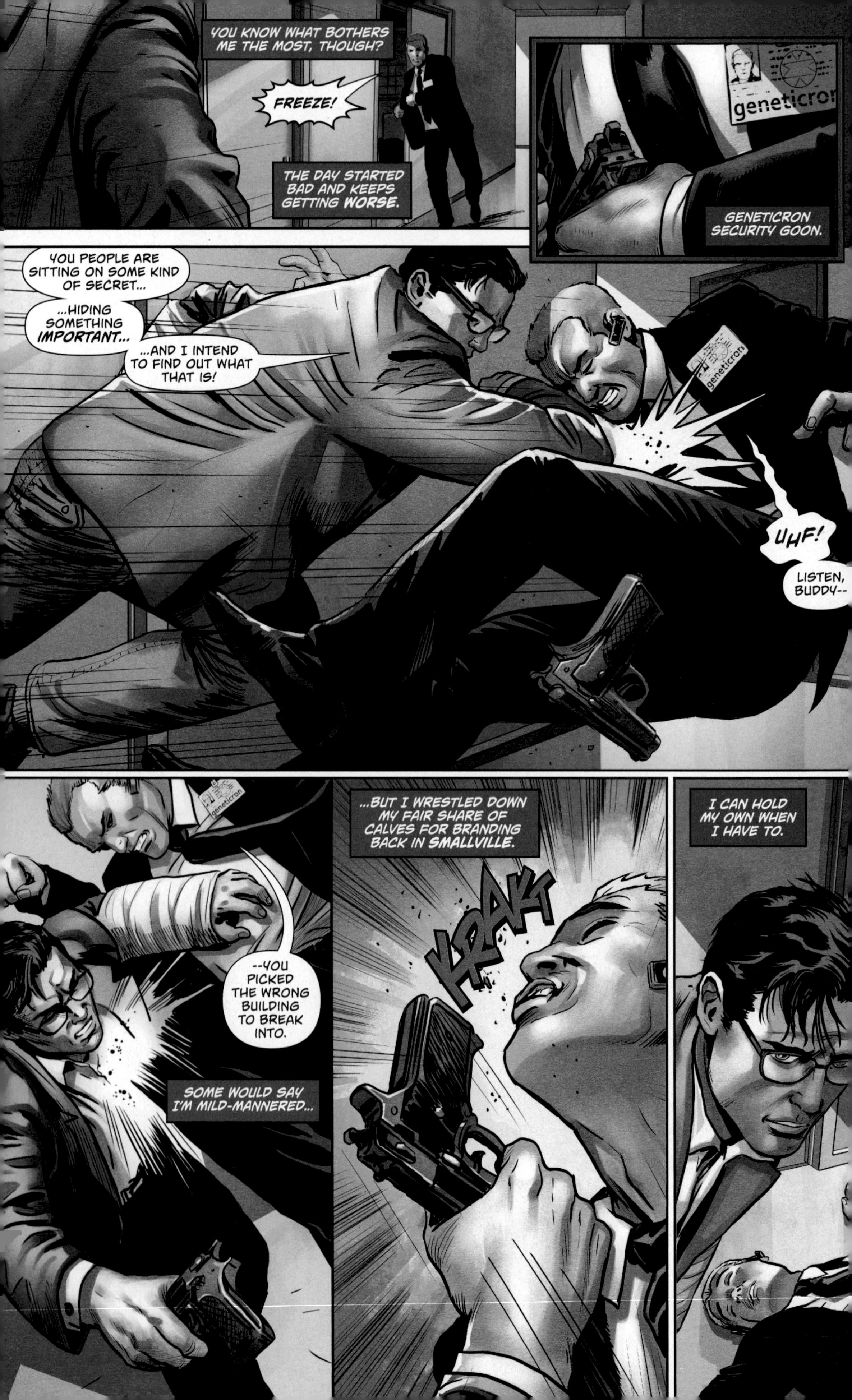
YOU KNOW WHAT BOTHERS ME THE MOST, THOUGH?
FREEZE!
THE DAY STARTED BAD AND KEEPS GETTING WORSE.
geneticron
GENETICRON SECURITY GOON.
YOU PEOPLE ARE SITTING ON SOME KIND OF SECRET...
...HIDING SOMETHING IMPORTANT...
...AND I INTEND TO FIND OUT WHAT THAT IS!
geneticron
UHF!
LISTEN, BUDDY--
geneticron
--YOU PICKED THE WRONG BUILDING TO BREAK INTO.
SOME WOULD SAY I'M MILD-MANNERED...
...BUT I WRESTLED DOWN MY FAIR SHARE OF CALVES FOR BRANDING BACK IN SMALLVILLE.
KRAKT
I CAN HOLD MY OWN WHEN I HAVE TO.

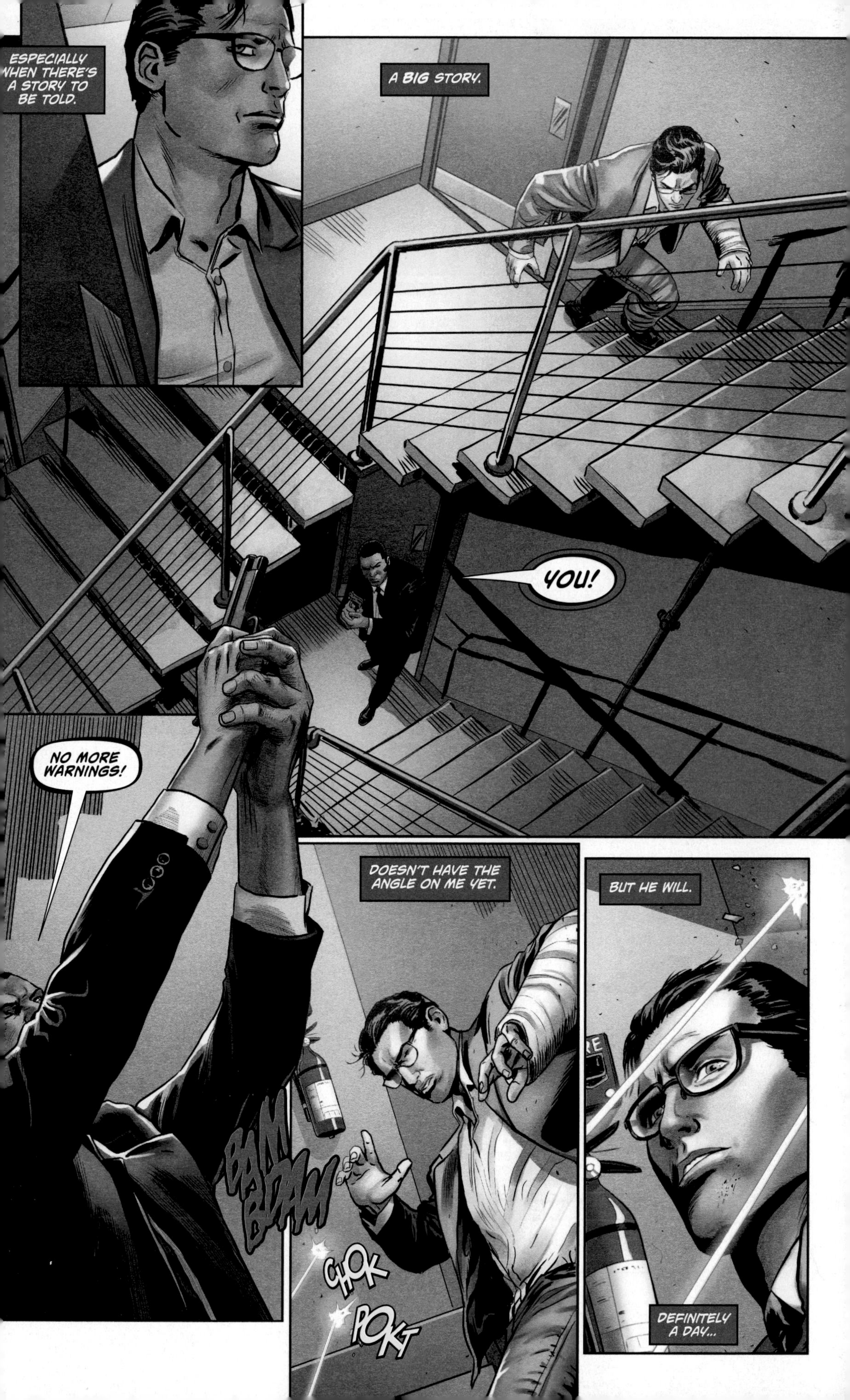

ESPECIALLY WHEN THERE'S A STORY TO BE TOLD.
A BIG STORY.
YOU!
NO MORE WARNINGS!
DOESN'T HAVE THE ANGLE ON ME YET.
BUT HE WILL.
BAM BLAM
CHOK
POKT
DEFINITELY A DAY...

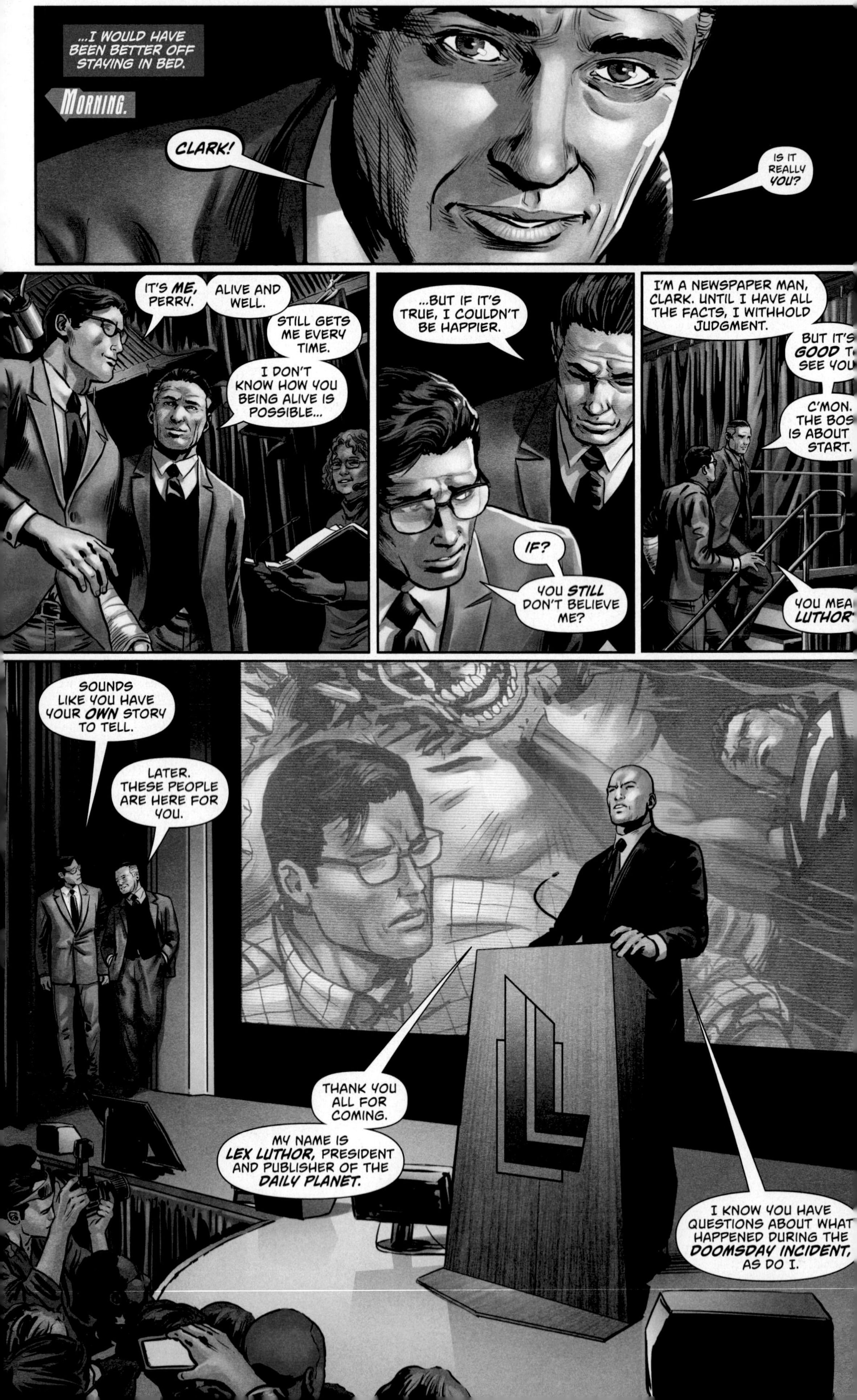
...I WOULD HAVE BEEN BETTER OFF STAYING IN BED.
MORNING.
CLARK!
IS IT REALLY YOU?
IT'S ME, PERRY.
ALIVE AND WELL.
STILL GETS ME EVERY TIME.
I DON'T KNOW HOW YOU BEING ALIVE IS POSSIBLE...
...BUT IF IT'S TRUE, I COULDN'T BE HAPPIER.
IF?
YOU STILL DON'T BELIEVE ME?
I'M A NEWSPAPER MAN, CLARK. UNTIL I HAVE ALL THE FACTS, I WITHHOLD JUDGMENT.
SOUNDS LIKE YOU HAVE YOUR OWN STORY TO TELL.
LATER. THESE PEOPLE ARE HERE FOR YOU.
THANK YOU ALL FOR COMING.
MY NAME IS LEX LUTHOR, PRESIDENT AND PUBLISHER OF THE DAILY PLANET.
I KNOW YOU HAVE QUESTIONS ABOUT WHAT HAPPENED DURING THE DOOMSDAY INCIDENT, AS DO I.

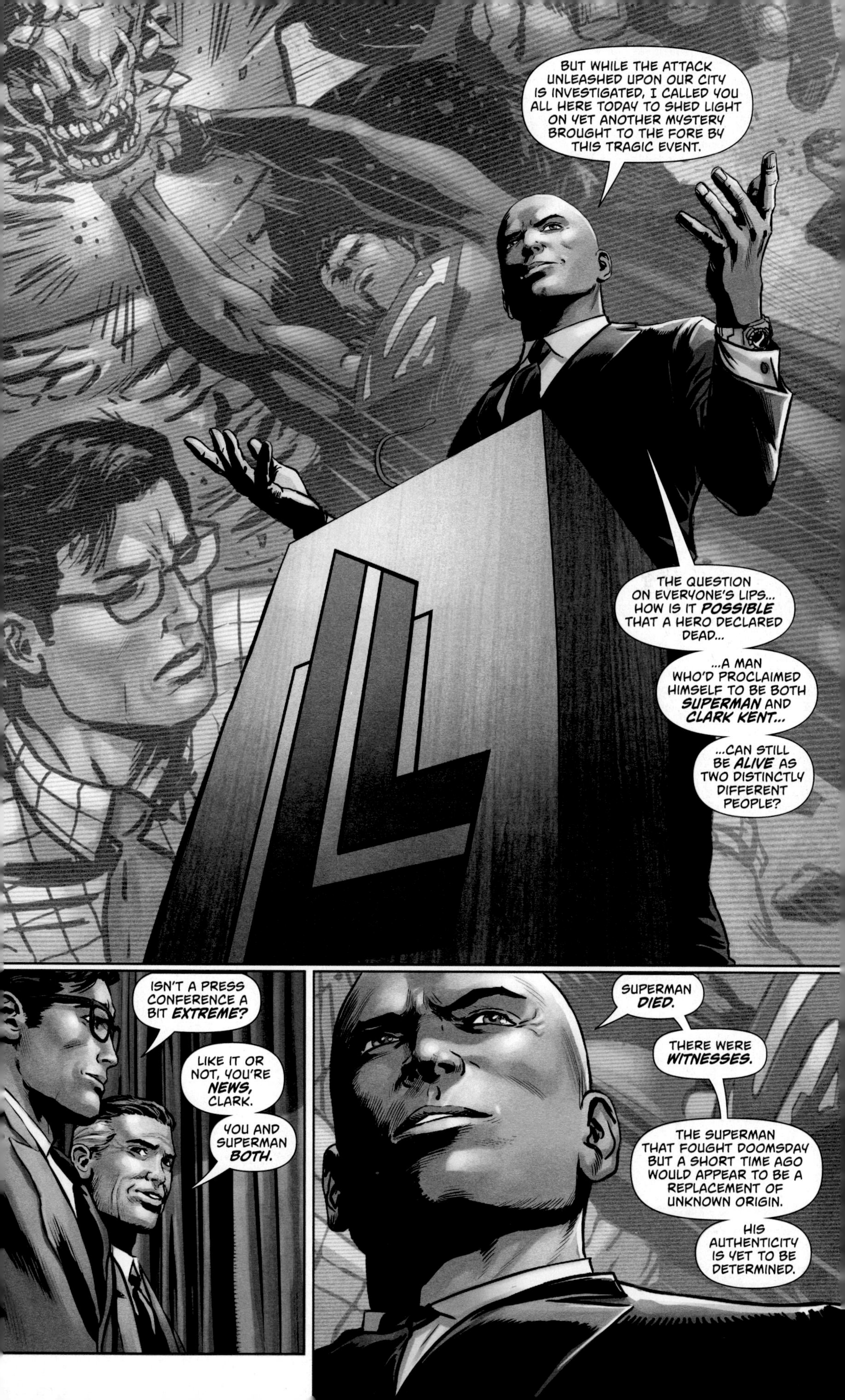

BUT WHILE THE ATTACK UNLEASHED UPON OUR CITY IS INVESTIGATED, I CALLED YOU ALL HERE TODAY TO SHED LIGHT ON YET ANOTHER MYSTERY BROUGHT TO THE FORE BY THIS TRAGIC EVENT.
THE QUESTION ON EVERYONE'S LIPS... HOW IS IT **POSSIBLE** THAT A HERO DECLARED DEAD...
...A MAN WHO'D PROCLAIMED HIMSELF TO BE BOTH **SUPERMAN** AND **CLARK KENT...**
...CAN STILL BE **ALIVE** AS TWO DISTINCTLY DIFFERENT PEOPLE?
ISN'T A PRESS CONFERENCE A BIT **EXTREME?**
LIKE IT OR NOT, YOU'RE **NEWS,** CLARK.
YOU AND SUPERMAN **BOTH.**
SUPERMAN **DIED.**
THERE WERE **WITNESSES.**
THE SUPERMAN THAT FOUGHT DOOMSDAY BUT A SHORT TIME AGO WOULD APPEAR TO BE A REPLACEMENT OF UNKNOWN ORIGIN.
HIS AUTHENTICITY IS YET TO BE DETERMINED.

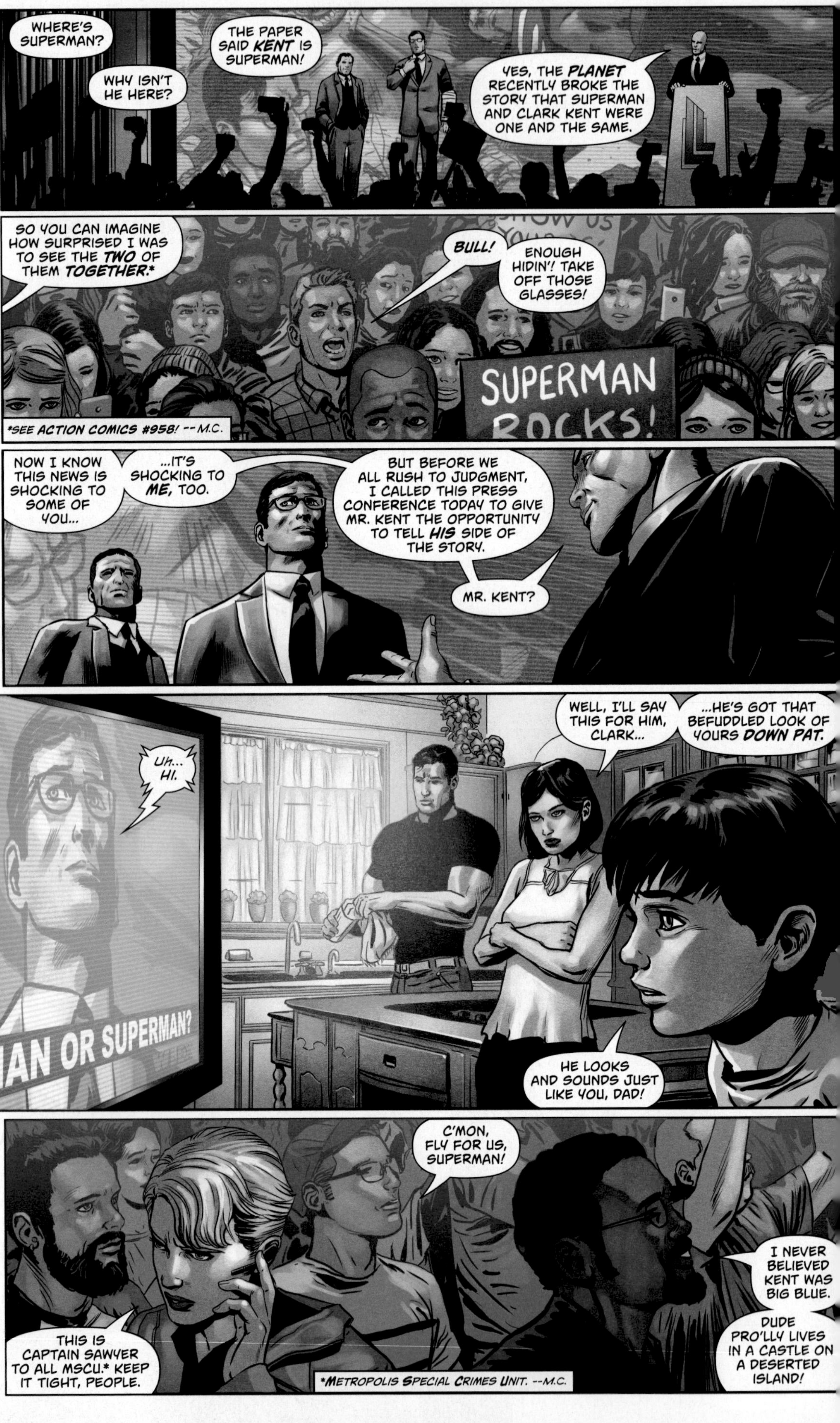
WHERE'S SUPERMAN?
WHY ISN'T HE HERE?
THE PAPER SAID KENT IS SUPERMAN!
YES, THE PLANET RECENTLY BROKE THE STORY THAT SUPERMAN AND CLARK KENT WERE ONE AND THE SAME.
SO YOU CAN IMAGINE HOW SURPRISED I WAS TO SEE THE TWO OF THEM TOGETHER.*
BULL!
ENOUGH HIDIN'! TAKE OFF THOSE GLASSES!
SUPERMAN ROCKS!
*SEE ACTION COMICS #958! --M.C.
NOW I KNOW THIS NEWS IS SHOCKING TO SOME OF YOU...
...IT'S SHOCKING TO ME, TOO.
BUT BEFORE WE ALL RUSH TO JUDGMENT, I CALLED THIS PRESS CONFERENCE TODAY TO GIVE MR. KENT THE OPPORTUNITY TO TELL HIS SIDE OF THE STORY.
MR. KENT?
Uh... HI.
MAN OR SUPERMAN?
WELL, I'LL SAY THIS FOR HIM, CLARK...
...HE'S GOT THAT BEFUDDLED LOOK OF YOURS DOWN PAT.
HE LOOKS AND SOUNDS JUST LIKE YOU, DAD!
C'MON, FLY FOR US, SUPERMAN!
I NEVER BELIEVED KENT WAS BIG BLUE.
DUDE PRO'LLY LIVES IN A CASTLE ON A DESERTED ISLAND!
THIS IS CAPTAIN SAWYER TO ALL MSCU.* KEEP IT TIGHT, PEOPLE.
*METROPOLIS SPECIAL CRIMES UNIT. --M.C.

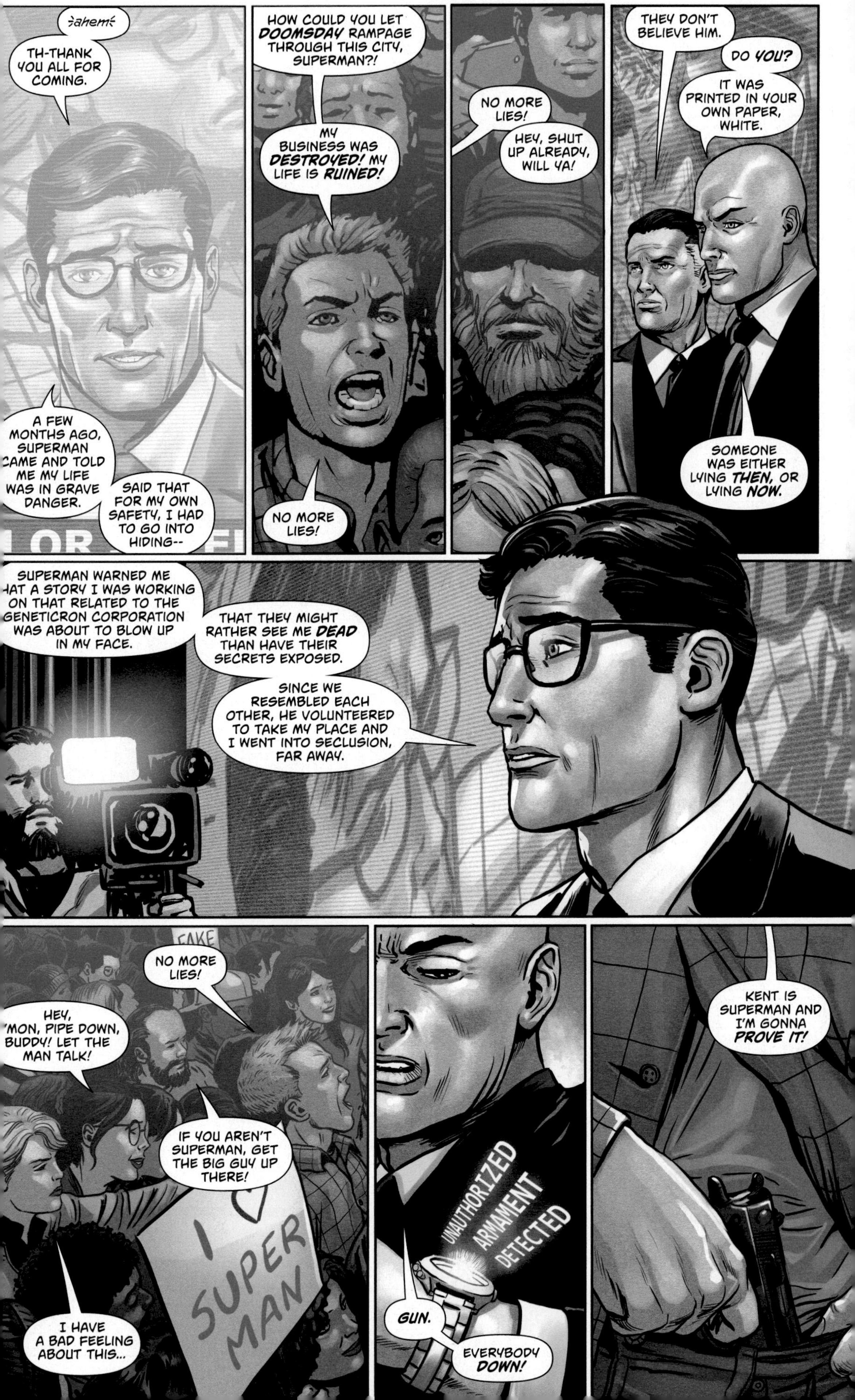

:ahem:
TH-THANK YOU ALL FOR COMING.
A FEW MONTHS AGO, SUPERMAN CAME AND TOLD ME MY LIFE WAS IN GRAVE DANGER.
SAID THAT FOR MY OWN SAFETY, I HAD TO GO INTO HIDING--
HOW COULD YOU LET DOOMSDAY RAMPAGE THROUGH THIS CITY, SUPERMAN?!
MY BUSINESS WAS DESTROYED! MY LIFE IS RUINED!
NO MORE LIES!
NO MORE LIES!
HEY, SHUT UP ALREADY, WILL YA!
THEY DON'T BELIEVE HIM.
DO YOU?
IT WAS PRINTED IN YOUR OWN PAPER, WHITE.
SOMEONE WAS EITHER LYING THEN, OR LYING NOW.
SUPERMAN WARNED ME THAT A STORY I WAS WORKING ON THAT RELATED TO THE GENETICRON CORPORATION WAS ABOUT TO BLOW UP IN MY FACE.
THAT THEY MIGHT RATHER SEE ME DEAD THAN HAVE THEIR SECRETS EXPOSED.
SINCE WE RESEMBLED EACH OTHER, HE VOLUNTEERED TO TAKE MY PLACE AND I WENT INTO SECLUSION, FAR AWAY.
FAKE
NO MORE LIES!
HEY, C'MON, PIPE DOWN, BUDDY! LET THE MAN TALK!
IF YOU AREN'T SUPERMAN, GET THE BIG GUY UP THERE!
I ♥ SUPER MAN
I HAVE A BAD FEELING ABOUT THIS...
UNAUTHORIZED ARMAMENT DETECTED
GUN.
EVERYBODY DOWN!
KENT IS SUPERMAN AND I'M GONNA PROVE IT!

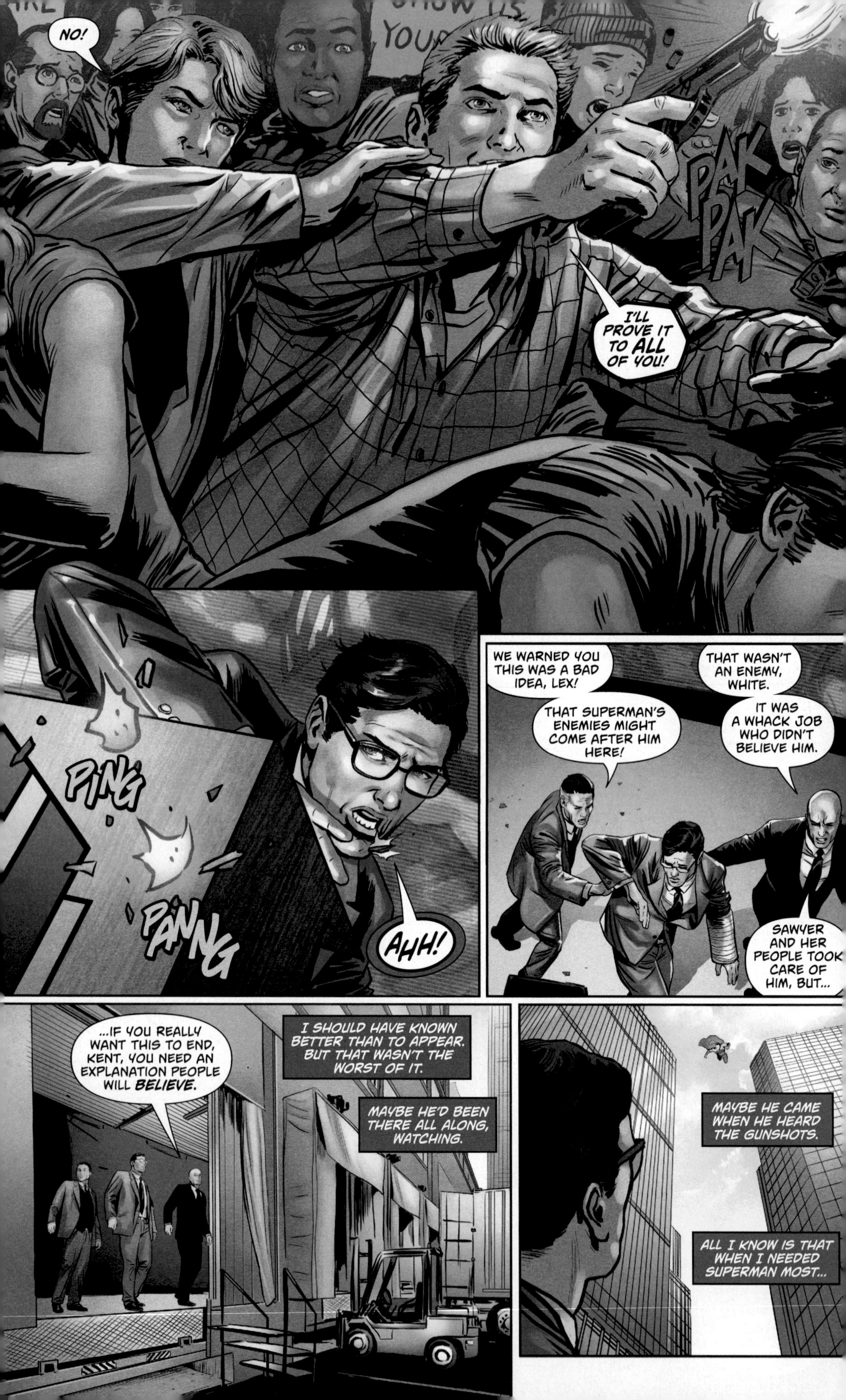
NO!
I'LL PROVE IT TO ALL OF YOU!
PAK PAK
PING
PANNG
AHH!
WE WARNED YOU THIS WAS A BAD IDEA, LEX!
THAT SUPERMAN'S ENEMIES MIGHT COME AFTER HIM HERE!
THAT WASN'T AN ENEMY, WHITE.
IT WAS A WHACK JOB WHO DIDN'T BELIEVE HIM.
SAWYER AND HER PEOPLE TOOK CARE OF HIM, BUT...
...IF YOU REALLY WANT THIS TO END, KENT, YOU NEED AN EXPLANATION PEOPLE WILL BELIEVE.
I SHOULD HAVE KNOWN BETTER THAN TO APPEAR. BUT THAT WASN'T THE WORST OF IT.
MAYBE HE'D BEEN THERE ALL ALONG, WATCHING.
MAYBE HE CAME WHEN HE HEARD THE GUNSHOTS.
ALL I KNOW IS THAT WHEN I NEEDED SUPERMAN MOST...

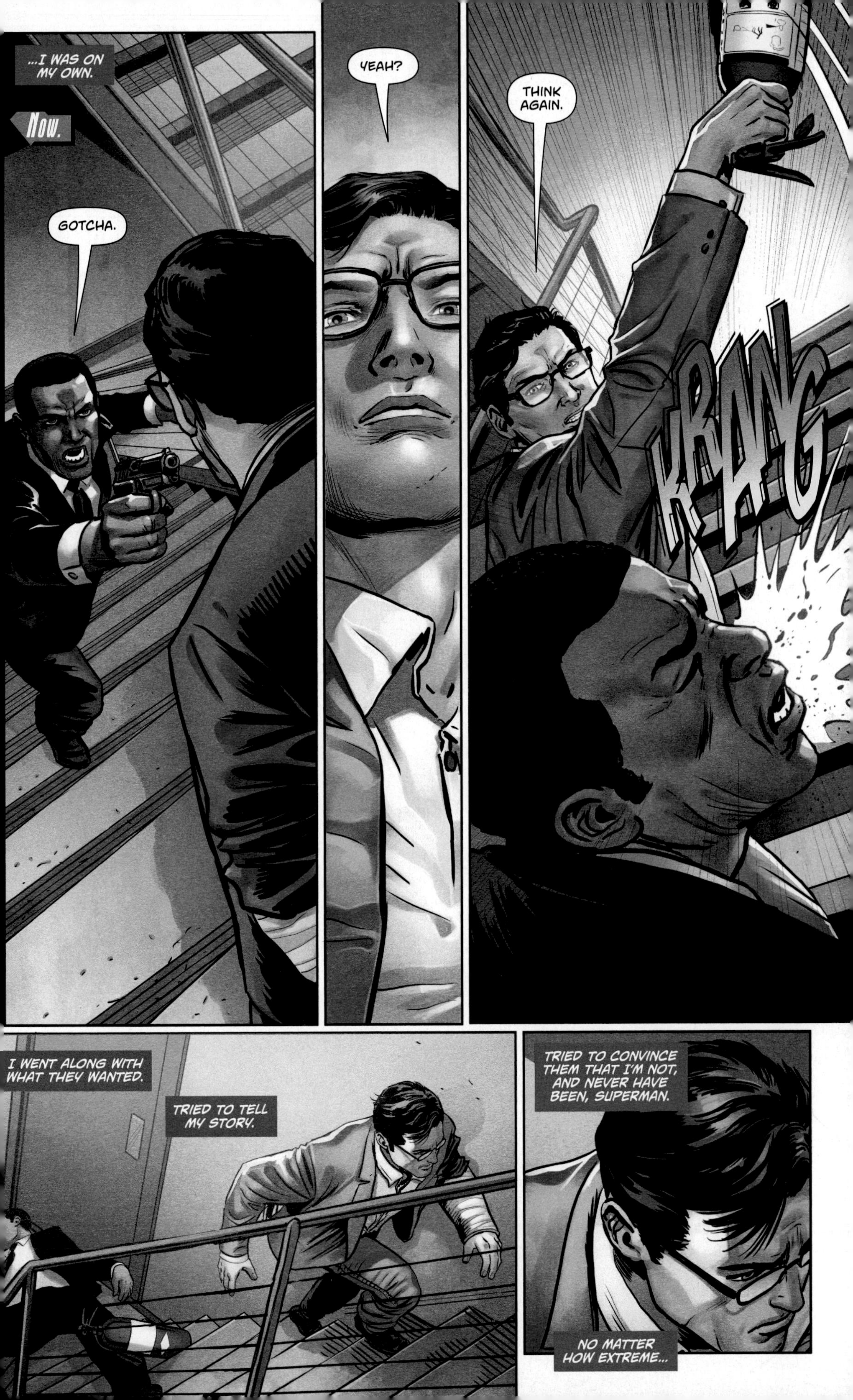
...I WAS ON MY OWN.
Now.
GOTCHA.
YEAH?
THINK AGAIN.
KRANG
I WENT ALONG WITH WHAT THEY WANTED.
TRIED TO TELL MY STORY.
TRIED TO CONVINCE THEM THAT I'M NOT, AND NEVER HAVE BEEN, SUPERMAN.
NO MATTER HOW EXTREME...

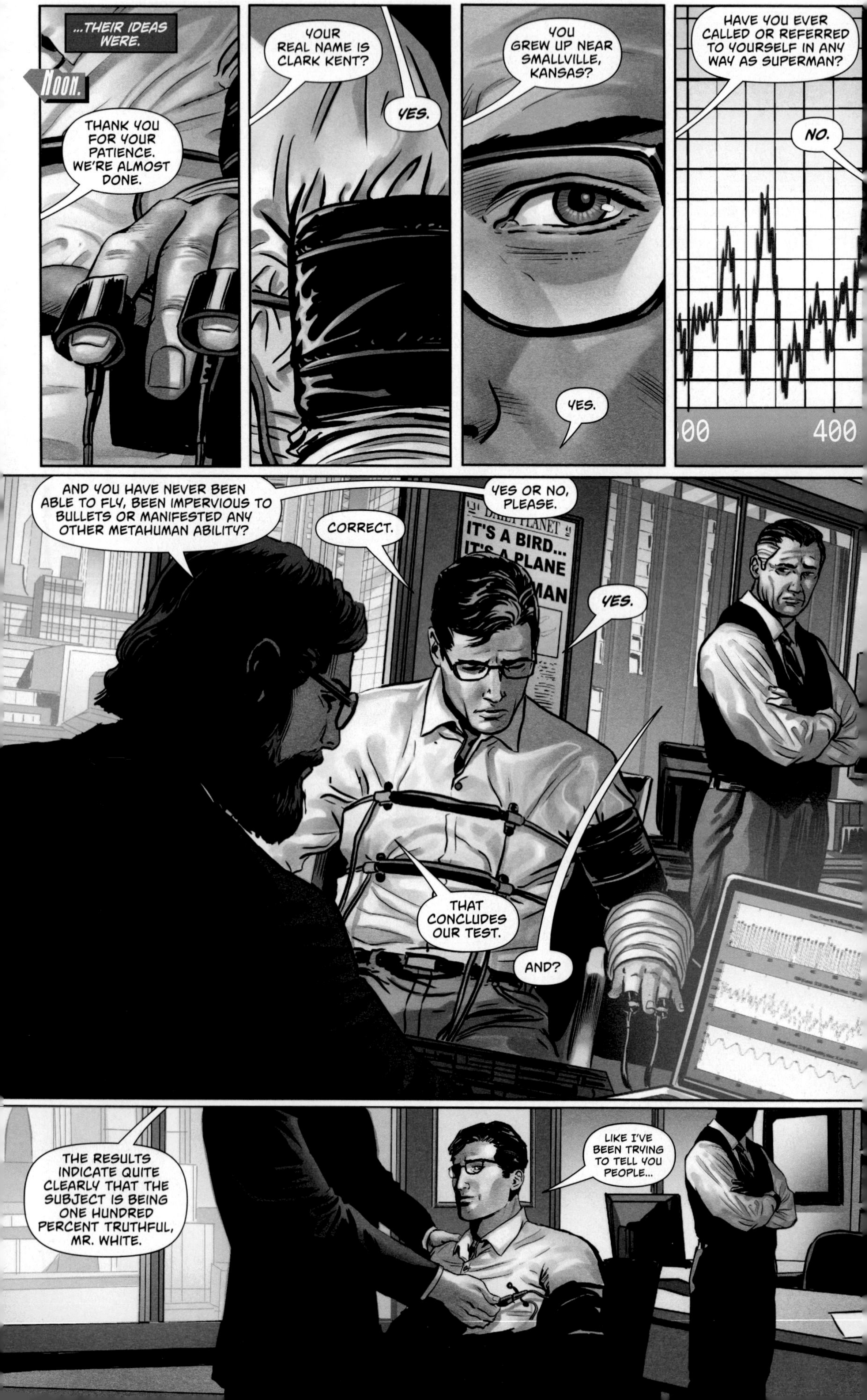

...THEIR IDEAS WERE.
NOON.
THANK YOU FOR YOUR PATIENCE. WE'RE ALMOST DONE.
YOUR REAL NAME IS CLARK KENT?
YES.
YOU GREW UP NEAR SMALLVILLE, KANSAS?
YES.
HAVE YOU EVER CALLED OR REFERRED TO YOURSELF IN ANY WAY AS SUPERMAN?
NO.
00
400
AND YOU HAVE NEVER BEEN ABLE TO FLY, BEEN IMPERVIOUS TO BULLETS OR MANIFESTED ANY OTHER METAHUMAN ABILITY?
YES OR NO, PLEASE.
CORRECT.
DAILY PLANET
IT'S A BIRD... IT'S A PLANE
MAN
YES.
THAT CONCLUDES OUR TEST.
AND?
THE RESULTS INDICATE QUITE CLEARLY THAT THE SUBJECT IS BEING ONE HUNDRED PERCENT TRUTHFUL, MR. WHITE.
LIKE I'VE BEEN TRYING TO TELL YOU PEOPLE...

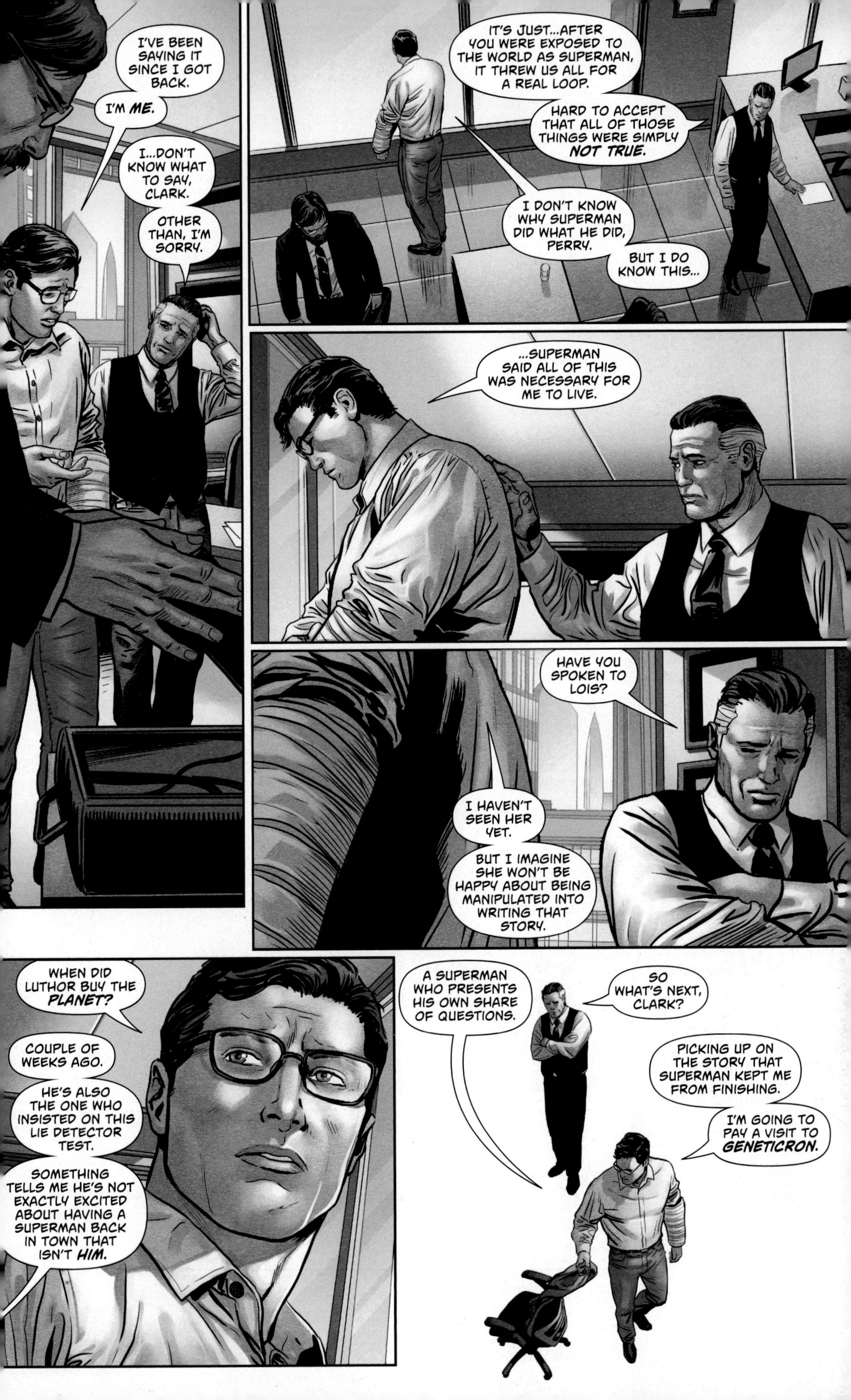
I'VE BEEN SAYING IT SINCE I GOT BACK.
I'M ME.
I...DON'T KNOW WHAT TO SAY, CLARK.
OTHER THAN, I'M SORRY.
IT'S JUST...AFTER YOU WERE EXPOSED TO THE WORLD AS SUPERMAN, IT THREW US ALL FOR A REAL LOOP.
HARD TO ACCEPT THAT ALL OF THOSE THINGS WERE SIMPLY NOT TRUE.
I DON'T KNOW WHY SUPERMAN DID WHAT HE DID, PERRY.
BUT I DO KNOW THIS...
...SUPERMAN SAID ALL OF THIS WAS NECESSARY FOR ME TO LIVE.
HAVE YOU SPOKEN TO LOIS?
I HAVEN'T SEEN HER YET.
BUT I IMAGINE SHE WON'T BE HAPPY ABOUT BEING MANIPULATED INTO WRITING THAT STORY.
WHEN DID LUTHOR BUY THE PLANET?
COUPLE OF WEEKS AGO.
HE'S ALSO THE ONE WHO INSISTED ON THIS LIE DETECTOR TEST.
SOMETHING TELLS ME HE'S NOT EXACTLY EXCITED ABOUT HAVING A SUPERMAN BACK IN TOWN THAT ISN'T HIM.
A SUPERMAN WHO PRESENTS HIS OWN SHARE OF QUESTIONS.
SO WHAT'S NEXT, CLARK?
PICKING UP ON THE STORY THAT SUPERMAN KEPT ME FROM FINISHING.
I'M GOING TO PAY A VISIT TO GENETICRON.

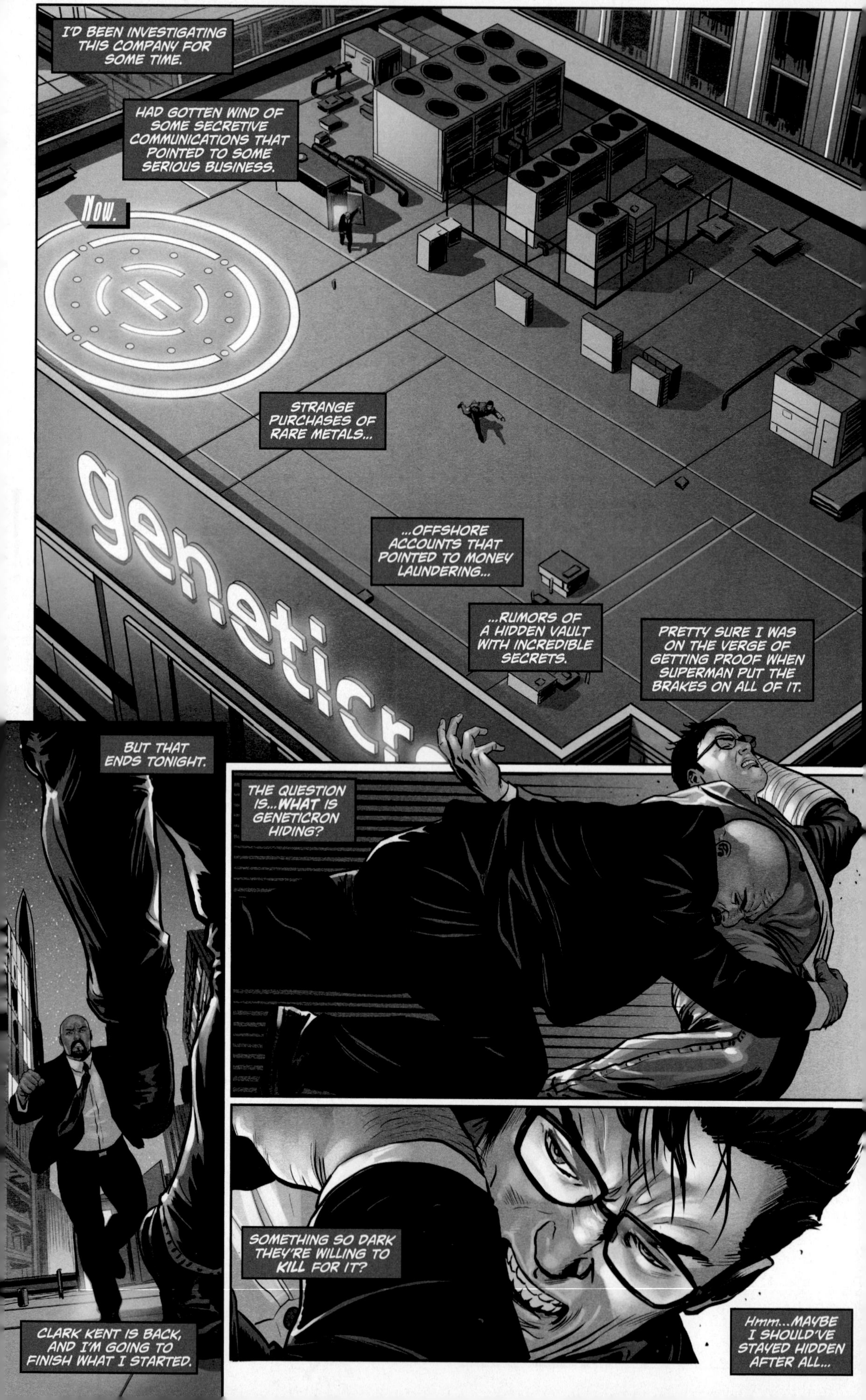
I'D BEEN INVESTIGATING THIS COMPANY FOR SOME TIME.
HAD GOTTEN WIND OF SOME SECRETIVE COMMUNICATIONS THAT POINTED TO SOME SERIOUS BUSINESS.
Now.
STRANGE PURCHASES OF RARE METALS...
...OFFSHORE ACCOUNTS THAT POINTED TO MONEY LAUNDERING...
...RUMORS OF A HIDDEN VAULT WITH INCREDIBLE SECRETS.
PRETTY SURE I WAS ON THE VERGE OF GETTING PROOF WHEN SUPERMAN PUT THE BRAKES ON ALL OF IT.
BUT THAT ENDS TONIGHT.
THE QUESTION IS...WHAT IS GENETICRON HIDING?
SOMETHING SO DARK THEY'RE WILLING TO KILL FOR IT?
CLARK KENT IS BACK, AND I'M GOING TO FINISH WHAT I STARTED.
Hmm...MAYBE I SHOULD'VE STAYED HIDDEN AFTER ALL...

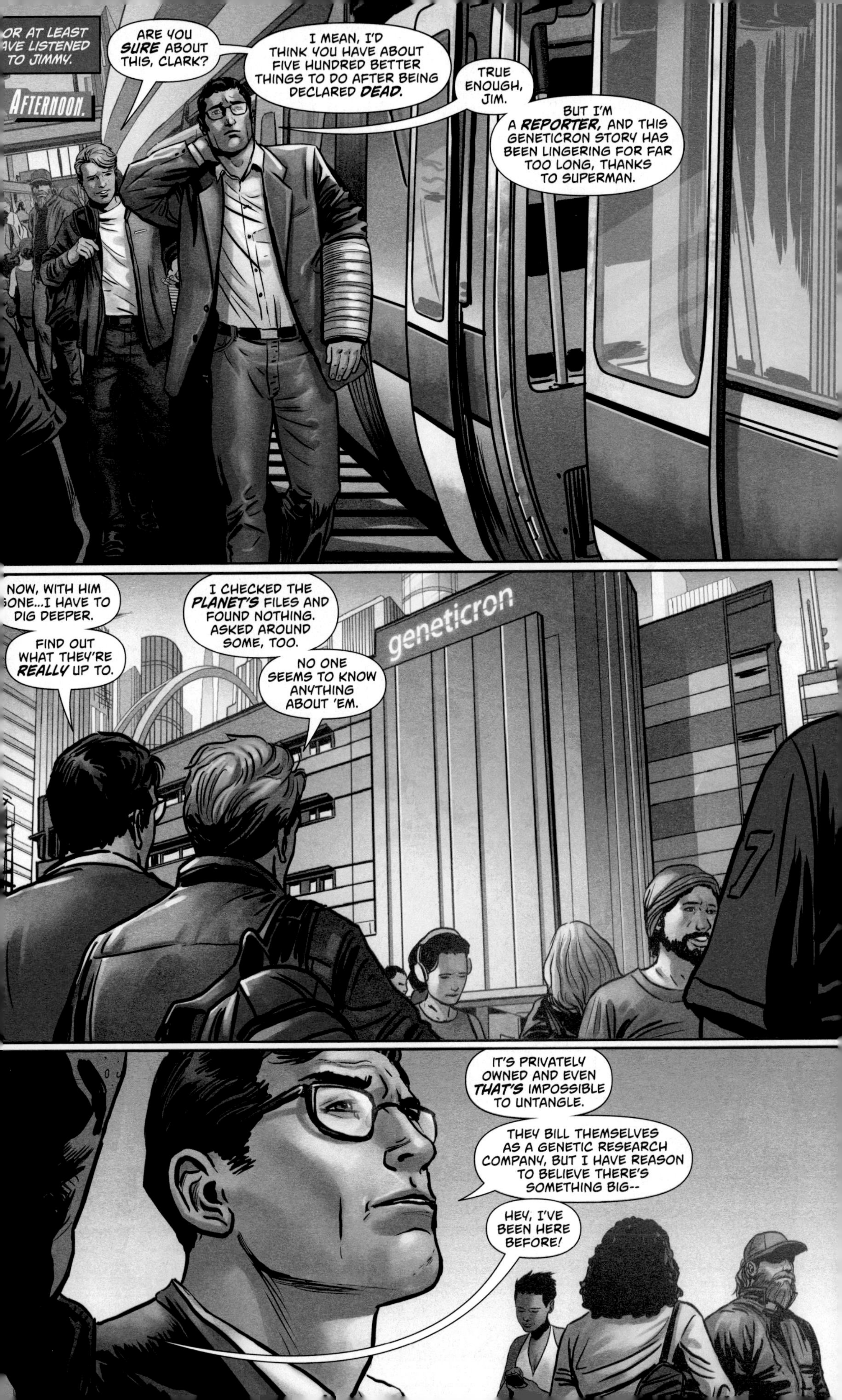

OR AT LEAST AVE LISTENED TO JIMMY.
AFTERNOON.
ARE YOU SURE ABOUT THIS, CLARK?
I MEAN, I'D THINK YOU HAVE ABOUT FIVE HUNDRED BETTER THINGS TO DO AFTER BEING DECLARED DEAD.
TRUE ENOUGH, JIM.
BUT I'M A REPORTER, AND THIS GENETICRON STORY HAS BEEN LINGERING FOR FAR TOO LONG, THANKS TO SUPERMAN.
NOW, WITH HIM GONE...I HAVE TO DIG DEEPER.
FIND OUT WHAT THEY'RE REALLY UP TO.
I CHECKED THE PLANET'S FILES AND FOUND NOTHING. ASKED AROUND SOME, TOO.
NO ONE SEEMS TO KNOW ANYTHING ABOUT 'EM.
geneticron
IT'S PRIVATELY OWNED AND EVEN THAT'S IMPOSSIBLE TO UNTANGLE.
THEY BILL THEMSELVES AS A GENETIC RESEARCH COMPANY, BUT I HAVE REASON TO BELIEVE THERE'S SOMETHING BIG--
HEY, I'VE BEEN HERE BEFORE!

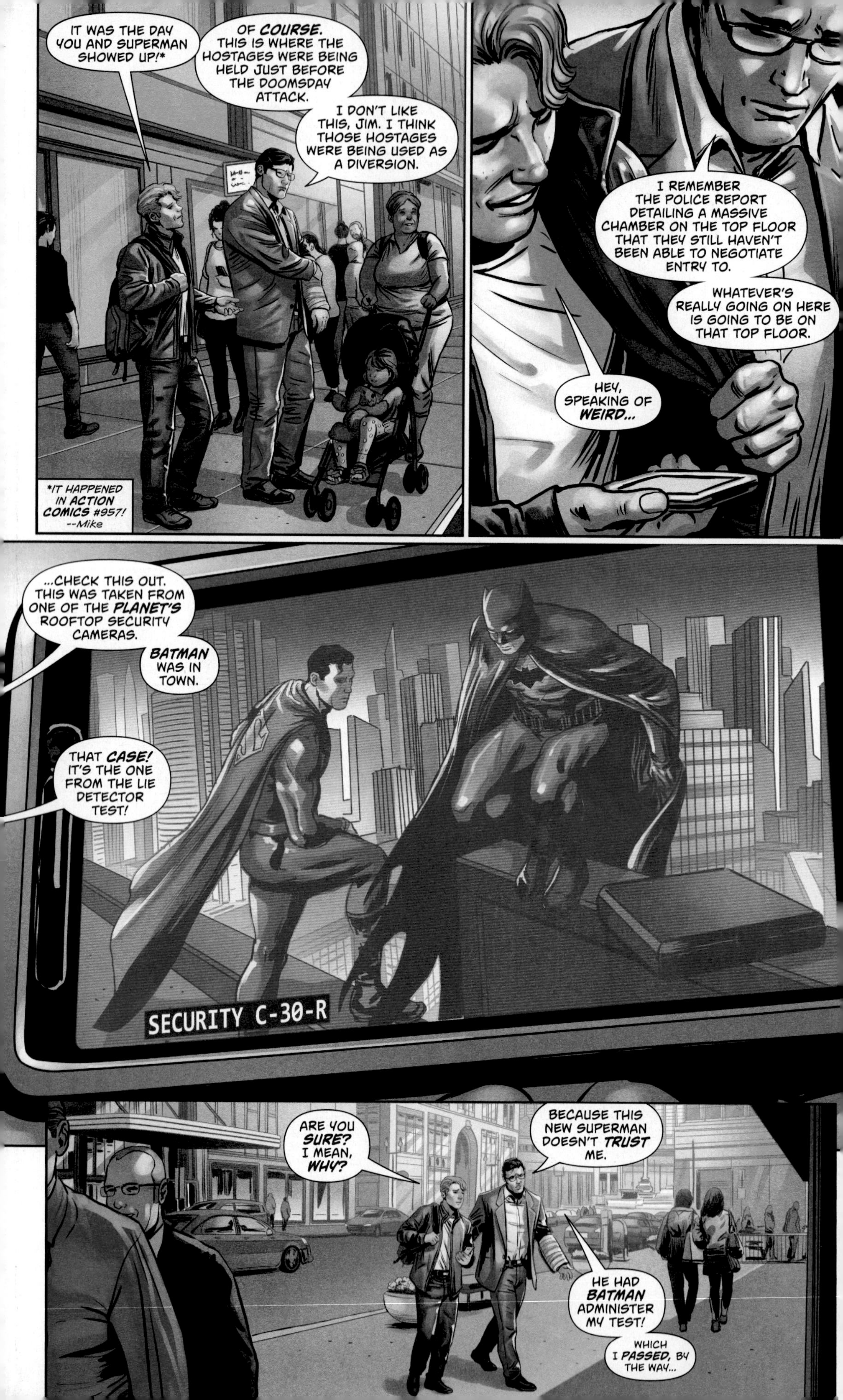
IT WAS THE DAY YOU AND SUPERMAN SHOWED UP!*
OF COURSE. THIS IS WHERE THE HOSTAGES WERE BEING HELD JUST BEFORE THE DOOMSDAY ATTACK.
I DON'T LIKE THIS, JIM. I THINK THOSE HOSTAGES WERE BEING USED AS A DIVERSION.
*IT HAPPENED IN ACTION COMICS #957! --Mike
I REMEMBER THE POLICE REPORT DETAILING A MASSIVE CHAMBER ON THE TOP FLOOR THAT THEY STILL HAVEN'T BEEN ABLE TO NEGOTIATE ENTRY TO.
WHATEVER'S REALLY GOING ON HERE IS GOING TO BE ON THAT TOP FLOOR.
HEY, SPEAKING OF WEIRD...
...CHECK THIS OUT. THIS WAS TAKEN FROM ONE OF THE PLANET'S ROOFTOP SECURITY CAMERAS.
BATMAN WAS IN TOWN.
THAT CASE! IT'S THE ONE FROM THE LIE DETECTOR TEST!
SECURITY C-30-R
ARE YOU SURE? I MEAN, WHY?
BECAUSE THIS NEW SUPERMAN DOESN'T TRUST ME.
HE HAD BATMAN ADMINISTER MY TEST!
WHICH I PASSED, BY THE WAY...

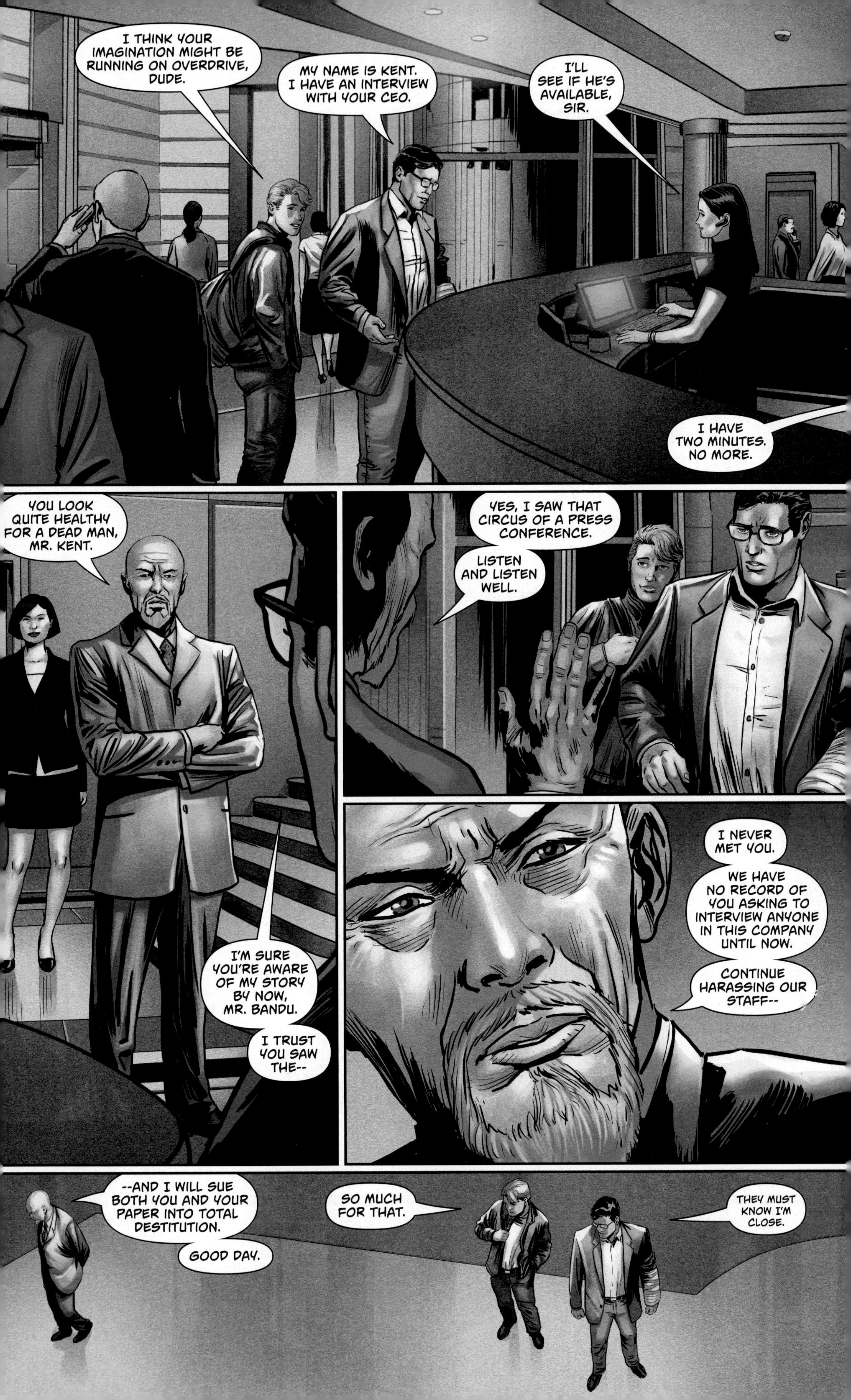
I THINK YOUR IMAGINATION MIGHT BE RUNNING ON OVERDRIVE, DUDE.
MY NAME IS KENT. I HAVE AN INTERVIEW WITH YOUR CEO.
I'LL SEE IF HE'S AVAILABLE, SIR.
I HAVE TWO MINUTES. NO MORE.
YOU LOOK QUITE HEALTHY FOR A DEAD MAN, MR. KENT.
I'M SURE YOU'RE AWARE OF MY STORY BY NOW, MR. BANDU.
I TRUST YOU SAW THE--
YES, I SAW THAT CIRCUS OF A PRESS CONFERENCE.
LISTEN AND LISTEN WELL.
I NEVER MET YOU.
WE HAVE NO RECORD OF YOU ASKING TO INTERVIEW ANYONE IN THIS COMPANY UNTIL NOW.
CONTINUE HARASSING OUR STAFF--
--AND I WILL SUE BOTH YOU AND YOUR PAPER INTO TOTAL DESTITUTION.
GOOD DAY.
SO MUCH FOR THAT.
THEY MUST KNOW I'M CLOSE.

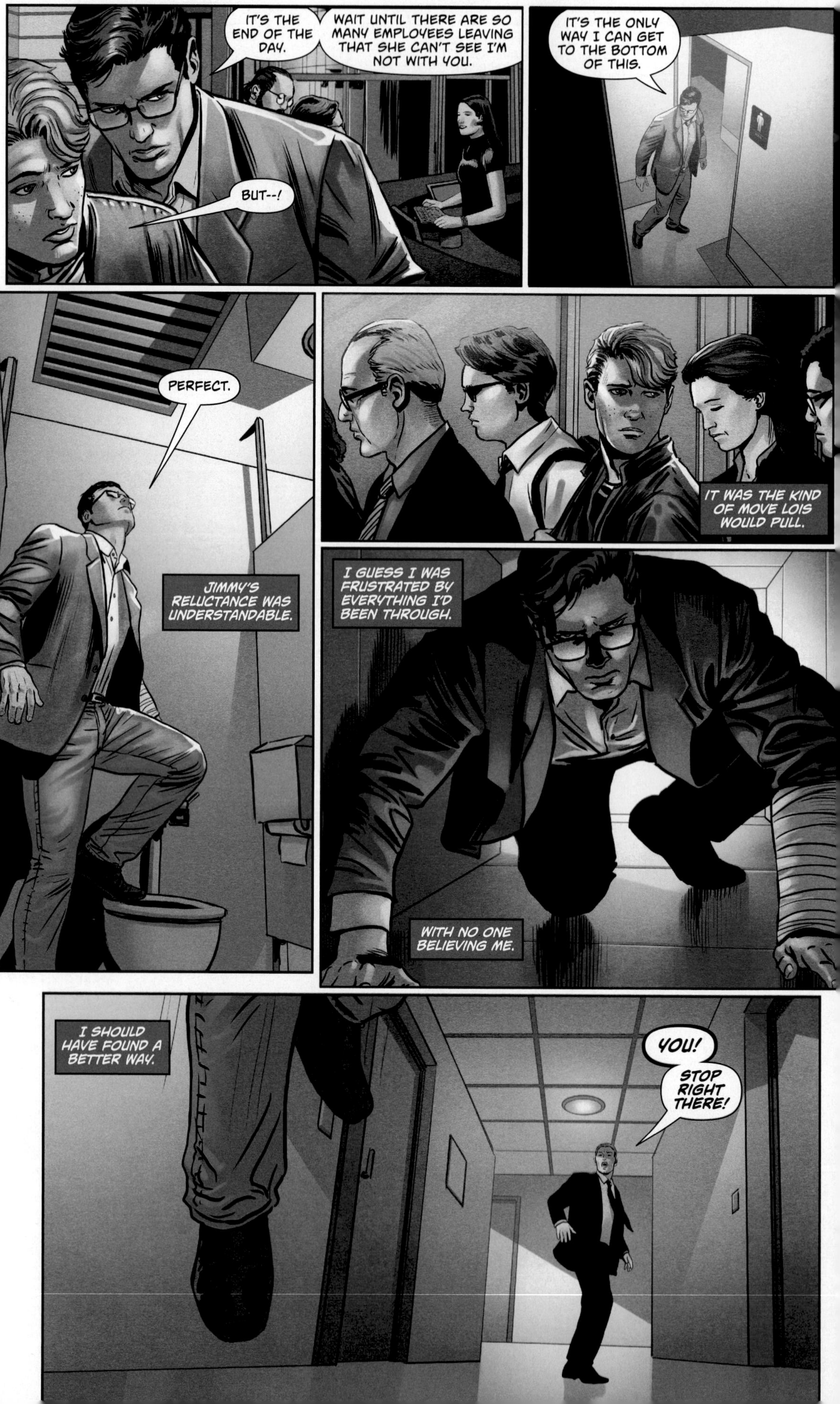
IT'S THE END OF THE DAY.
WAIT UNTIL THERE ARE SO MANY EMPLOYEES LEAVING THAT SHE CAN'T SEE I'M NOT WITH YOU.
BUT--!
IT'S THE ONLY WAY I CAN GET TO THE BOTTOM OF THIS.
PERFECT.
JIMMY'S RELUCTANCE WAS UNDERSTANDABLE.
IT WAS THE KIND OF MOVE LOIS WOULD PULL.
I GUESS I WAS FRUSTRATED BY EVERYTHING I'D BEEN THROUGH.
WITH NO ONE BELIEVING ME.
I SHOULD HAVE FOUND A BETTER WAY.
YOU!
STOP RIGHT THERE!

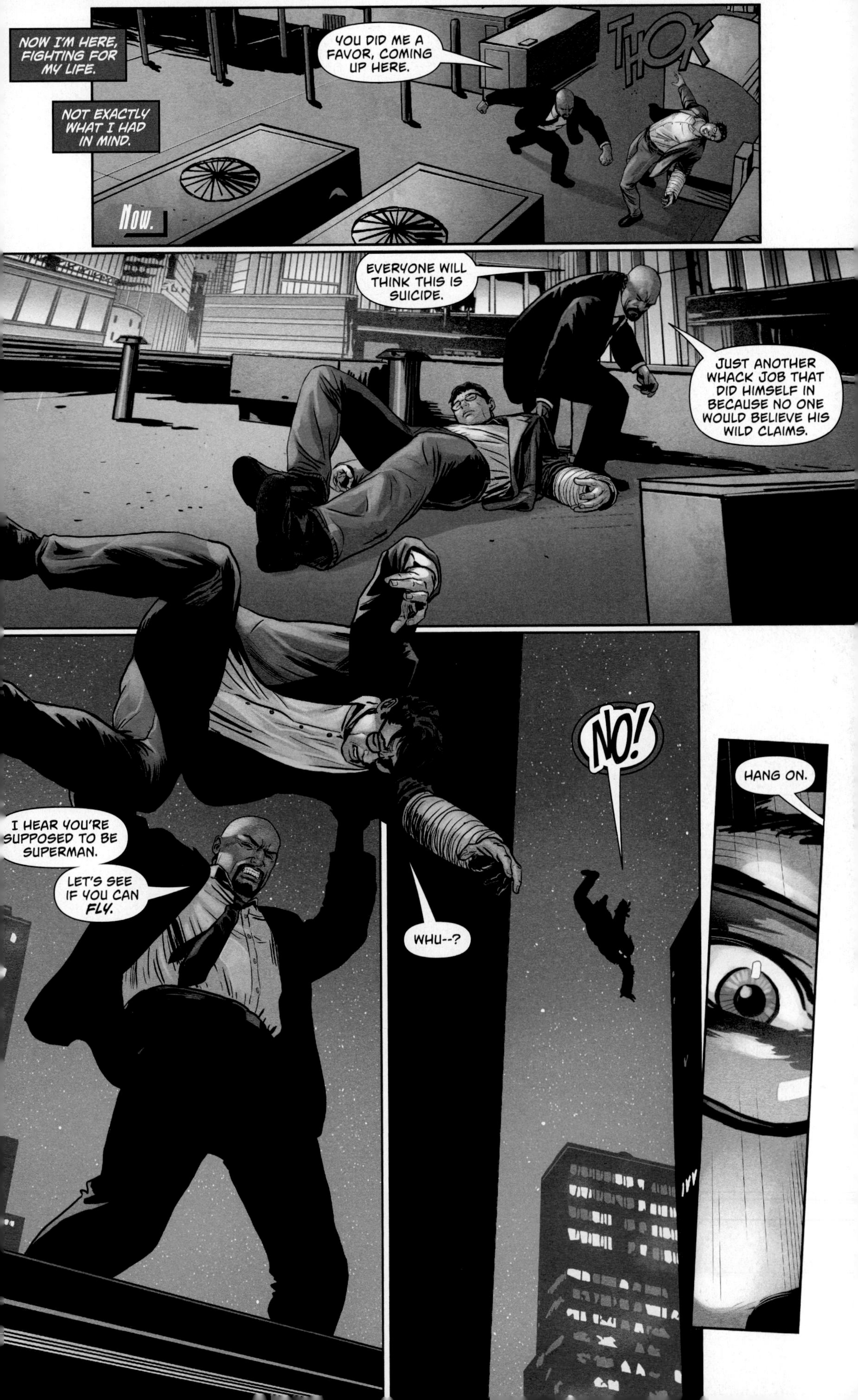
NOW I'M HERE, FIGHTING FOR MY LIFE.
NOT EXACTLY WHAT I HAD IN MIND.
Now.
YOU DID ME A FAVOR, COMING UP HERE.
THOK
EVERYONE WILL THINK THIS IS SUICIDE.
JUST ANOTHER WHACK JOB THAT DID HIMSELF IN BECAUSE NO ONE WOULD BELIEVE HIS WILD CLAIMS.
I HEAR YOU'RE SUPPOSED TO BE SUPERMAN.
LET'S SEE IF YOU CAN FLY.
WHU--?
NO!
HANG ON.

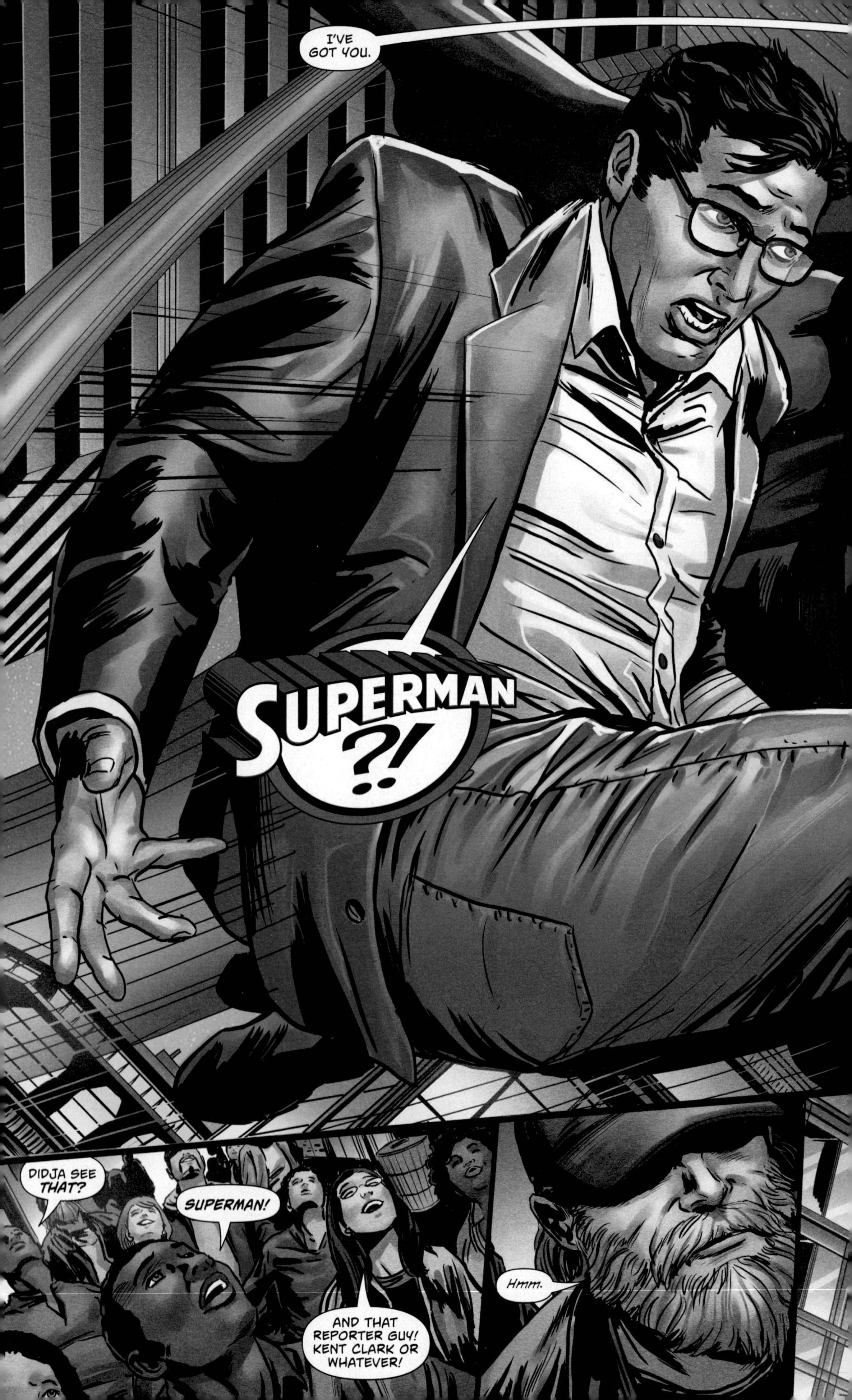
I'VE GOT YOU.
SUPERMAN ?!
DIDJA SEE THAT?
SUPERMAN!
AND THAT REPORTER GUY! KENT CLARK OR WHATEVER!
Hmm.

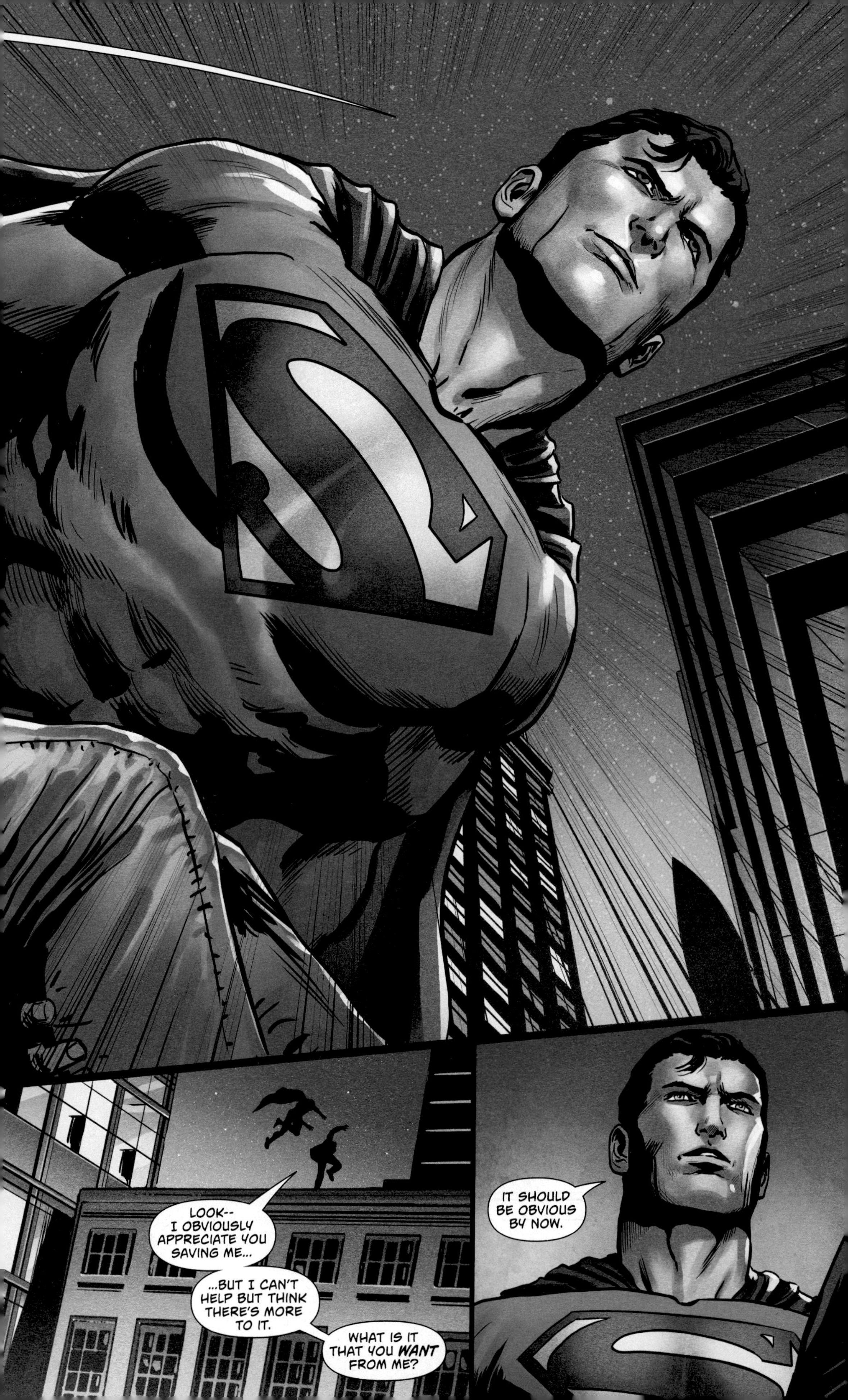
LOOK-- I OBVIOUSLY APPRECIATE YOU SAVING ME...
...BUT I CAN'T HELP BUT THINK THERE'S MORE TO IT.
WHAT IS IT THAT YOU *WANT* FROM ME?
IT SHOULD BE OBVIOUS BY NOW.

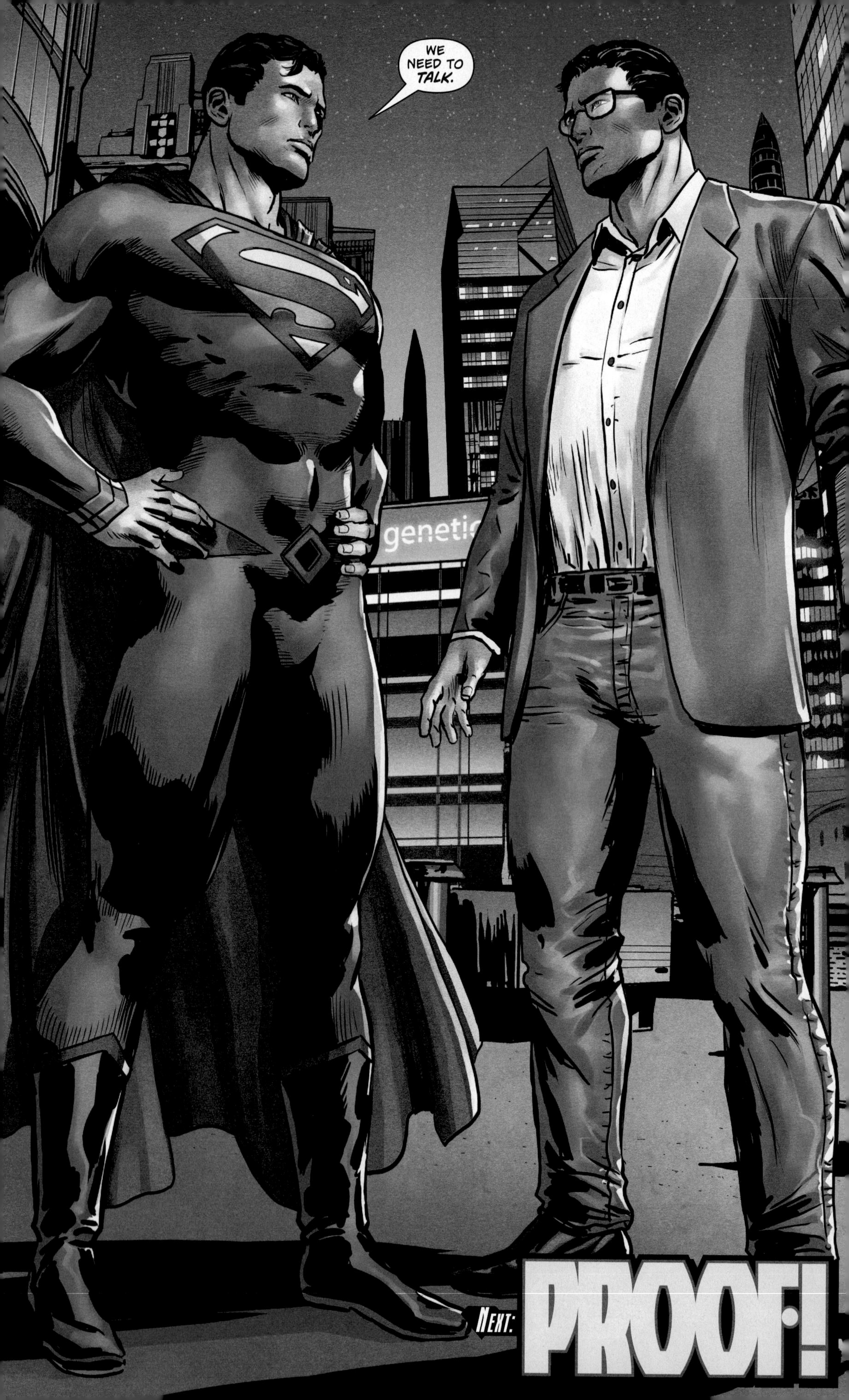
WE NEED TO TALK.
genetic
NEXT: PROOF!

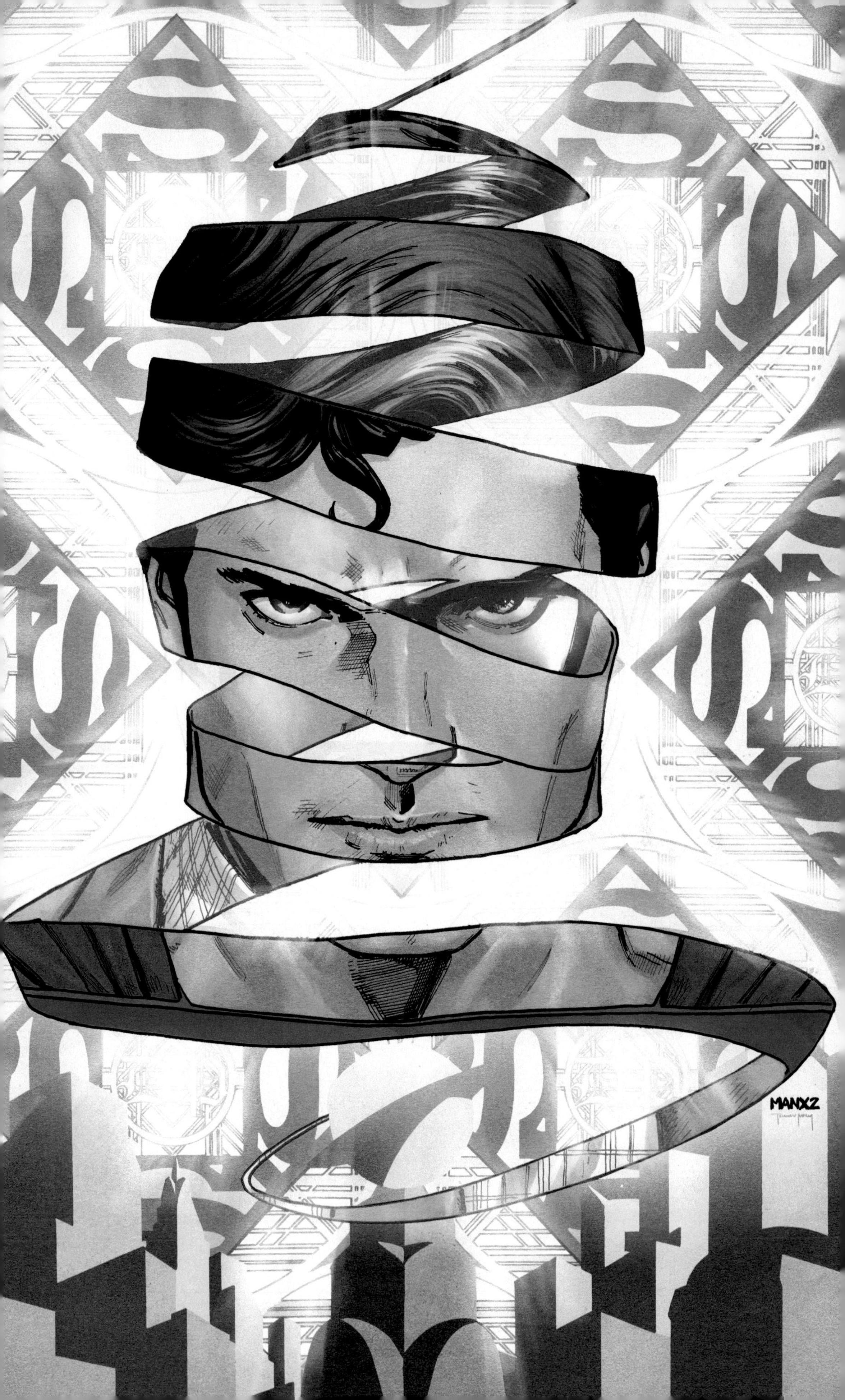
MANX2

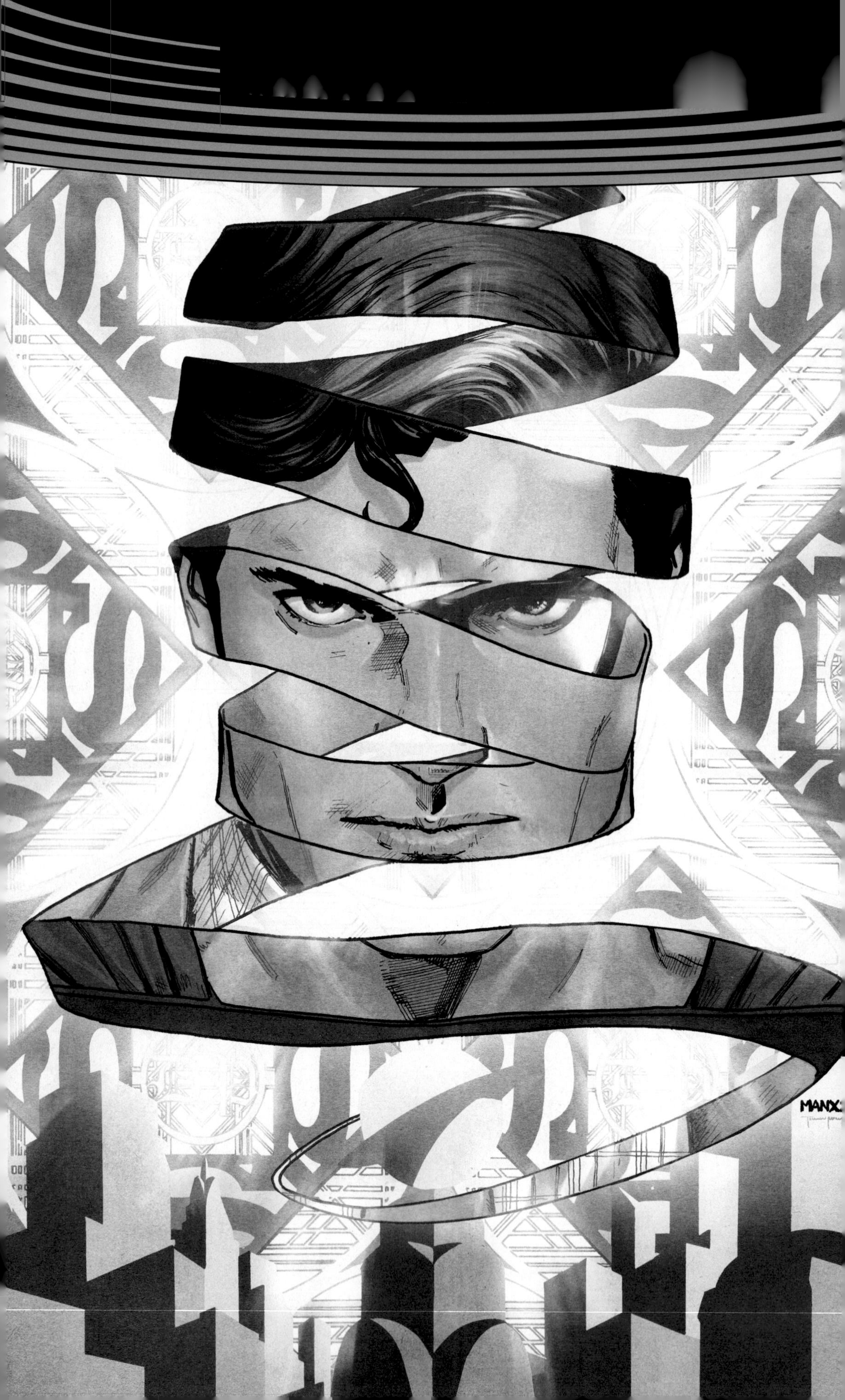
MANX

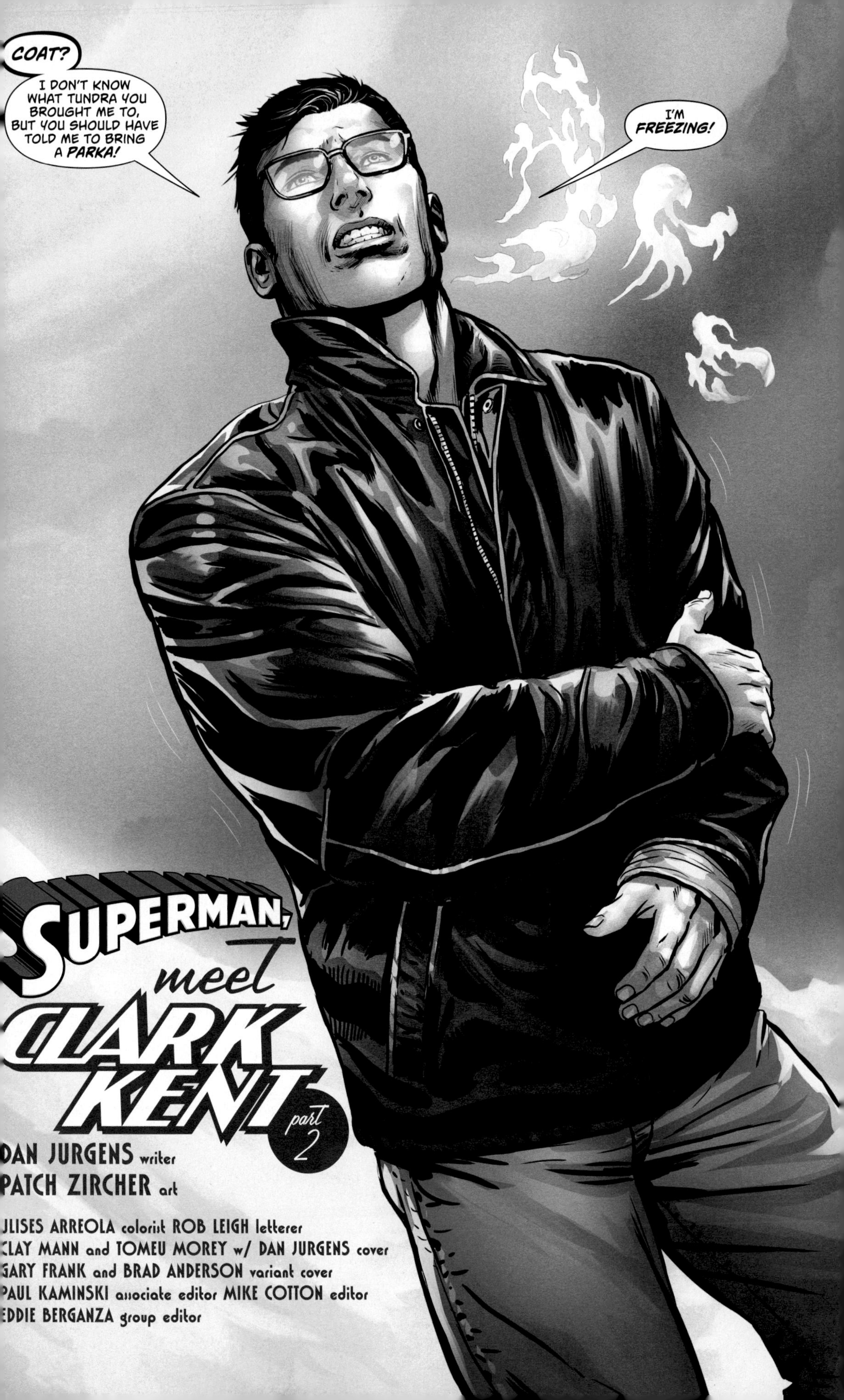
COAT?
I DON'T KNOW WHAT TUNDRA YOU BROUGHT ME TO, BUT YOU SHOULD HAVE TOLD ME TO BRING A PARKA!
I'M FREEZING!
SUPERMAN, meet CLARK KENT part 2
DAN JURGENS writer
PATCH ZIRCHER art
ULISES ARREOLA colorist ROB LEIGH letterer
CLAY MANN and TOMEU MOREY w/ DAN JURGENS cover
GARY FRANK and BRAD ANDERSON variant cover
PAUL KAMINSKI associate editor MIKE COTTON editor
EDDIE BERGANZA group editor

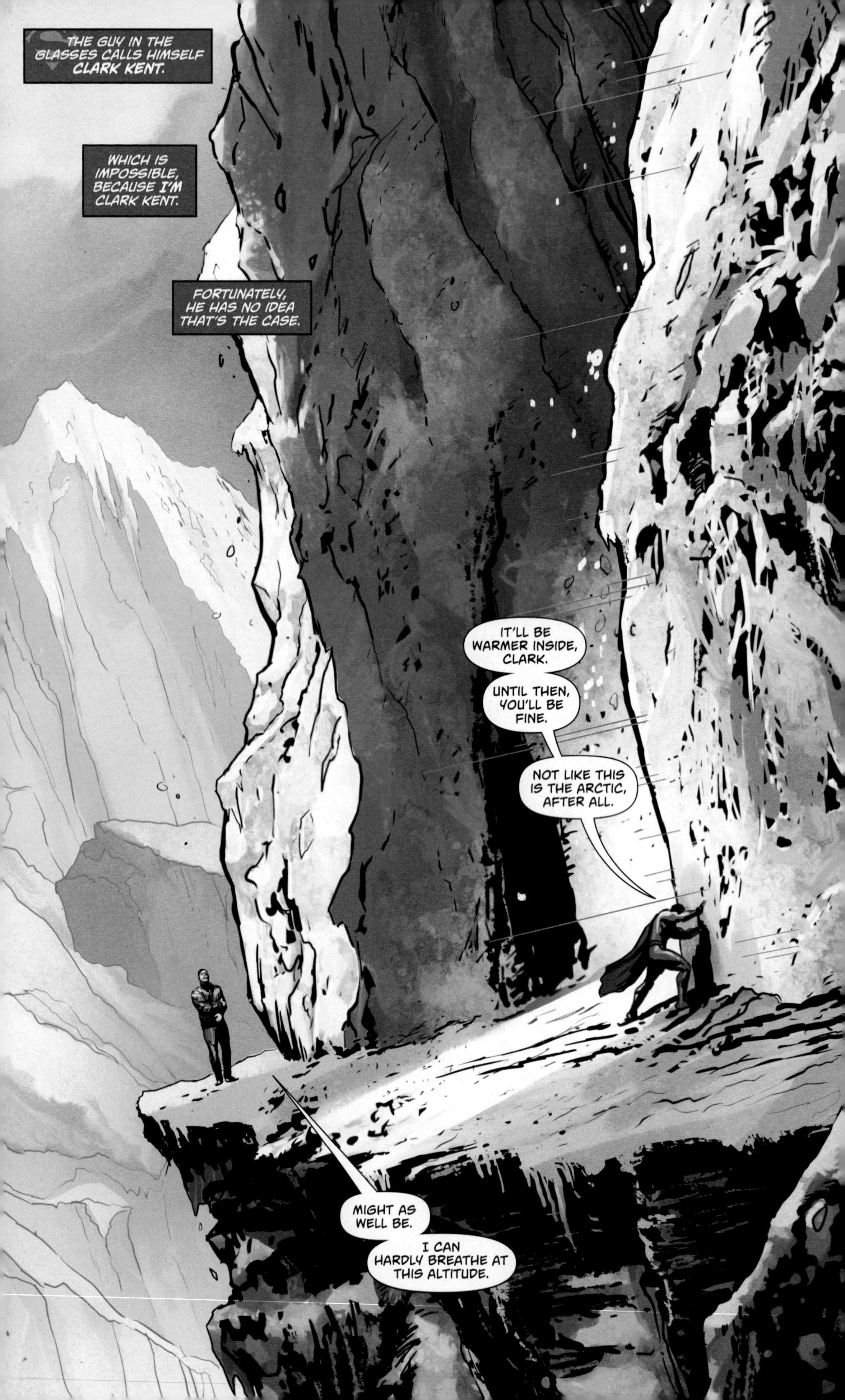

THE GUY IN THE GLASSES CALLS HIMSELF **CLARK KENT.**
WHICH IS IMPOSSIBLE, BECAUSE ***I'M*** CLARK KENT.
FORTUNATELY, HE HAS NO IDEA THAT'S THE CASE.
IT'LL BE WARMER INSIDE, CLARK.
UNTIL THEN, YOU'LL BE FINE.
NOT LIKE THIS IS THE ARCTIC, AFTER ALL.
MIGHT AS WELL BE.
I CAN HARDLY BREATHE AT THIS ALTITUDE.

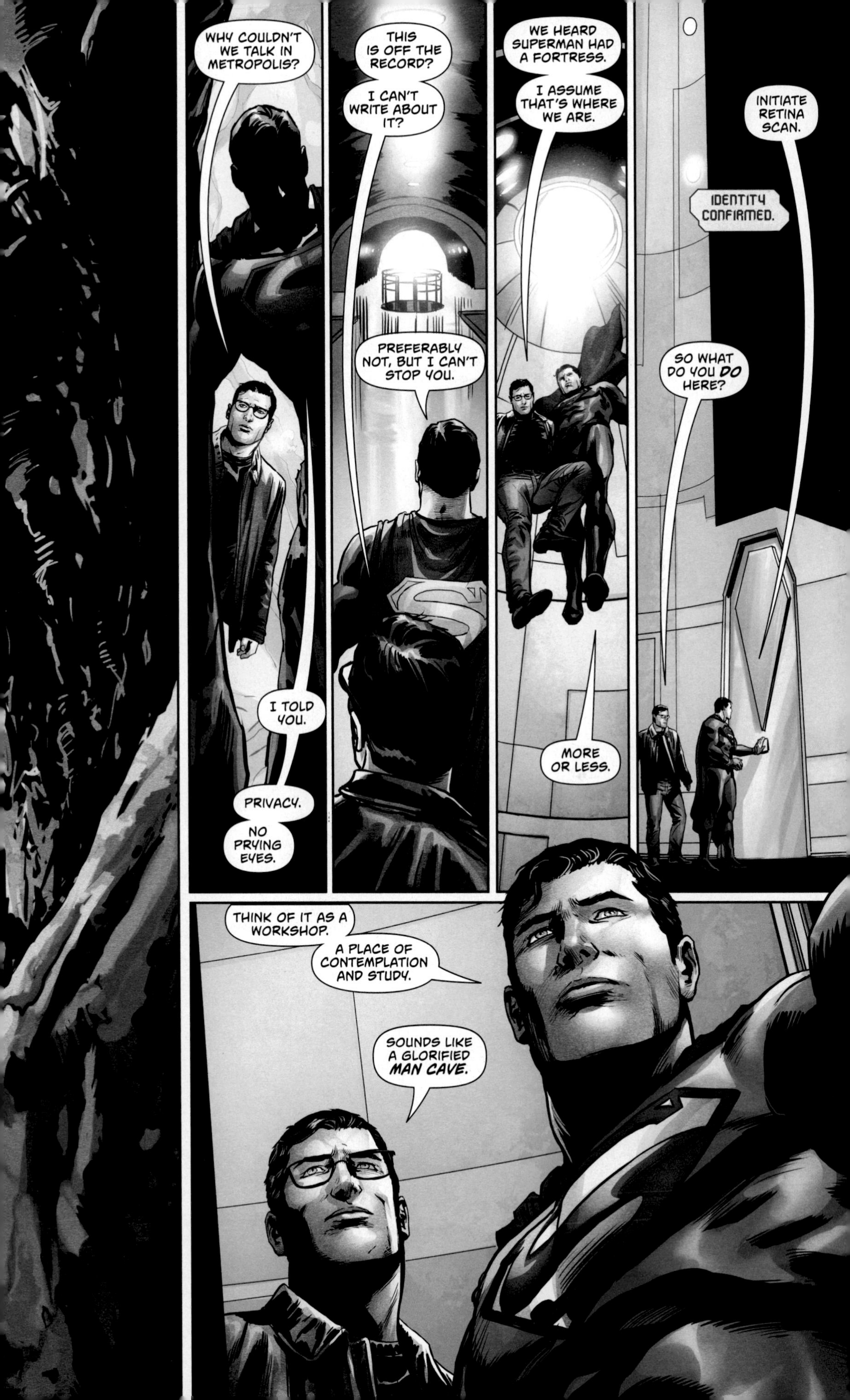
WHY COULDN'T WE TALK IN METROPOLIS?
I TOLD YOU.
PRIVACY.
NO PRYING EYES.
THIS IS OFF THE RECORD?
I CAN'T WRITE ABOUT IT?
PREFERABLY NOT, BUT I CAN'T STOP YOU.
WE HEARD SUPERMAN HAD A FORTRESS.
I ASSUME THAT'S WHERE WE ARE.
MORE OR LESS.
INITIATE RETINA SCAN.
IDENTITY CONFIRMED.
SO WHAT DO YOU *DO* HERE?
THINK OF IT AS A WORKSHOP.
A PLACE OF CONTEMPLATION AND STUDY.
SOUNDS LIKE A GLORIFIED *MAN CAVE.*

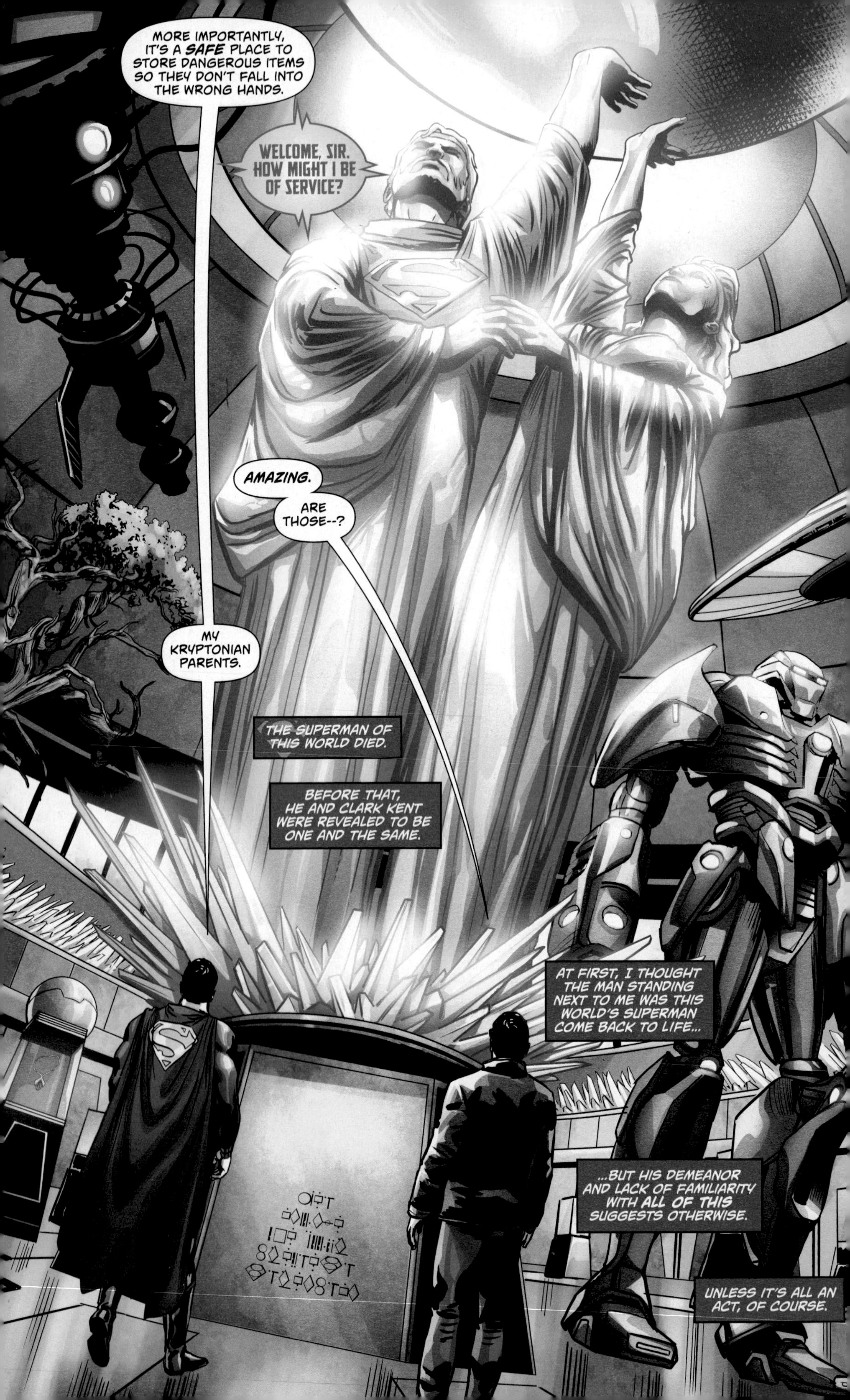
MORE IMPORTANTLY, IT'S A SAFE PLACE TO STORE DANGEROUS ITEMS SO THEY DON'T FALL INTO THE WRONG HANDS.
WELCOME, SIR. HOW MIGHT I BE OF SERVICE?
AMAZING.
ARE THOSE--?
MY KRYPTONIAN PARENTS.
THE SUPERMAN OF THIS WORLD DIED.
BEFORE THAT, HE AND CLARK KENT WERE REVEALED TO BE ONE AND THE SAME.
AT FIRST, I THOUGHT THE MAN STANDING NEXT TO ME WAS THIS WORLD'S SUPERMAN COME BACK TO LIFE...
...BUT HIS DEMEANOR AND LACK OF FAMILIARITY WITH ALL OF THIS SUGGESTS OTHERWISE.
UNLESS IT'S ALL AN ACT, OF COURSE.

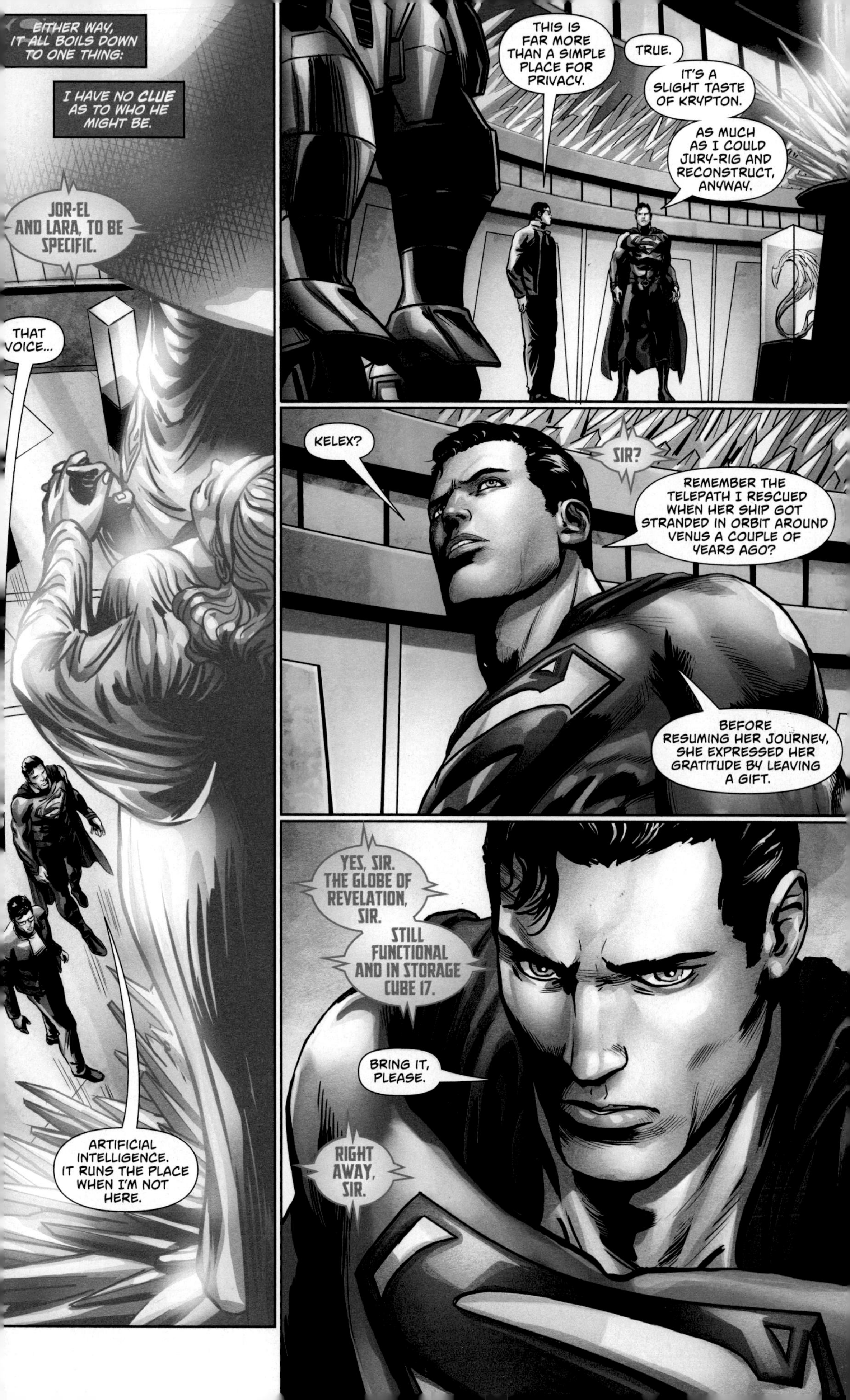
EITHER WAY, IT ALL BOILS DOWN TO ONE THING:
I HAVE NO CLUE AS TO WHO HE MIGHT BE.
JOR-EL AND LARA, TO BE SPECIFIC.
THAT VOICE...
ARTIFICIAL INTELLIGENCE. IT RUNS THE PLACE WHEN I'M NOT HERE.
THIS IS FAR MORE THAN A SIMPLE PLACE FOR PRIVACY.
TRUE.
IT'S A SLIGHT TASTE OF KRYPTON.
AS MUCH AS I COULD JURY-RIG AND RECONSTRUCT, ANYWAY.
KELEX?
SIR?
REMEMBER THE TELEPATH I RESCUED WHEN HER SHIP GOT STRANDED IN ORBIT AROUND VENUS A COUPLE OF YEARS AGO?
BEFORE RESUMING HER JOURNEY, SHE EXPRESSED HER GRATITUDE BY LEAVING A GIFT.
YES, SIR. THE GLOBE OF REVELATION, SIR.
STILL FUNCTIONAL AND IN STORAGE CUBE 17.
BRING IT, PLEASE.
RIGHT AWAY, SIR.

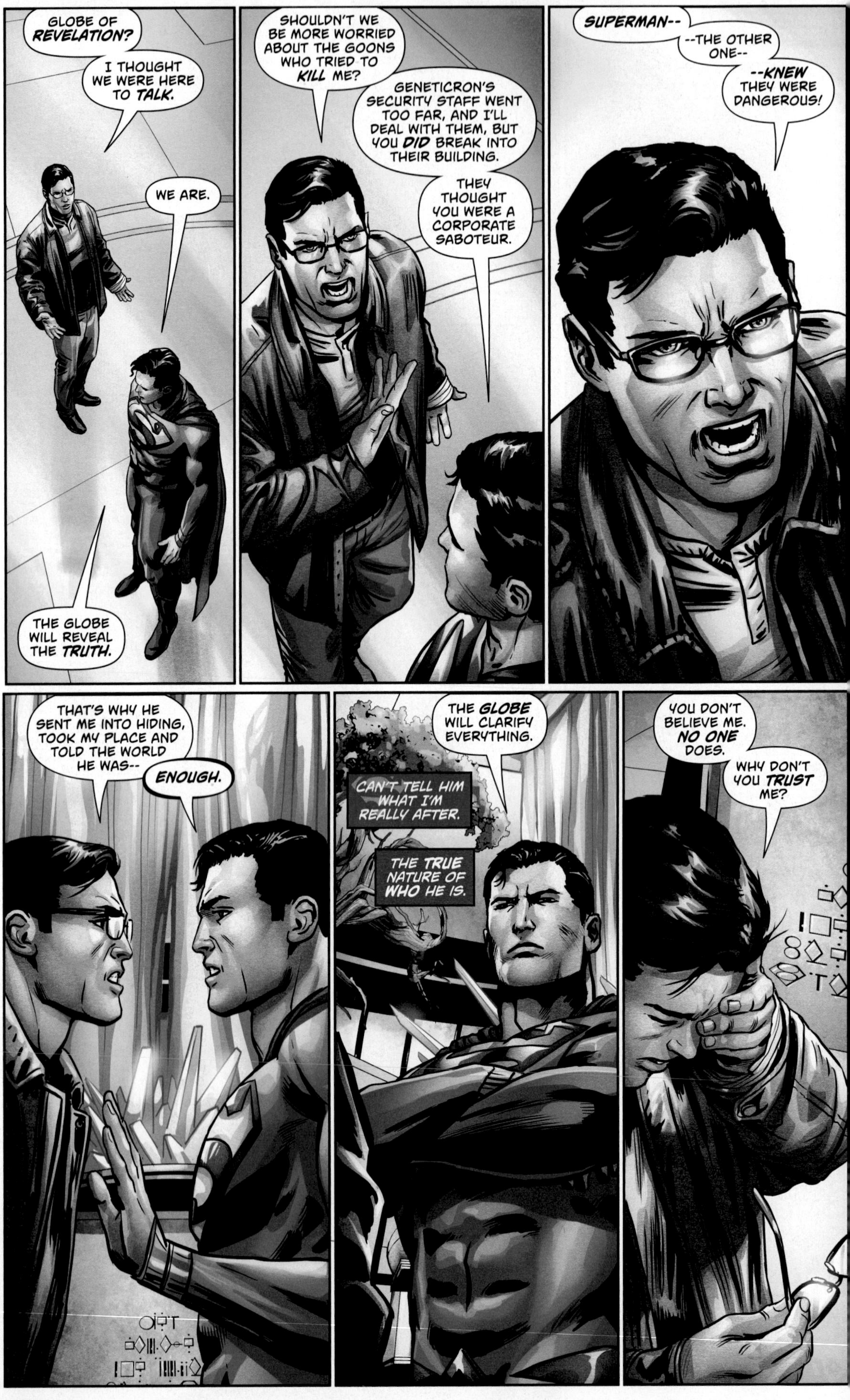
GLOBE OF *REVELATION?*
I THOUGHT WE WERE HERE TO *TALK.*
WE ARE.
THE GLOBE WILL REVEAL THE *TRUTH.*
SHOULDN'T WE BE MORE WORRIED ABOUT THE GOONS WHO TRIED TO *KILL* ME?
GENETICRON'S SECURITY STAFF WENT TOO FAR, AND I'LL DEAL WITH THEM, BUT YOU *DID* BREAK INTO THEIR BUILDING.
THEY THOUGHT YOU WERE A CORPORATE SABOTEUR.
SUPERMAN--
--THE OTHER ONE--
--KNEW THEY WERE DANGEROUS!
THAT'S WHY HE SENT ME INTO HIDING, TOOK MY PLACE AND TOLD THE WORLD HE WAS--
ENOUGH.
THE *GLOBE* WILL CLARIFY EVERYTHING.
CAN'T TELL HIM WHAT I'M REALLY AFTER.
THE *TRUE* NATURE OF *WHO* HE IS.
YOU DON'T BELIEVE ME. *NO ONE* DOES.
WHY DON'T YOU *TRUST* ME?

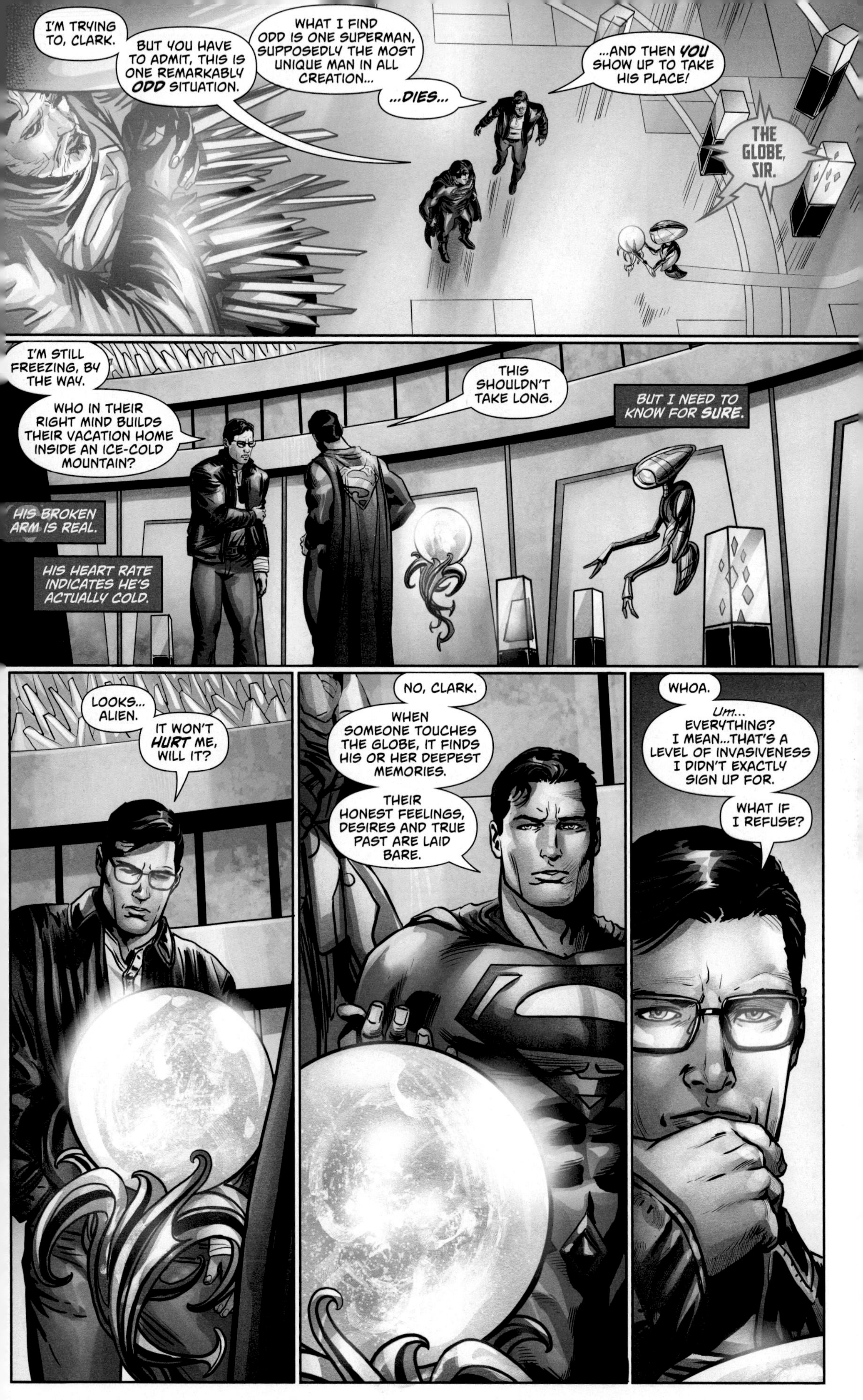
I'M TRYING TO, CLARK.
BUT YOU HAVE TO ADMIT, THIS IS ONE REMARKABLY ODD SITUATION.
WHAT I FIND ODD IS ONE SUPERMAN, SUPPOSEDLY THE MOST UNIQUE MAN IN ALL CREATION...
...DIES...
...AND THEN YOU SHOW UP TO TAKE HIS PLACE!
THE GLOBE, SIR.
I'M STILL FREEZING, BY THE WAY.
WHO IN THEIR RIGHT MIND BUILDS THEIR VACATION HOME INSIDE AN ICE-COLD MOUNTAIN?
THIS SHOULDN'T TAKE LONG.
BUT I NEED TO KNOW FOR SURE.
HIS BROKEN ARM IS REAL.
HIS HEART RATE INDICATES HE'S ACTUALLY COLD.
LOOKS... ALIEN.
IT WON'T HURT ME, WILL IT?
NO, CLARK.
WHEN SOMEONE TOUCHES THE GLOBE, IT FINDS HIS OR HER DEEPEST MEMORIES.
THEIR HONEST FEELINGS, DESIRES AND TRUE PAST ARE LAID BARE.
WHOA.
Um... EVERYTHING? I MEAN...THAT'S A LEVEL OF INVASIVENESS I DIDN'T EXACTLY SIGN UP FOR.
WHAT IF I REFUSE?

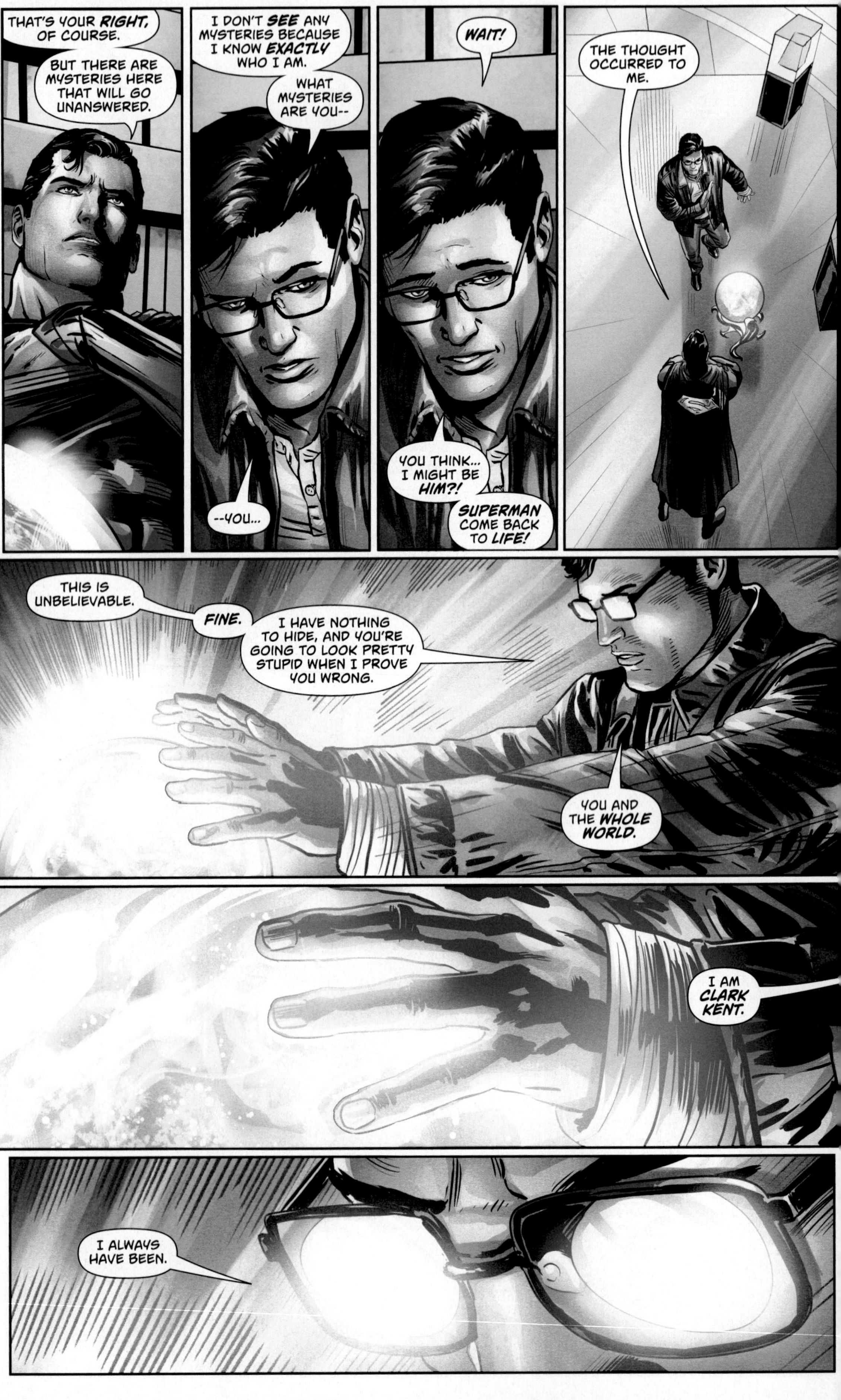
THAT'S YOUR RIGHT, OF COURSE.
BUT THERE ARE MYSTERIES HERE THAT WILL GO UNANSWERED.
I DON'T SEE ANY MYSTERIES BECAUSE I KNOW EXACTLY WHO I AM.
WHAT MYSTERIES ARE YOU--
--YOU...
WAIT!
YOU THINK... I MIGHT BE HIM?!
SUPERMAN COME BACK TO LIFE!
THE THOUGHT OCCURRED TO ME.
THIS IS UNBELIEVABLE.
FINE.
I HAVE NOTHING TO HIDE, AND YOU'RE GOING TO LOOK PRETTY STUPID WHEN I PROVE YOU WRONG.
YOU AND THE WHOLE WORLD.
I AM CLARK KENT.
I ALWAYS HAVE BEEN.

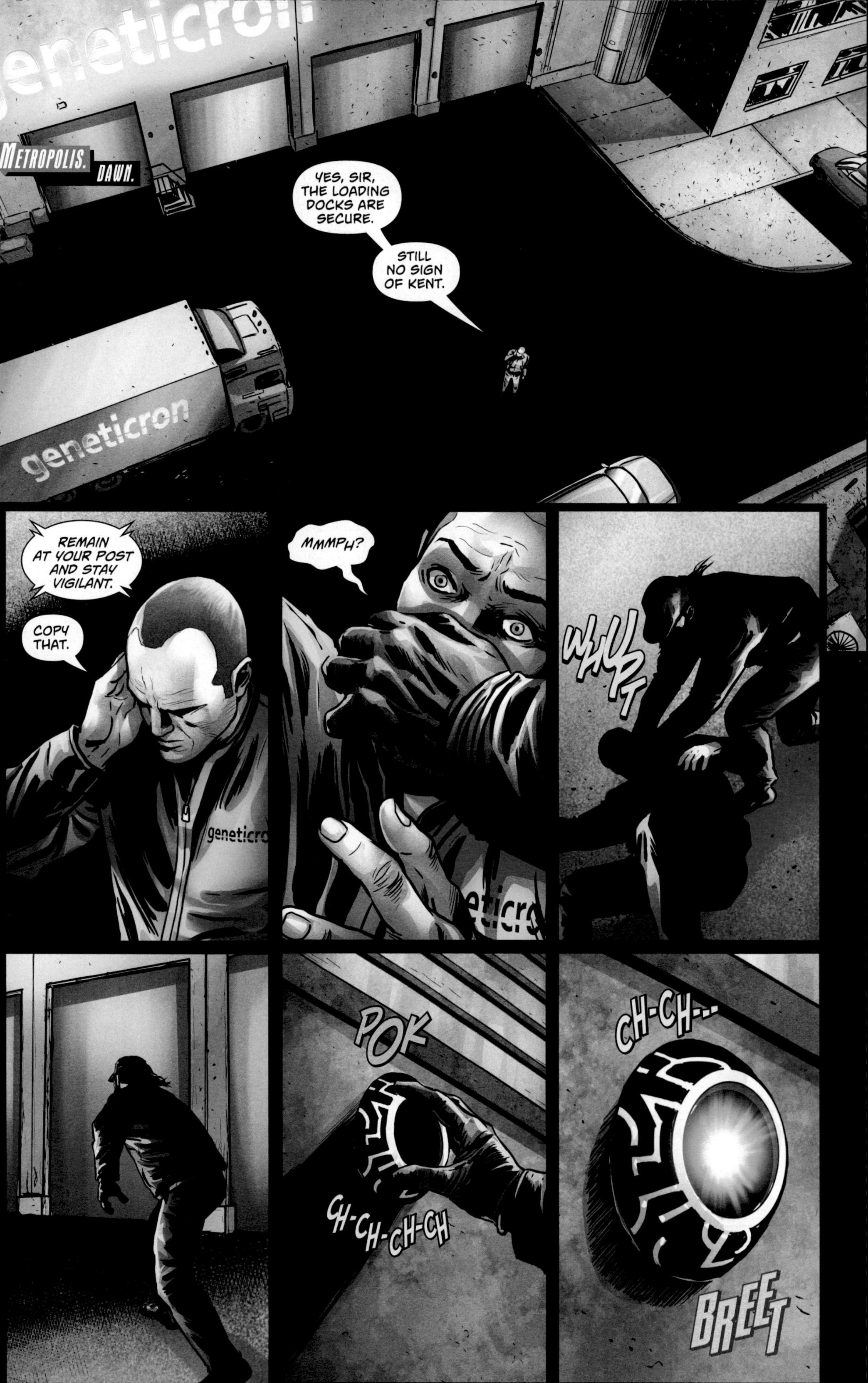
geneticron
METROPOLIS. DAWN.
YES, SIR, THE LOADING DOCKS ARE SECURE.
STILL NO SIGN OF KENT.
geneticron
REMAIN AT YOUR POST AND STAY VIGILANT.
COPY THAT.
geneticron
MMMPH?
WHUPT
POK
CH-CH-CH-CH
CH-CH--
BREET

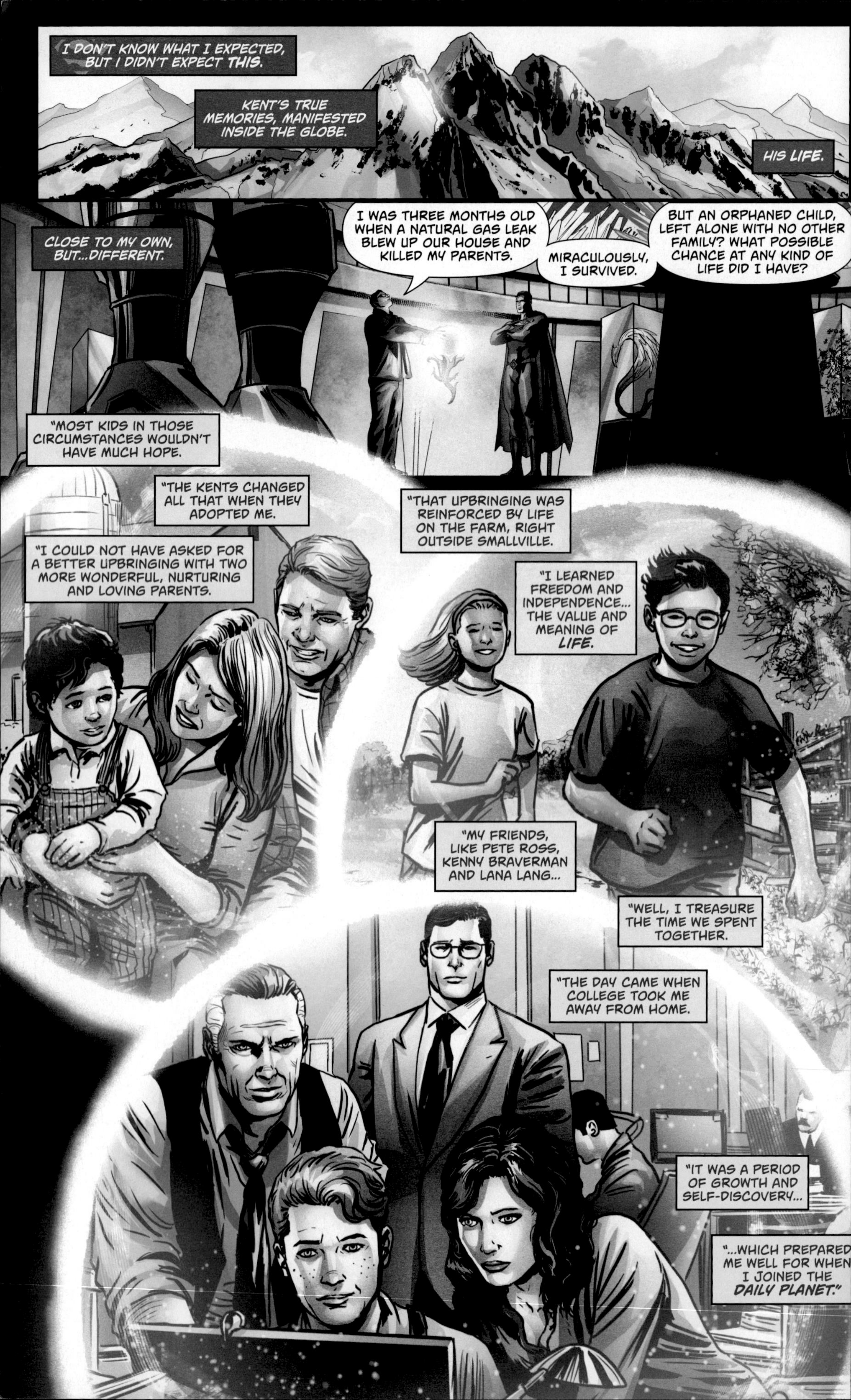
I DON'T KNOW WHAT I EXPECTED, BUT I DIDN'T EXPECT THIS.
KENT'S TRUE MEMORIES, MANIFESTED INSIDE THE GLOBE.
HIS LIFE.
CLOSE TO MY OWN, BUT...DIFFERENT.
I WAS THREE MONTHS OLD WHEN A NATURAL GAS LEAK BLEW UP OUR HOUSE AND KILLED MY PARENTS.
MIRACULOUSLY, I SURVIVED.
BUT AN ORPHANED CHILD, LEFT ALONE WITH NO OTHER FAMILY? WHAT POSSIBLE CHANCE AT ANY KIND OF LIFE DID I HAVE?
"MOST KIDS IN THOSE CIRCUMSTANCES WOULDN'T HAVE MUCH HOPE.
"THE KENTS CHANGED ALL THAT WHEN THEY ADOPTED ME.
"I COULD NOT HAVE ASKED FOR A BETTER UPBRINGING WITH TWO MORE WONDERFUL, NURTURING AND LOVING PARENTS.
"THAT UPBRINGING WAS REINFORCED BY LIFE ON THE FARM, RIGHT OUTSIDE SMALLVILLE.
"I LEARNED FREEDOM AND INDEPENDENCE... THE VALUE AND MEANING OF LIFE.
"MY FRIENDS, LIKE PETE ROSS, KENNY BRAVERMAN AND LANA LANG...
"WELL, I TREASURE THE TIME WE SPENT TOGETHER.
"THE DAY CAME WHEN COLLEGE TOOK ME AWAY FROM HOME.
"IT WAS A PERIOD OF GROWTH AND SELF-DISCOVERY...
"...WHICH PREPARED ME WELL FOR WHEN I JOINED THE DAILY PLANET."

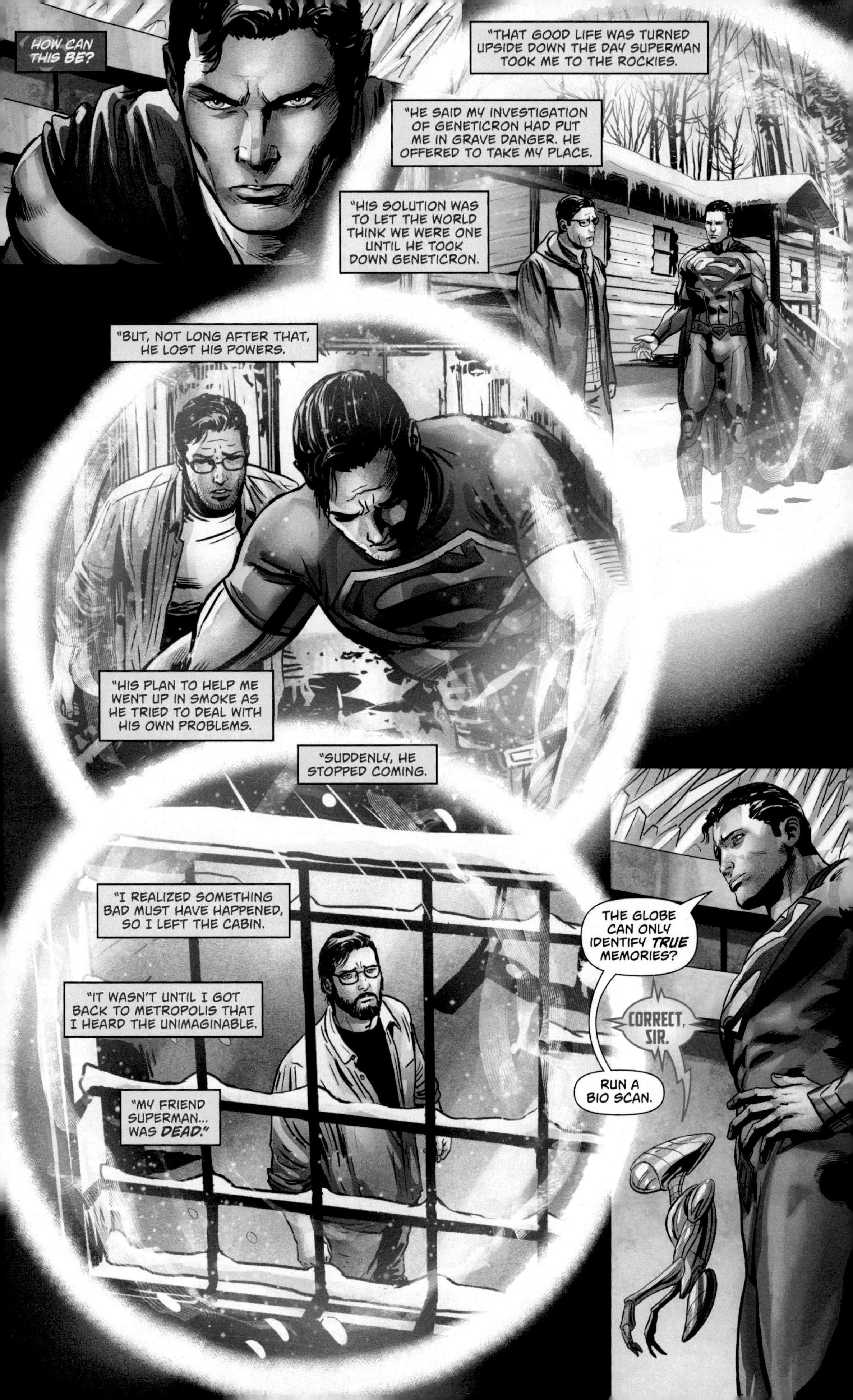
HOW CAN THIS BE?
"THAT GOOD LIFE WAS TURNED UPSIDE DOWN THE DAY SUPERMAN TOOK ME TO THE ROCKIES.
"HE SAID MY INVESTIGATION OF GENETICRON HAD PUT ME IN GRAVE DANGER. HE OFFERED TO TAKE MY PLACE.
"HIS SOLUTION WAS TO LET THE WORLD THINK WE WERE ONE UNTIL HE TOOK DOWN GENETICRON.
"BUT, NOT LONG AFTER THAT, HE LOST HIS POWERS.
"HIS PLAN TO HELP ME WENT UP IN SMOKE AS HE TRIED TO DEAL WITH HIS OWN PROBLEMS.
"SUDDENLY, HE STOPPED COMING.
"I REALIZED SOMETHING BAD MUST HAVE HAPPENED, SO I LEFT THE CABIN.
"IT WASN'T UNTIL I GOT BACK TO METROPOLIS THAT I HEARD THE UNIMAGINABLE.
"MY FRIEND SUPERMAN... WAS *DEAD.*"
THE GLOBE CAN ONLY IDENTIFY *TRUE* MEMORIES?
CORRECT, SIR.
RUN A BIO SCAN.

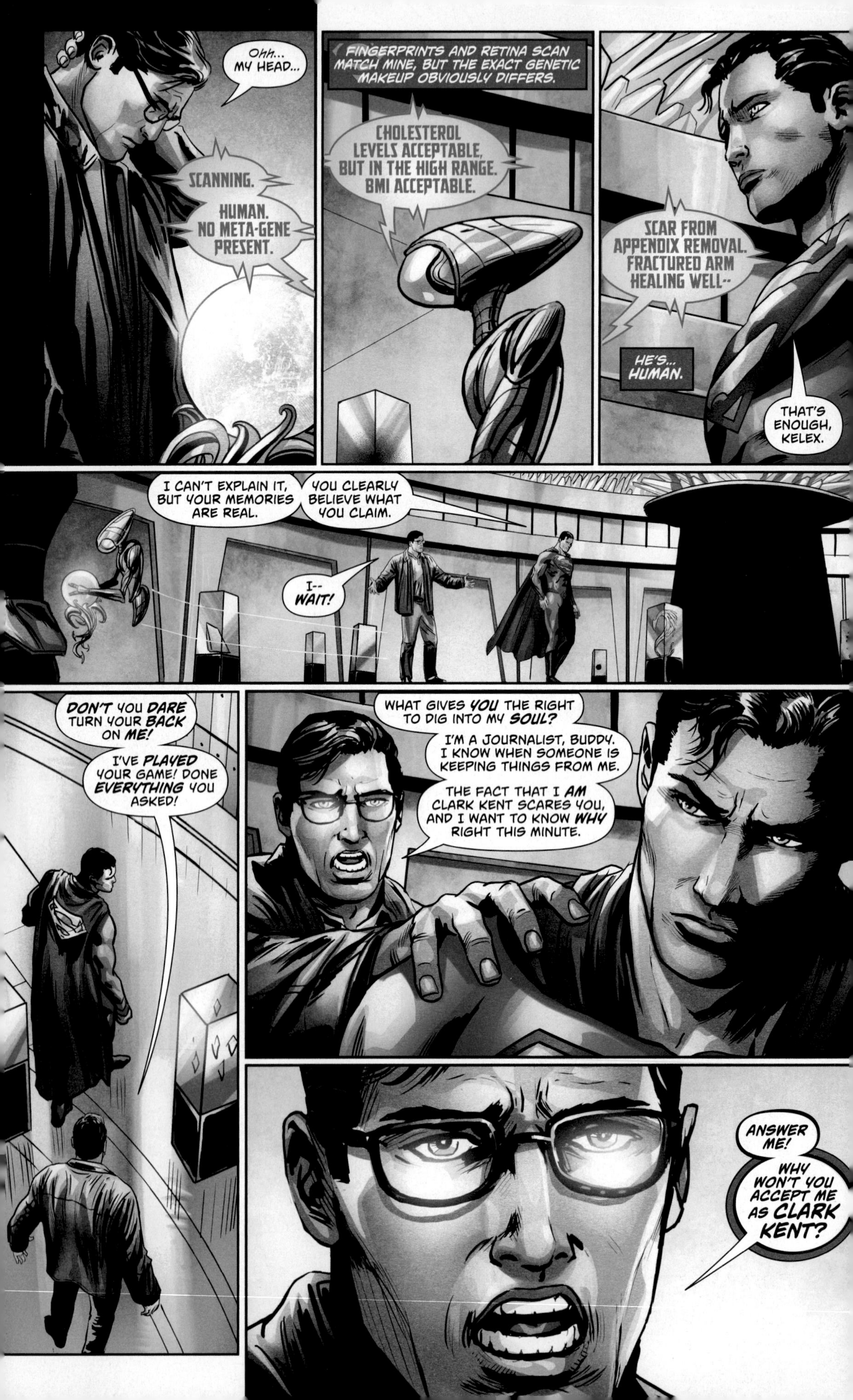

Ohh... MY HEAD...
SCANNING.
HUMAN. NO META-GENE PRESENT.
FINGERPRINTS AND RETINA SCAN MATCH MINE, BUT THE EXACT GENETIC MAKEUP OBVIOUSLY DIFFERS.
CHOLESTEROL LEVELS ACCEPTABLE, BUT IN THE HIGH RANGE. BMI ACCEPTABLE.
SCAR FROM APPENDIX REMOVAL. FRACTURED ARM HEALING WELL--
HE'S... HUMAN.
THAT'S ENOUGH, KELEX.
I CAN'T EXPLAIN IT, BUT YOUR MEMORIES ARE REAL.
YOU CLEARLY BELIEVE WHAT YOU CLAIM.
I-- WAIT!
DON'T YOU DARE TURN YOUR BACK ON ME!
I'VE PLAYED YOUR GAME! DONE EVERYTHING YOU ASKED!
WHAT GIVES YOU THE RIGHT TO DIG INTO MY SOUL?
I'M A JOURNALIST, BUDDY. I KNOW WHEN SOMEONE IS KEEPING THINGS FROM ME.
THE FACT THAT I AM CLARK KENT SCARES YOU, AND I WANT TO KNOW WHY RIGHT THIS MINUTE.
ANSWER ME!
WHY WON'T YOU ACCEPT ME AS CLARK KENT?

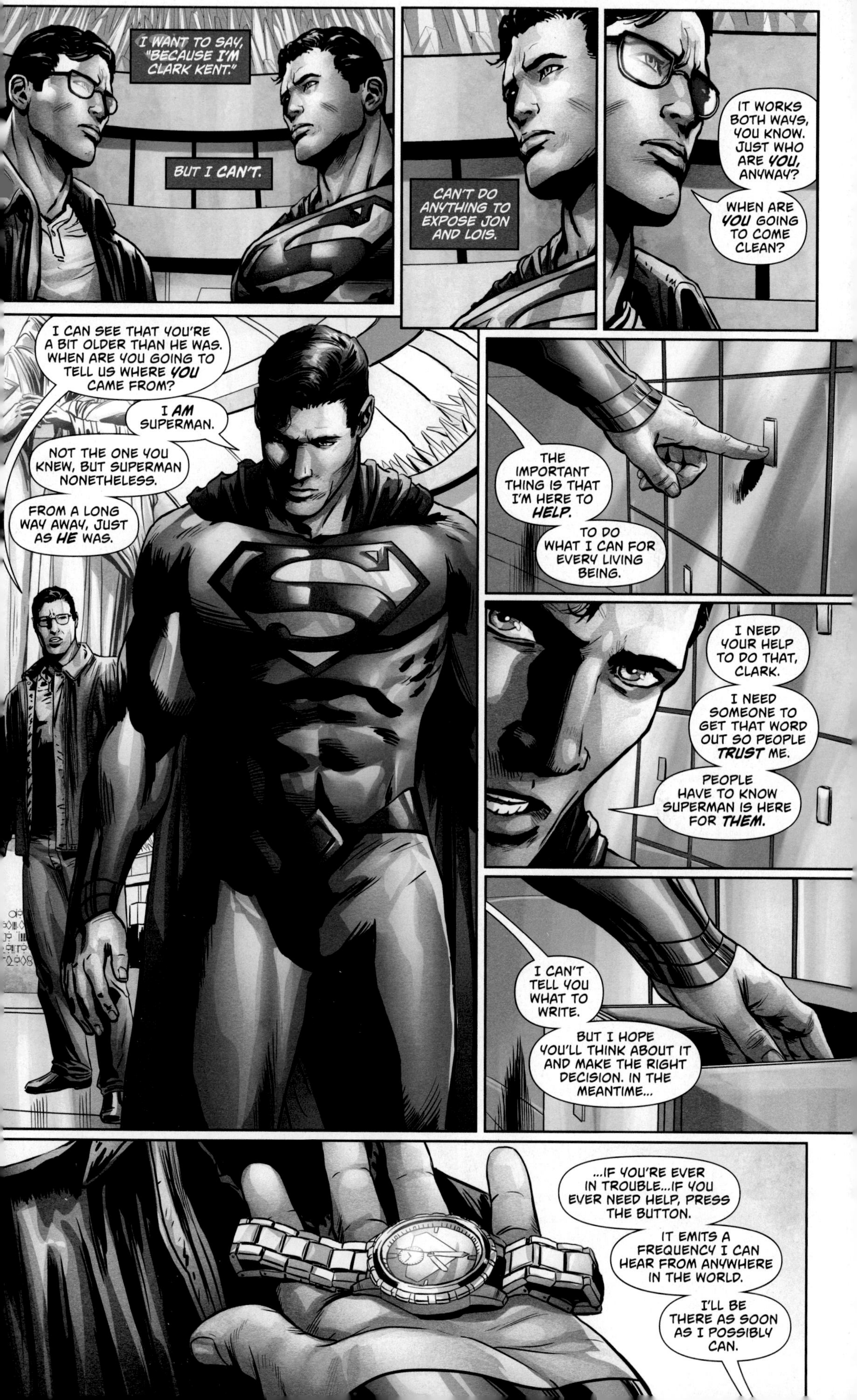
I WANT TO SAY, "BECAUSE I'M CLARK KENT."
BUT I CAN'T.
CAN'T DO ANYTHING TO EXPOSE JON AND LOIS.
IT WORKS BOTH WAYS, YOU KNOW. JUST WHO ARE YOU, ANYWAY?
WHEN ARE YOU GOING TO COME CLEAN?
I CAN SEE THAT YOU'RE A BIT OLDER THAN HE WAS. WHEN ARE YOU GOING TO TELL US WHERE YOU CAME FROM?
I AM SUPERMAN.
NOT THE ONE YOU KNEW, BUT SUPERMAN NONETHELESS.
FROM A LONG WAY AWAY, JUST AS HE WAS.
THE IMPORTANT THING IS THAT I'M HERE TO HELP.
TO DO WHAT I CAN FOR EVERY LIVING BEING.
I NEED YOUR HELP TO DO THAT, CLARK.
I NEED SOMEONE TO GET THAT WORD OUT SO PEOPLE TRUST ME.
PEOPLE HAVE TO KNOW SUPERMAN IS HERE FOR THEM.
I CAN'T TELL YOU WHAT TO WRITE.
BUT I HOPE YOU'LL THINK ABOUT IT AND MAKE THE RIGHT DECISION. IN THE MEANTIME...
...IF YOU'RE EVER IN TROUBLE...IF YOU EVER NEED HELP, PRESS THE BUTTON.
IT EMITS A FREQUENCY I CAN HEAR FROM ANYWHERE IN THE WORLD.
I'LL BE THERE AS SOON AS I POSSIBLY CAN.

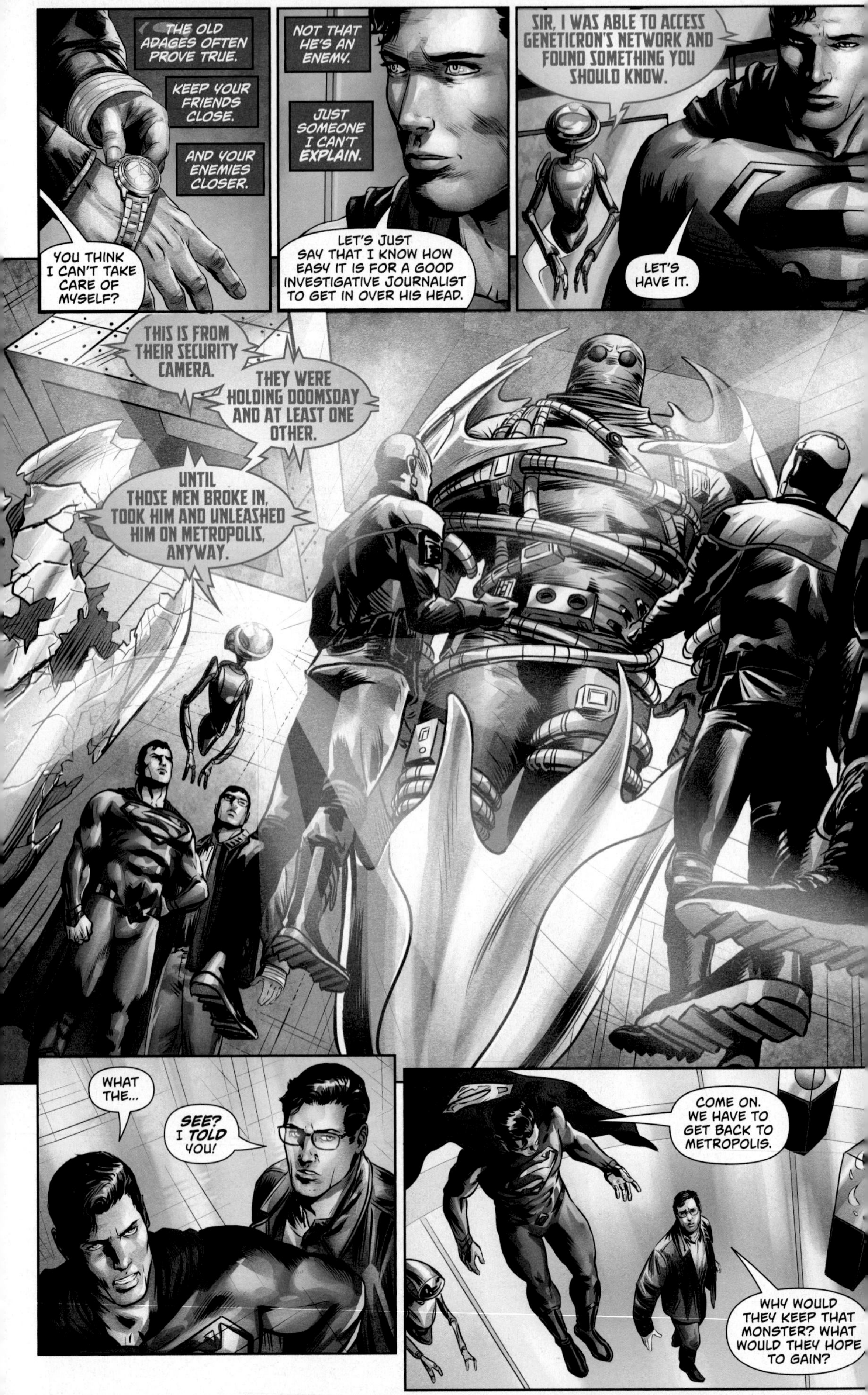
THE OLD ADAGES OFTEN PROVE TRUE.
KEEP YOUR FRIENDS CLOSE.
AND YOUR ENEMIES CLOSER.
YOU THINK I CAN'T TAKE CARE OF MYSELF?
NOT THAT HE'S AN ENEMY.
JUST SOMEONE I CAN'T EXPLAIN.
LET'S JUST SAY THAT I KNOW HOW EASY IT IS FOR A GOOD INVESTIGATIVE JOURNALIST TO GET IN OVER HIS HEAD.
SIR, I WAS ABLE TO ACCESS GENETICRON'S NETWORK AND FOUND SOMETHING YOU SHOULD KNOW.
LET'S HAVE IT.
THIS IS FROM THEIR SECURITY CAMERA.
THEY WERE HOLDING DOOMSDAY AND AT LEAST ONE OTHER.
UNTIL THOSE MEN BROKE IN, TOOK HIM AND UNLEASHED HIM ON METROPOLIS, ANYWAY.
WHAT THE...
SEE? I TOLD YOU!
COME ON. WE HAVE TO GET BACK TO METROPOLIS.
WHY WOULD THEY KEEP THAT MONSTER? WHAT WOULD THEY HOPE TO GAIN?

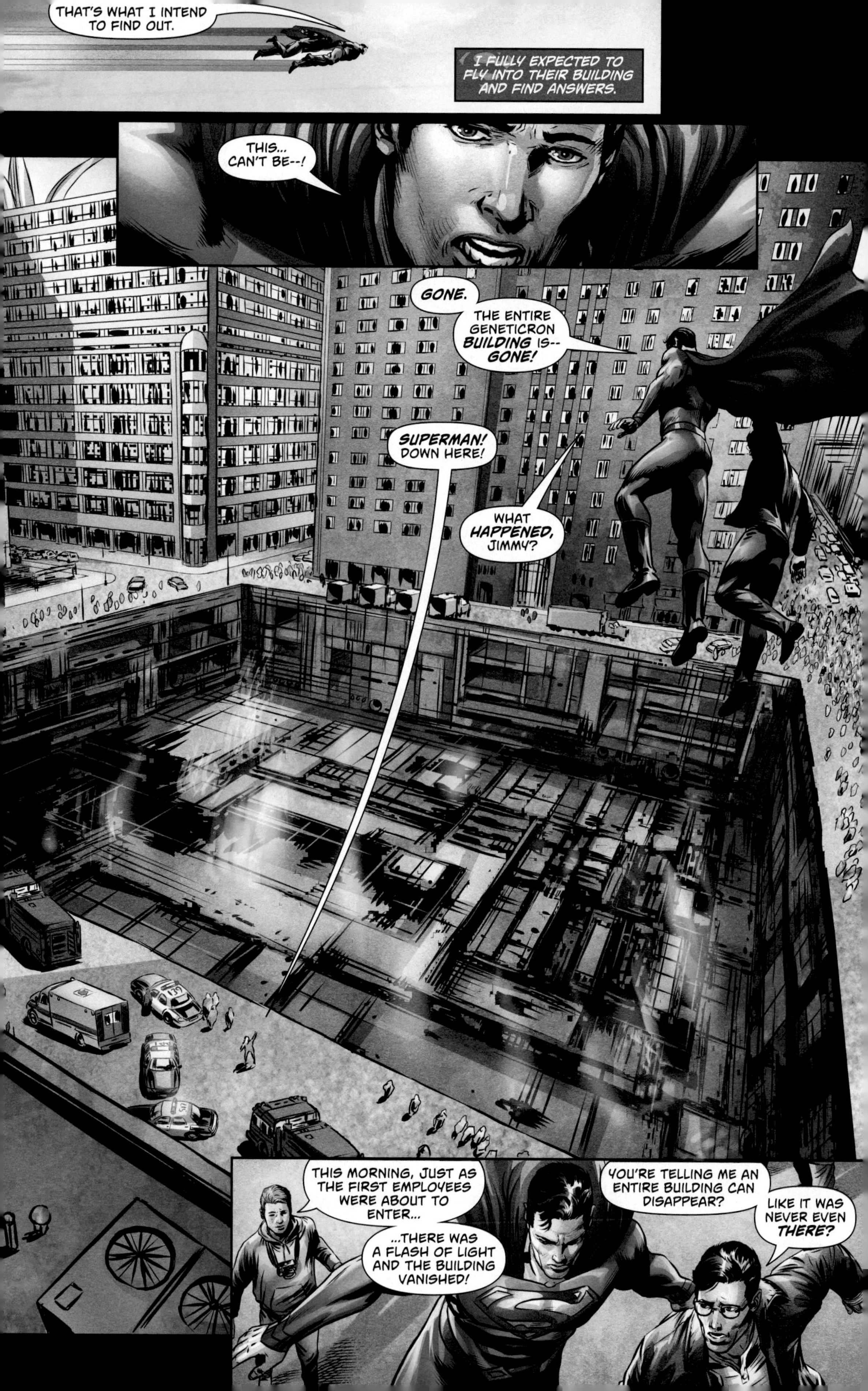
THAT'S WHAT I INTEND TO FIND OUT.
I FULLY EXPECTED TO FLY INTO THEIR BUILDING AND FIND ANSWERS.
THIS... CAN'T BE--!
GONE.
THE ENTIRE GENETICRON BUILDING IS-- GONE!
SUPERMAN! DOWN HERE!
WHAT HAPPENED, JIMMY?
THIS MORNING, JUST AS THE FIRST EMPLOYEES WERE ABOUT TO ENTER...
...THERE WAS A FLASH OF LIGHT AND THE BUILDING VANISHED!
YOU'RE TELLING ME AN ENTIRE BUILDING CAN DISAPPEAR?
LIKE IT WAS NEVER EVEN THERE?

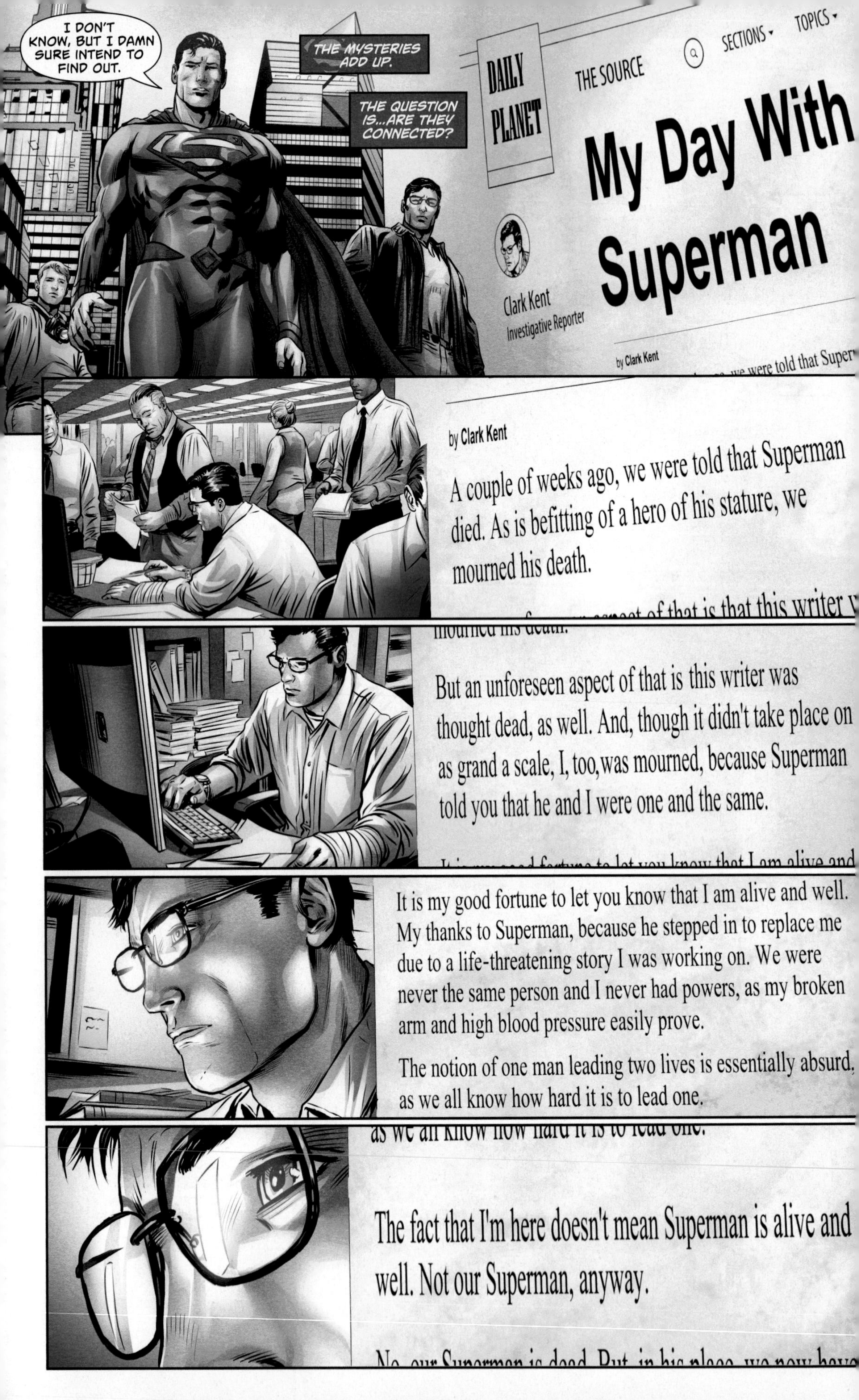
I DON'T KNOW, BUT I DAMN SURE INTEND TO FIND OUT.
THE MYSTERIES ADD UP.
THE QUESTION IS...ARE THEY CONNECTED?
DAILY PLANET
THE SOURCE
SECTIONS
TOPICS
My Day With Superman
Clark Kent
Investigative Reporter
by Clark Kent
by Clark Kent
A couple of weeks ago, we were told that Superman died. As is befitting of a hero of his stature, we mourned his death.
But an unforeseen aspect of that is this writer was thought dead, as well. And, though it didn't take place on as grand a scale, I, too, was mourned, because Superman told you that he and I were one and the same.
It is my good fortune to let you know that I am alive and well. My thanks to Superman, because he stepped in to replace me due to a life-threatening story I was working on. We were never the same person and I never had powers, as my broken arm and high blood pressure easily prove.
The notion of one man leading two lives is essentially absurd, as we all know how hard it is to lead one.
The fact that I'm here doesn't mean Superman is alive and well. Not our Superman, anyway.

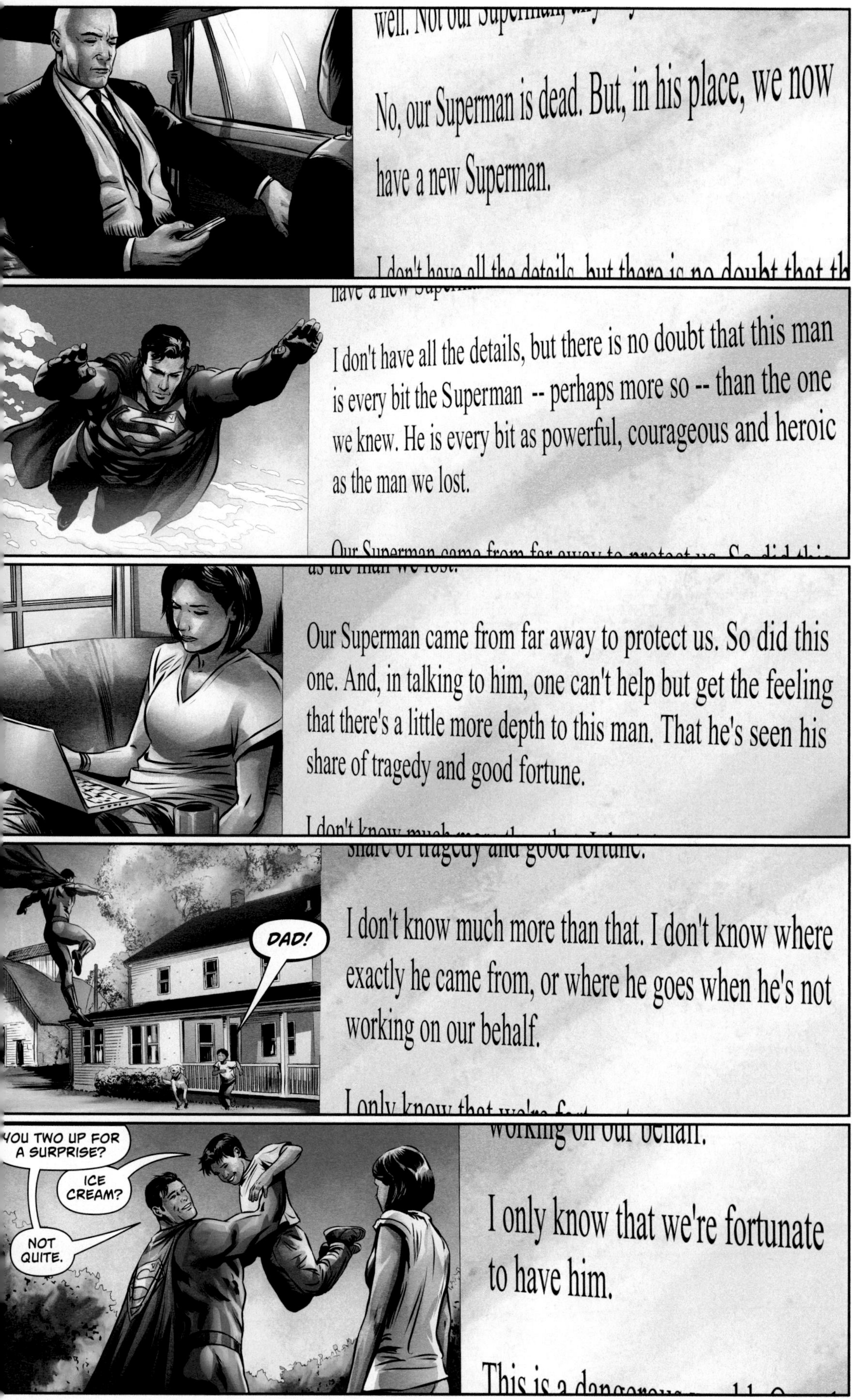

well. Not our Superman, any...

No, our Superman is dead. But, in his place, we now have a new Superman.

I don't have all the details, but there is no doubt that th...

I don't have all the details, but there is no doubt that this man is every bit the Superman -- perhaps more so -- than the one we knew. He is every bit as powerful, courageous and heroic as the man we lost.

Our Superman came from far away to protect us. So did this...

Our Superman came from far away to protect us. So did this one. And, in talking to him, one can't help but get the feeling that there's a little more depth to this man. That he's seen his share of tragedy and good fortune.

I don't know much more than that. I don't...

DAD!

I don't know much more than that. I don't know where exactly he came from, or where he goes when he's not working on our behalf.

I only know that we're f... working on our behalf.

YOU TWO UP FOR A SURPRISE?

ICE CREAM?

NOT QUITE.

I only know that we're fortunate to have him.

This is a dangerous...

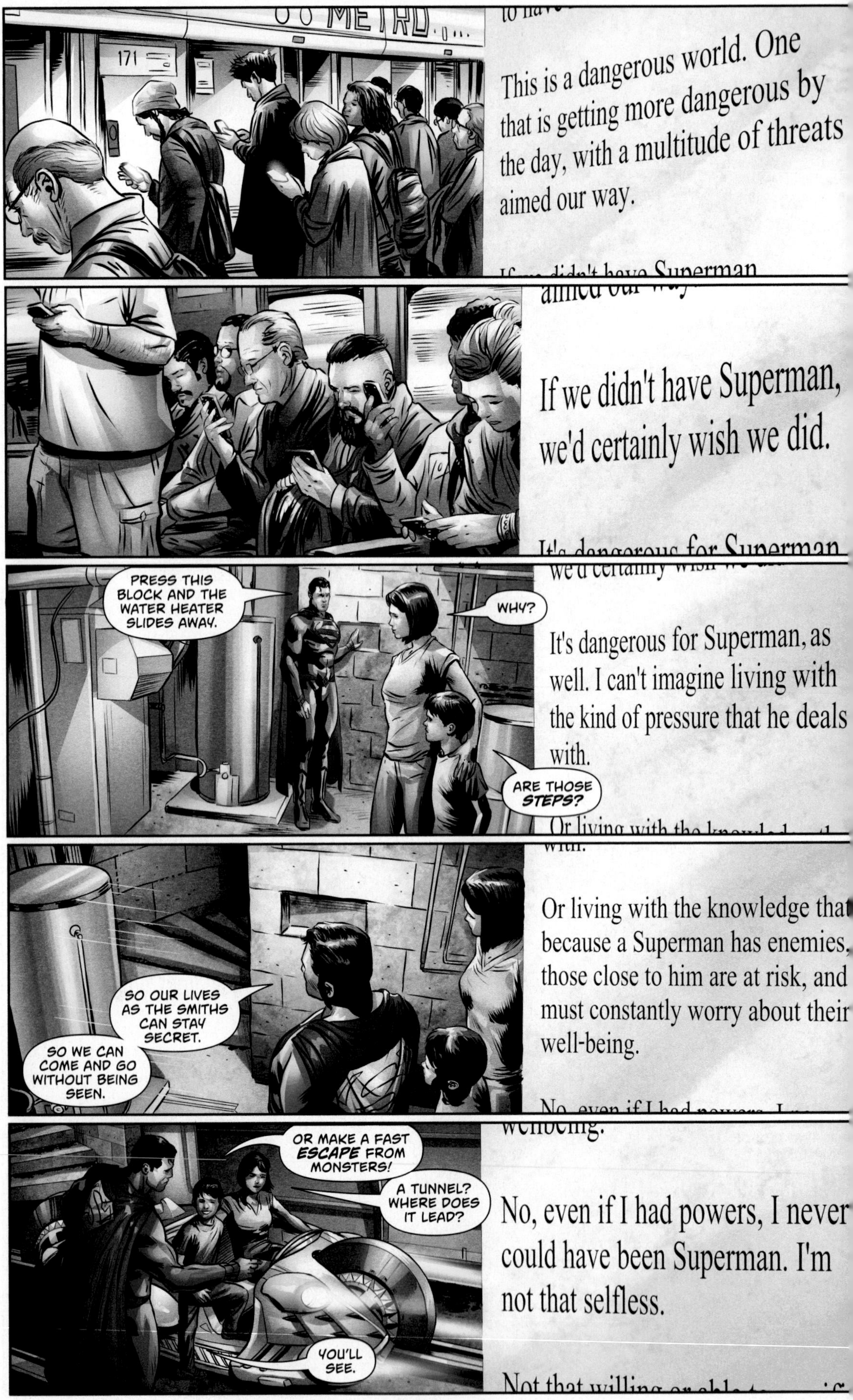
METRO
171
This is a dangerous world. One that is getting more dangerous by the day, with a multitude of threats aimed our way.
If we didn't have Superman, we'd certainly wish we did.
PRESS THIS BLOCK AND THE WATER HEATER SLIDES AWAY.
WHY?
It's dangerous for Superman, as well. I can't imagine living with the kind of pressure that he deals with.
ARE THOSE *STEPS?*
SO OUR LIVES AS THE SMITHS CAN STAY SECRET.
SO WE CAN COME AND GO WITHOUT BEING SEEN.
Or living with the knowledge that because a Superman has enemies, those close to him are at risk, and must constantly worry about their well-being.
OR MAKE A FAST *ESCAPE* FROM MONSTERS!
A TUNNEL? WHERE DOES IT LEAD?
YOU'LL SEE.
No, even if I had powers, I never could have been Superman. I'm not that selfless.

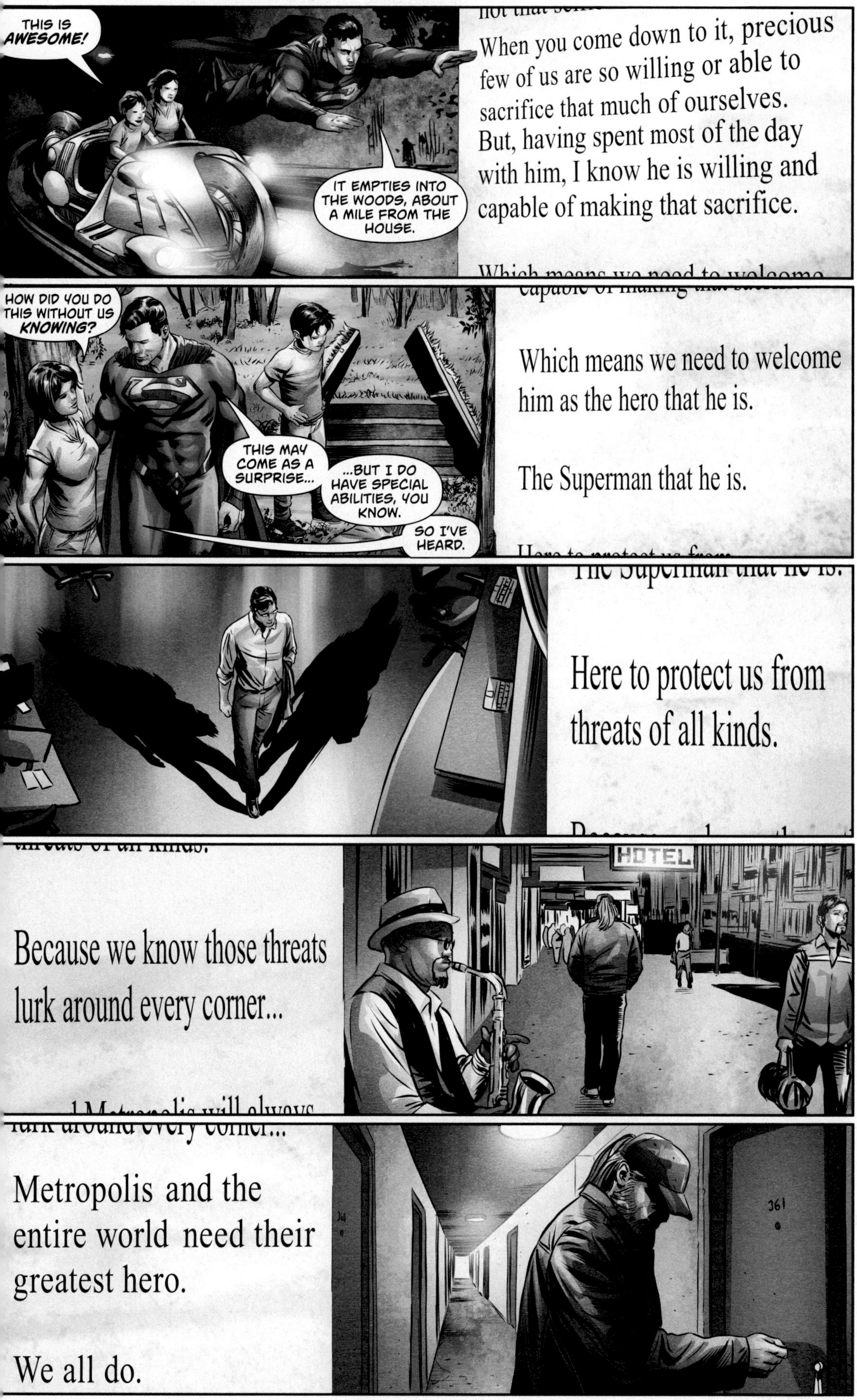
THIS IS AWESOME!
IT EMPTIES INTO THE WOODS, ABOUT A MILE FROM THE HOUSE.
When you come down to it, precious few of us are so willing or able to sacrifice that much of ourselves.
But, having spent most of the day with him, I know he is willing and capable of making that sacrifice.
HOW DID YOU DO THIS WITHOUT US KNOWING?
THIS MAY COME AS A SURPRISE...
...BUT I DO HAVE SPECIAL ABILITIES, YOU KNOW.
SO I'VE HEARD.
Which means we need to welcome him as the hero that he is.
The Superman that he is.
Here to protect us from threats of all kinds.
Because we know those threats lurk around every corner...
HOTEL
Metropolis and the entire world need their greatest hero.
We all do.
361

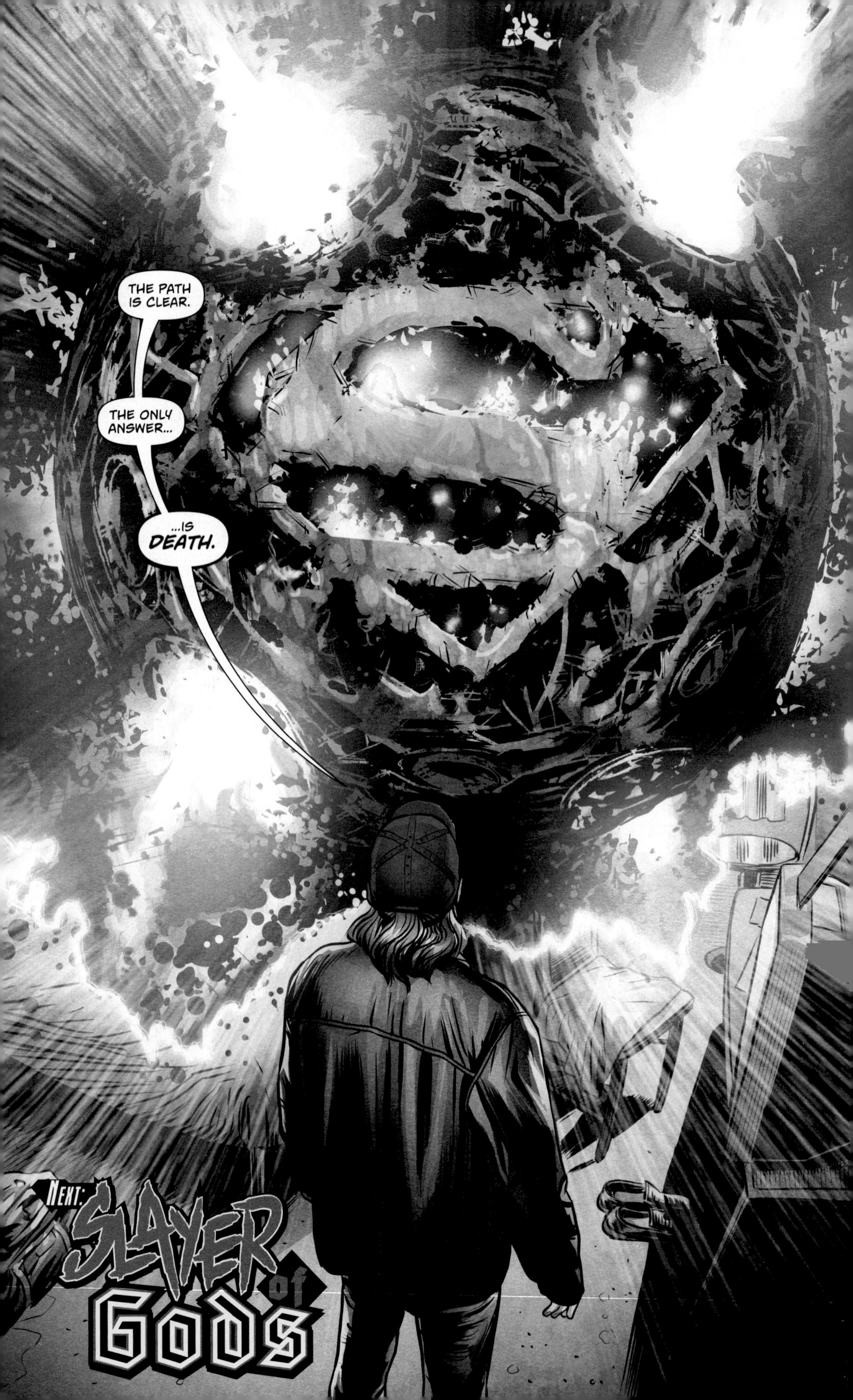
THE PATH IS CLEAR.
THE ONLY ANSWER...
...IS DEATH.
NEXT: SLAYER of GODS

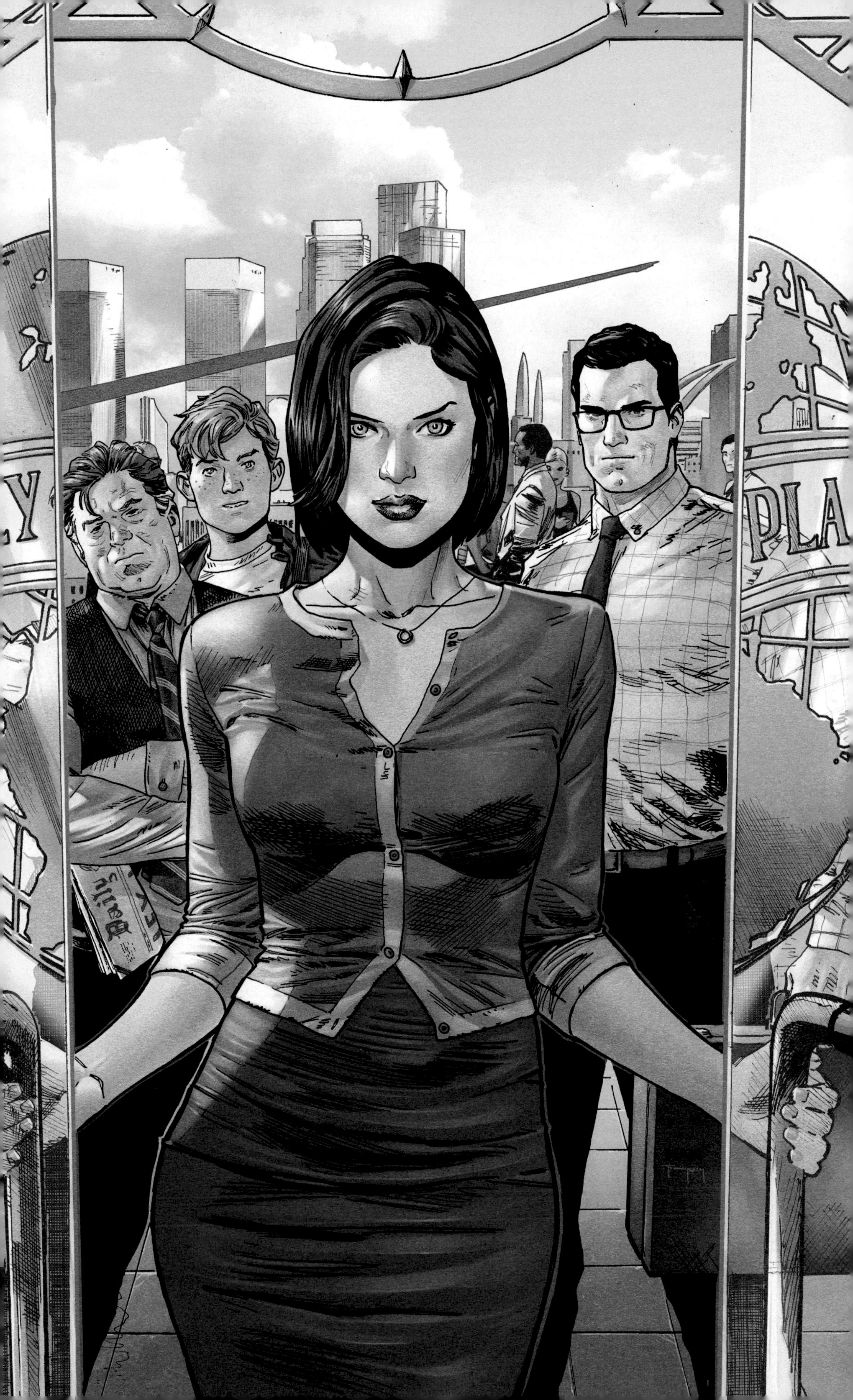
LY
PLA
Daily

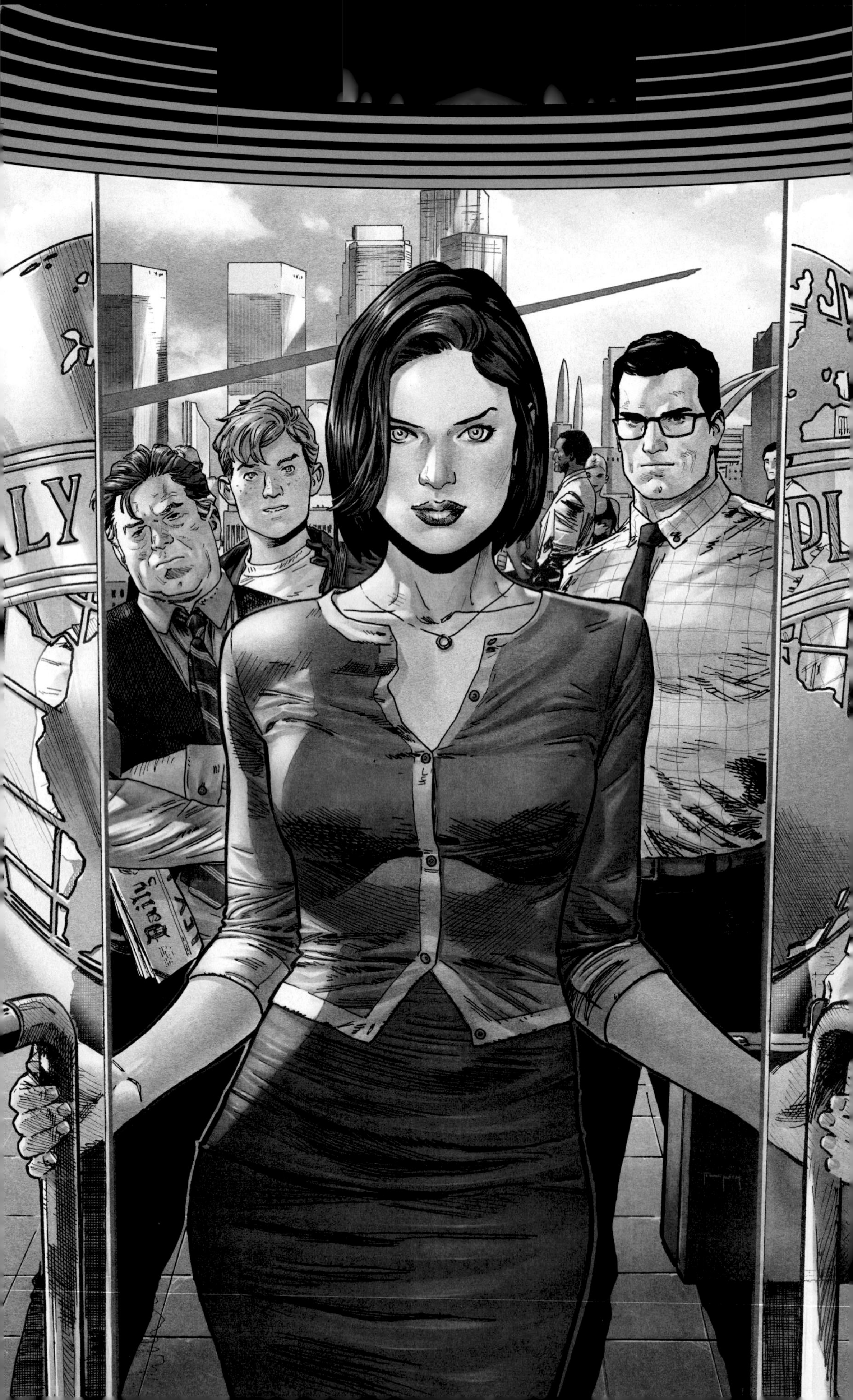

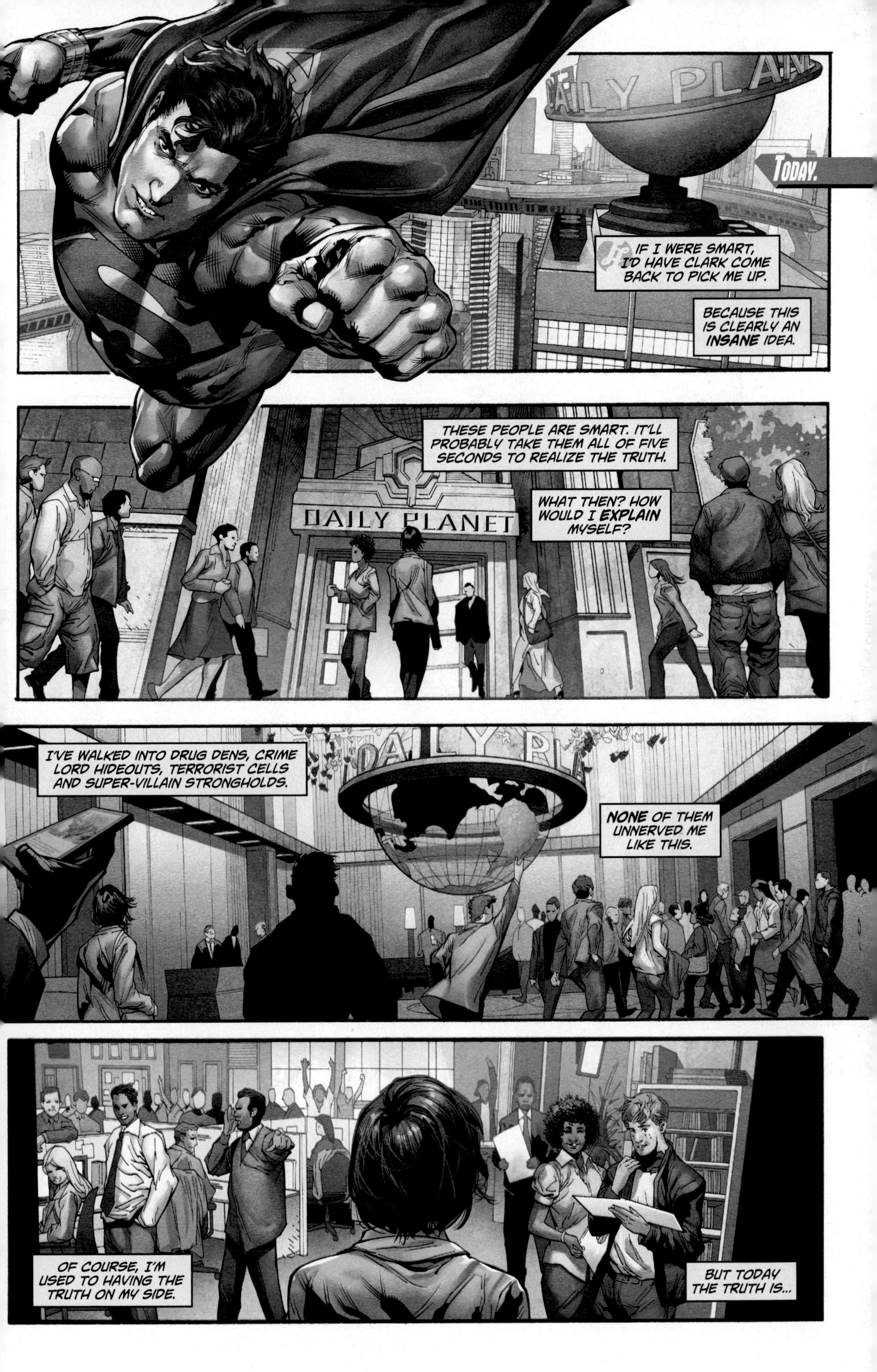
DAILY PLANET
TODAY.
IF I WERE SMART, I'D HAVE CLARK COME BACK TO PICK ME UP.
BECAUSE THIS IS CLEARLY AN INSANE IDEA.
THESE PEOPLE ARE SMART. IT'LL PROBABLY TAKE THEM ALL OF FIVE SECONDS TO REALIZE THE TRUTH.
DAILY PLANET
WHAT THEN? HOW WOULD I EXPLAIN MYSELF?
I'VE WALKED INTO DRUG DENS, CRIME LORD HIDEOUTS, TERRORIST CELLS AND SUPER-VILLAIN STRONGHOLDS.
NONE OF THEM UNNERVED ME LIKE THIS.
OF COURSE, I'M USED TO HAVING THE TRUTH ON MY SIDE.
BUT TODAY THE TRUTH IS...

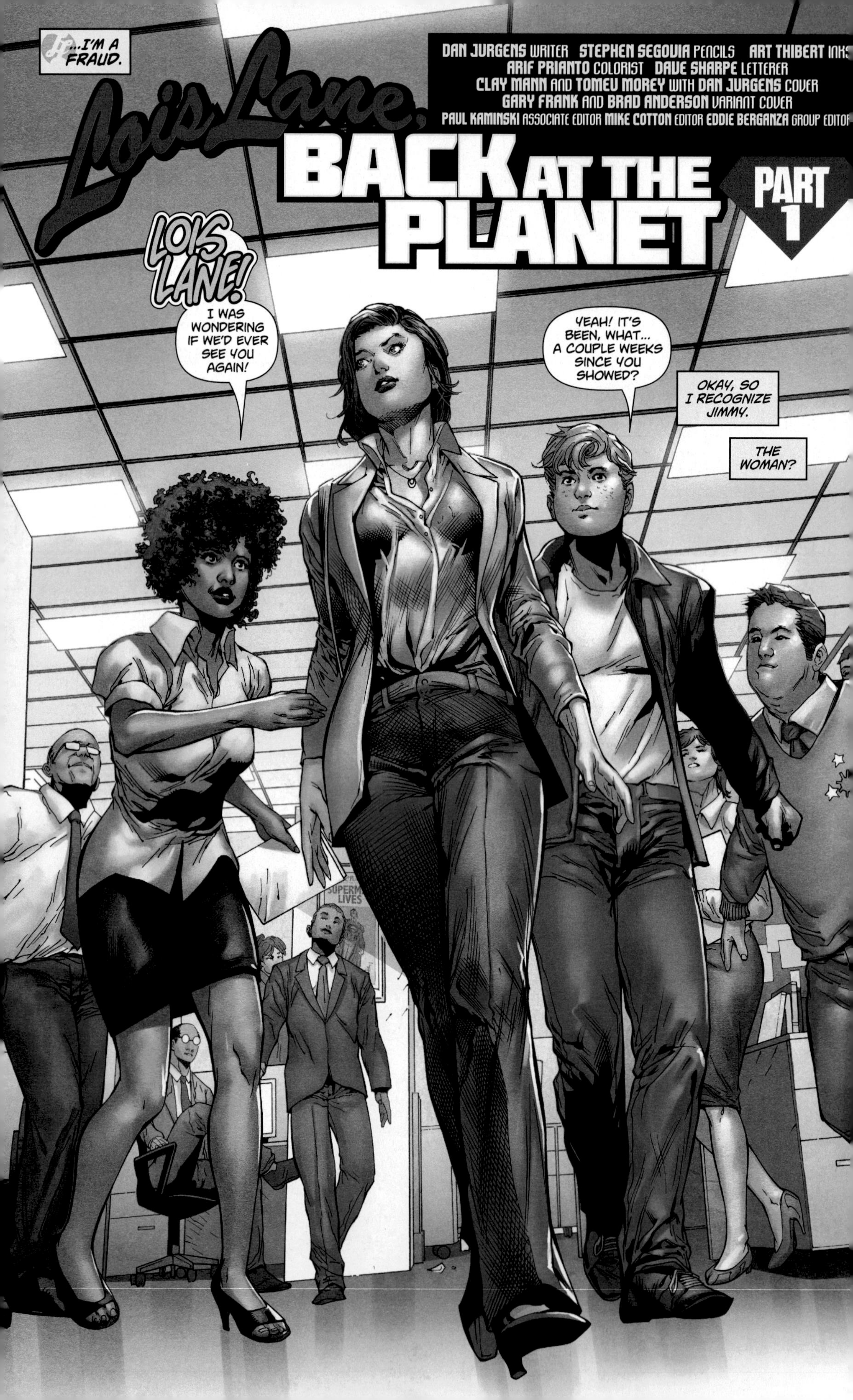
...I'M A FRAUD.
Lois Lane,
DAN JURGENS WRITER STEPHEN SEGOVIA PENCILS ART THIBERT INKS
ARIF PRIANTO COLORIST DAVE SHARPE LETTERER
CLAY MANN AND TOMEU MOREY WITH DAN JURGENS COVER
GARY FRANK AND BRAD ANDERSON VARIANT COVER
PAUL KAMINSKI ASSOCIATE EDITOR MIKE COTTON EDITOR EDDIE BERGANZA GROUP EDITOR
BACK AT THE PLANET
PART 1
LOIS LANE! I WAS WONDERING IF WE'D EVER SEE YOU AGAIN!
YEAH! IT'S BEEN, WHAT... A COUPLE WEEKS SINCE YOU SHOWED?
OKAY, SO I RECOGNIZE JIMMY.
THE WOMAN?
SUPERMAN LIVES

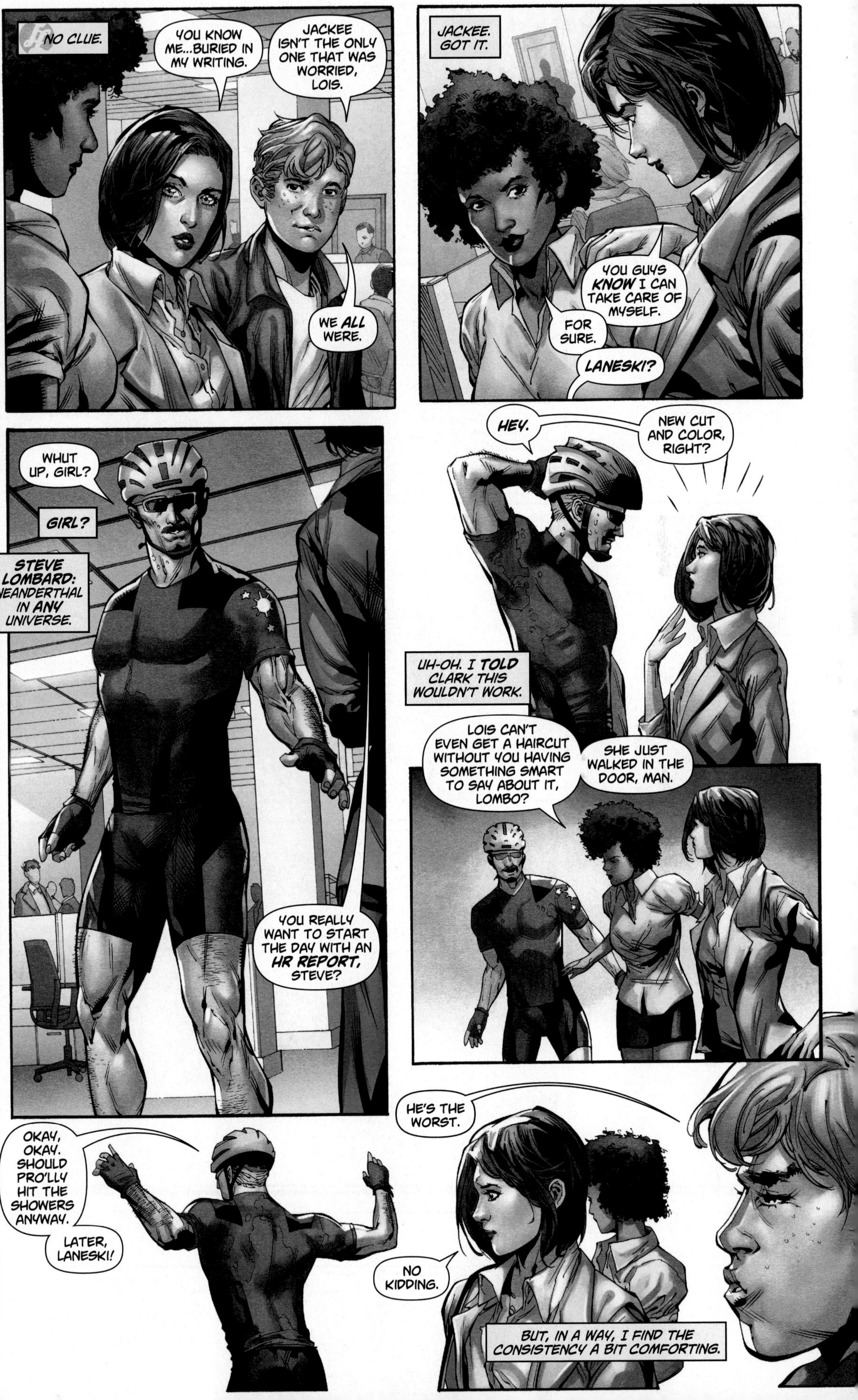
NO CLUE.
YOU KNOW ME...BURIED IN MY WRITING.
JACKEE ISN'T THE ONLY ONE THAT WAS WORRIED, LOIS.
WE ALL WERE.
JACKEE. GOT IT.
YOU GUYS KNOW I CAN TAKE CARE OF MYSELF.
FOR SURE.
LANESKI?
WHUT UP, GIRL?
GIRL?
STEVE LOMBARD: NEANDERTHAL IN ANY UNIVERSE.
YOU REALLY WANT TO START THE DAY WITH AN HR REPORT, STEVE?
HEY.
NEW CUT AND COLOR, RIGHT?
UH-OH. I TOLD CLARK THIS WOULDN'T WORK.
LOIS CAN'T EVEN GET A HAIRCUT WITHOUT YOU HAVING SOMETHING SMART TO SAY ABOUT IT, LOMBO?
SHE JUST WALKED IN THE DOOR, MAN.
OKAY, OKAY. SHOULD PRO'LLY HIT THE SHOWERS ANYWAY.
LATER, LANESKI!
HE'S THE WORST.
NO KIDDING.
BUT, IN A WAY, I FIND THE CONSISTENCY A BIT COMFORTING.

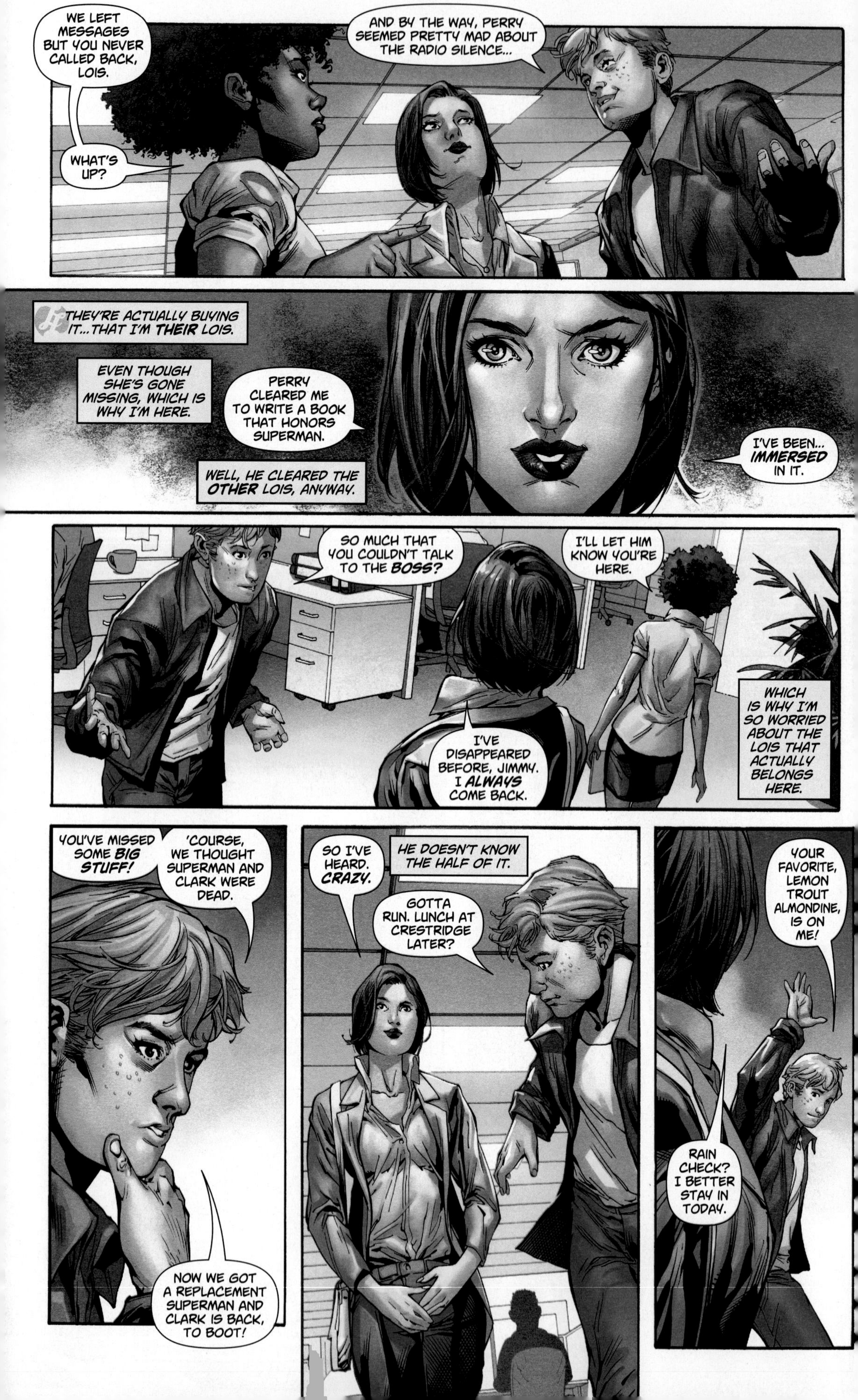
WE LEFT MESSAGES BUT YOU NEVER CALLED BACK, LOIS.
WHAT'S UP?
AND BY THE WAY, PERRY SEEMED PRETTY MAD ABOUT THE RADIO SILENCE...
THEY'RE ACTUALLY BUYING IT...THAT I'M THEIR LOIS.
EVEN THOUGH SHE'S GONE MISSING, WHICH IS WHY I'M HERE.
PERRY CLEARED ME TO WRITE A BOOK THAT HONORS SUPERMAN.
WELL, HE CLEARED THE OTHER LOIS, ANYWAY.
I'VE BEEN... IMMERSED IN IT.
SO MUCH THAT YOU COULDN'T TALK TO THE BOSS?
I'LL LET HIM KNOW YOU'RE HERE.
I'VE DISAPPEARED BEFORE, JIMMY. I ALWAYS COME BACK.
WHICH IS WHY I'M SO WORRIED ABOUT THE LOIS THAT ACTUALLY BELONGS HERE.
YOU'VE MISSED SOME BIG STUFF!
'COURSE, WE THOUGHT SUPERMAN AND CLARK WERE DEAD.
NOW WE GOT A REPLACEMENT SUPERMAN AND CLARK IS BACK, TO BOOT!
SO I'VE HEARD. CRAZY.
HE DOESN'T KNOW THE HALF OF IT.
GOTTA RUN. LUNCH AT CRESTRIDGE LATER?
YOUR FAVORITE, LEMON TROUT ALMONDINE, IS ON ME!
RAIN CHECK? I BETTER STAY IN TODAY.

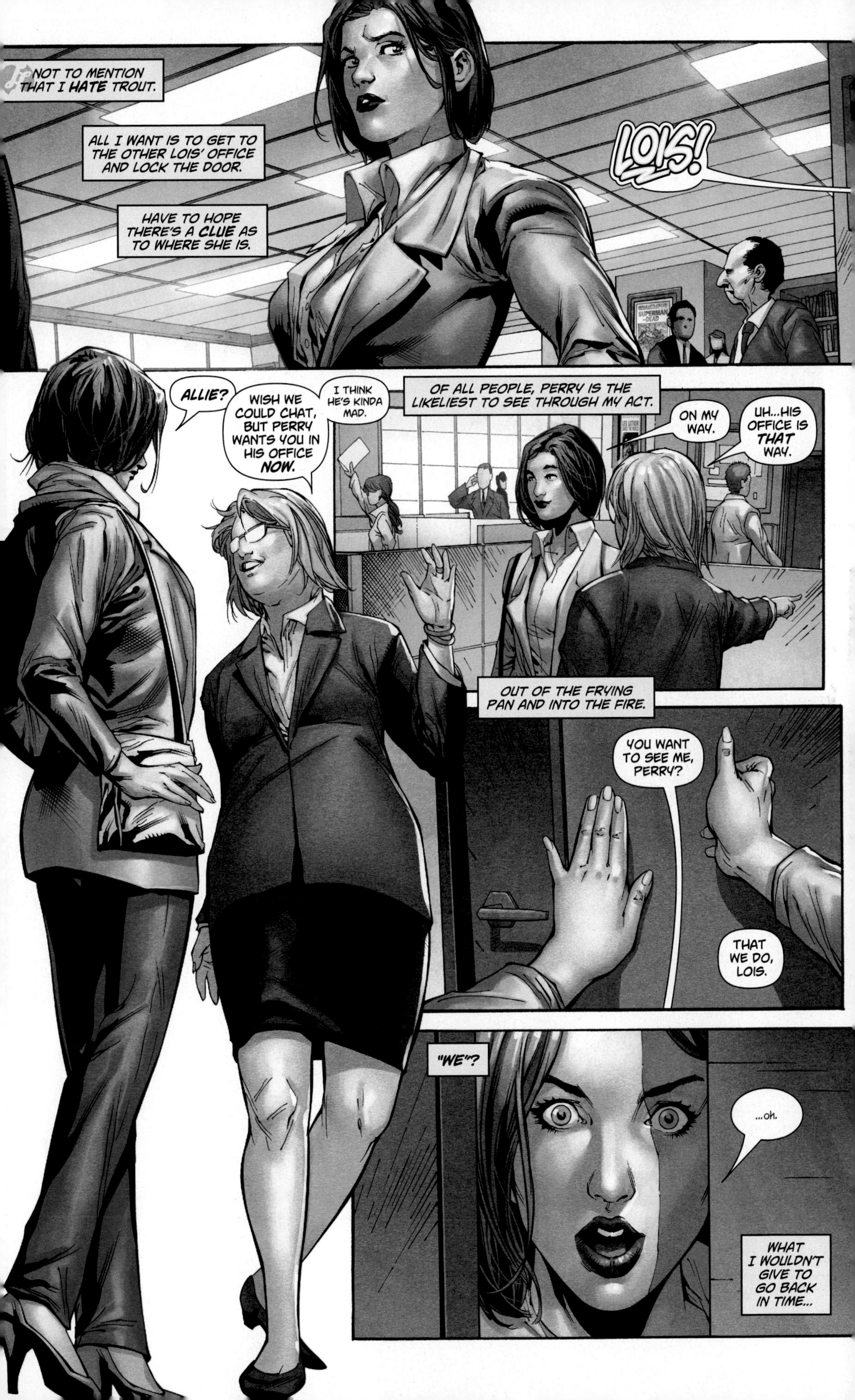
NOT TO MENTION THAT I HATE TROUT.
ALL I WANT IS TO GET TO THE OTHER LOIS' OFFICE AND LOCK THE DOOR.
HAVE TO HOPE THERE'S A CLUE AS TO WHERE SHE IS.
LOIS!
SUPERMAN DEAD
ALLIE?
WISH WE COULD CHAT, BUT PERRY WANTS YOU IN HIS OFFICE NOW.
I THINK HE'S KINDA MAD.
OF ALL PEOPLE, PERRY IS THE LIKELIEST TO SEE THROUGH MY ACT.
ON MY WAY.
UH...HIS OFFICE IS THAT WAY.
OUT OF THE FRYING PAN AND INTO THE FIRE.
YOU WANT TO SEE ME, PERRY?
THAT WE DO, LOIS.
"WE"?
...oh.
WHAT I WOULDN'T GIVE TO GO BACK IN TIME...

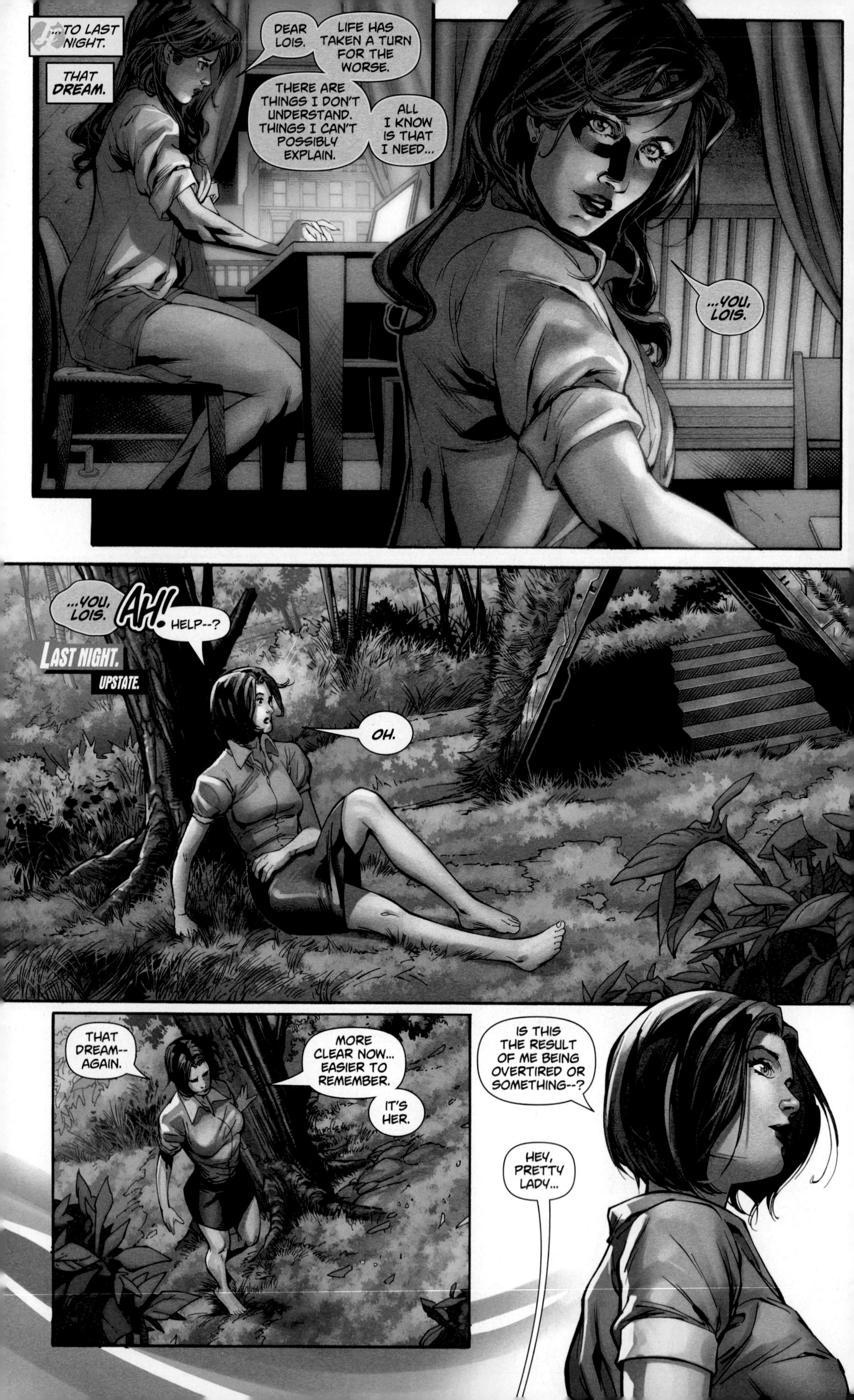

...TO LAST NIGHT.
THAT DREAM.
DEAR LOIS.
LIFE HAS TAKEN A TURN FOR THE WORSE.
THERE ARE THINGS I DON'T UNDERSTAND. THINGS I CAN'T POSSIBLY EXPLAIN.
ALL I KNOW IS THAT I NEED...
...YOU, LOIS.
...YOU, LOIS.
AH!
HELP--?
LAST NIGHT.
UPSTATE.
OH.
THAT DREAM-- AGAIN.
MORE CLEAR NOW... EASIER TO REMEMBER.
IT'S HER.
IS THIS THE RESULT OF ME BEING OVERTIRED OR SOMETHING--?
HEY, PRETTY LADY...

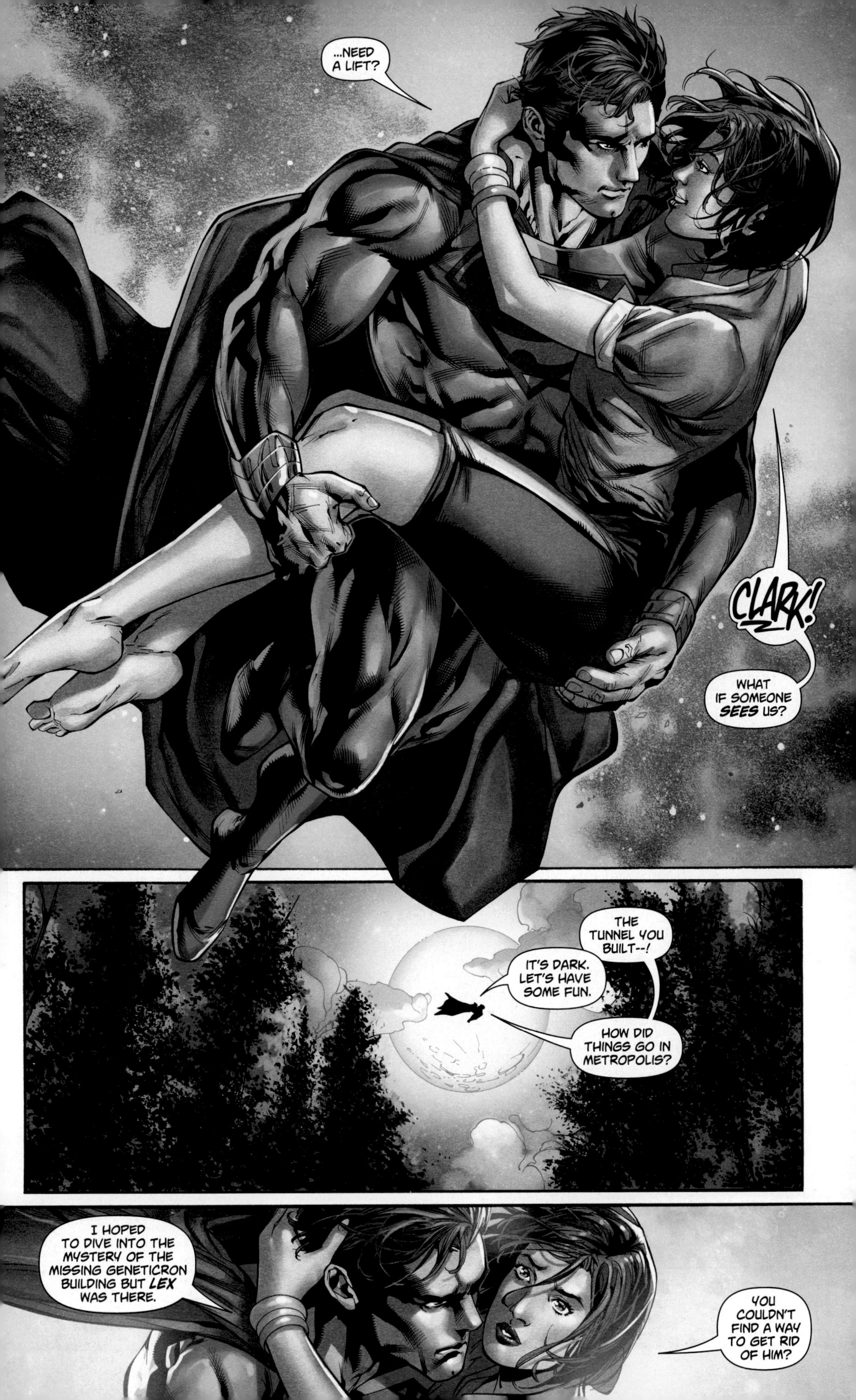
...NEED A LIFT?
CLARK!
WHAT IF SOMEONE SEES US?
IT'S DARK. LET'S HAVE SOME FUN.
THE TUNNEL YOU BUILT--!
HOW DID THINGS GO IN METROPOLIS?
I HOPED TO DIVE INTO THE MYSTERY OF THE MISSING GENETICRON BUILDING BUT LEX WAS THERE.
YOU COULDN'T FIND A WAY TO GET RID OF HIM?

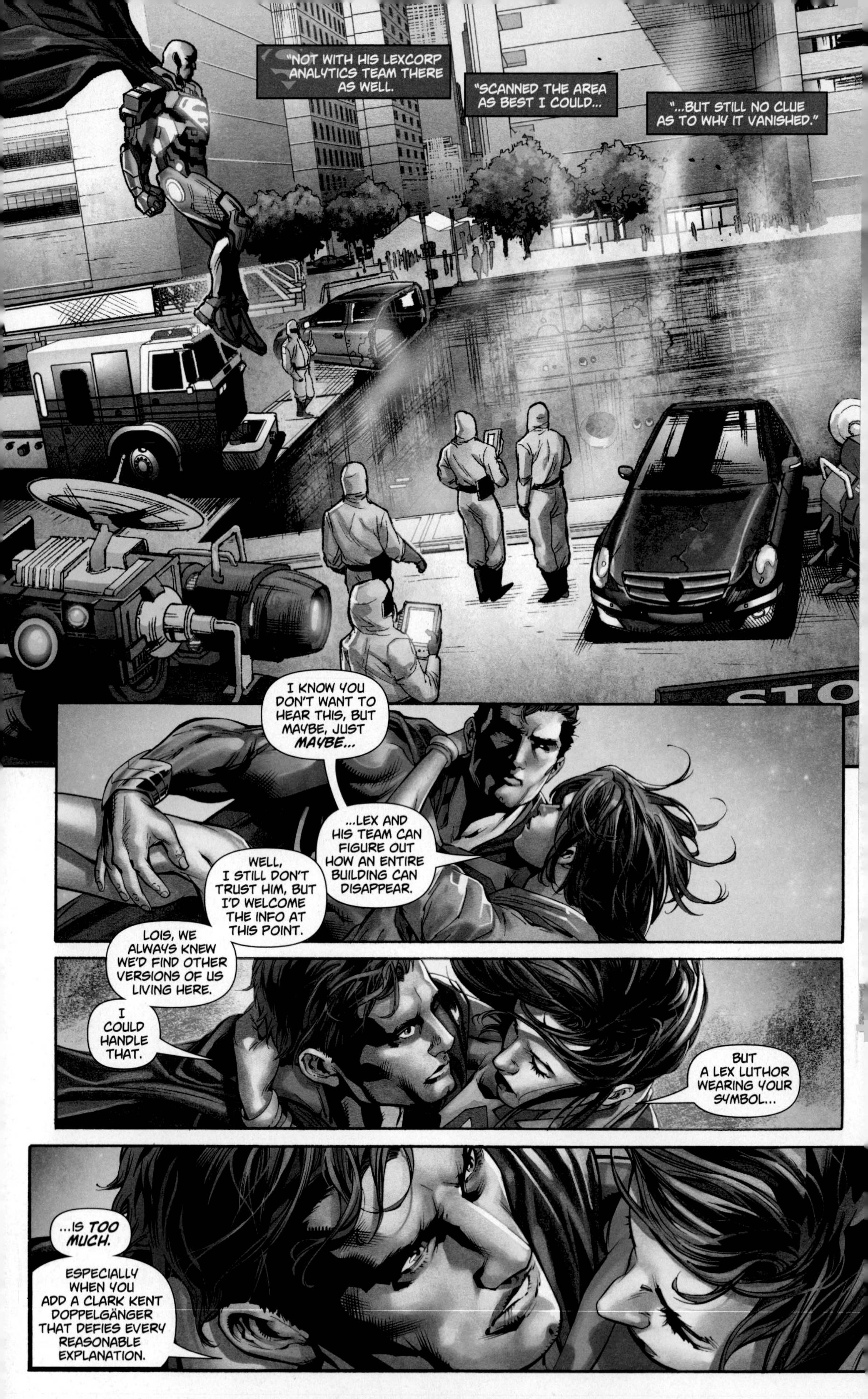
"NOT WITH HIS LEXCORP ANALYTICS TEAM THERE AS WELL.
"SCANNED THE AREA AS BEST I COULD...
"...BUT STILL NO CLUE AS TO WHY IT VANISHED."
I KNOW YOU DON'T WANT TO HEAR THIS, BUT MAYBE, JUST *MAYBE*...
...LEX AND HIS TEAM CAN FIGURE OUT HOW AN ENTIRE BUILDING CAN DISAPPEAR.
WELL, I STILL DON'T TRUST HIM, BUT I'D WELCOME THE INFO AT THIS POINT.
LOIS, WE ALWAYS KNEW WE'D FIND OTHER VERSIONS OF US LIVING HERE.
I COULD HANDLE THAT.
BUT A LEX LUTHOR WEARING YOUR SYMBOL...
...IS *TOO MUCH*.
ESPECIALLY WHEN YOU ADD A CLARK KENT DOPPELGÄNGER THAT DEFIES EVERY REASONABLE EXPLANATION.

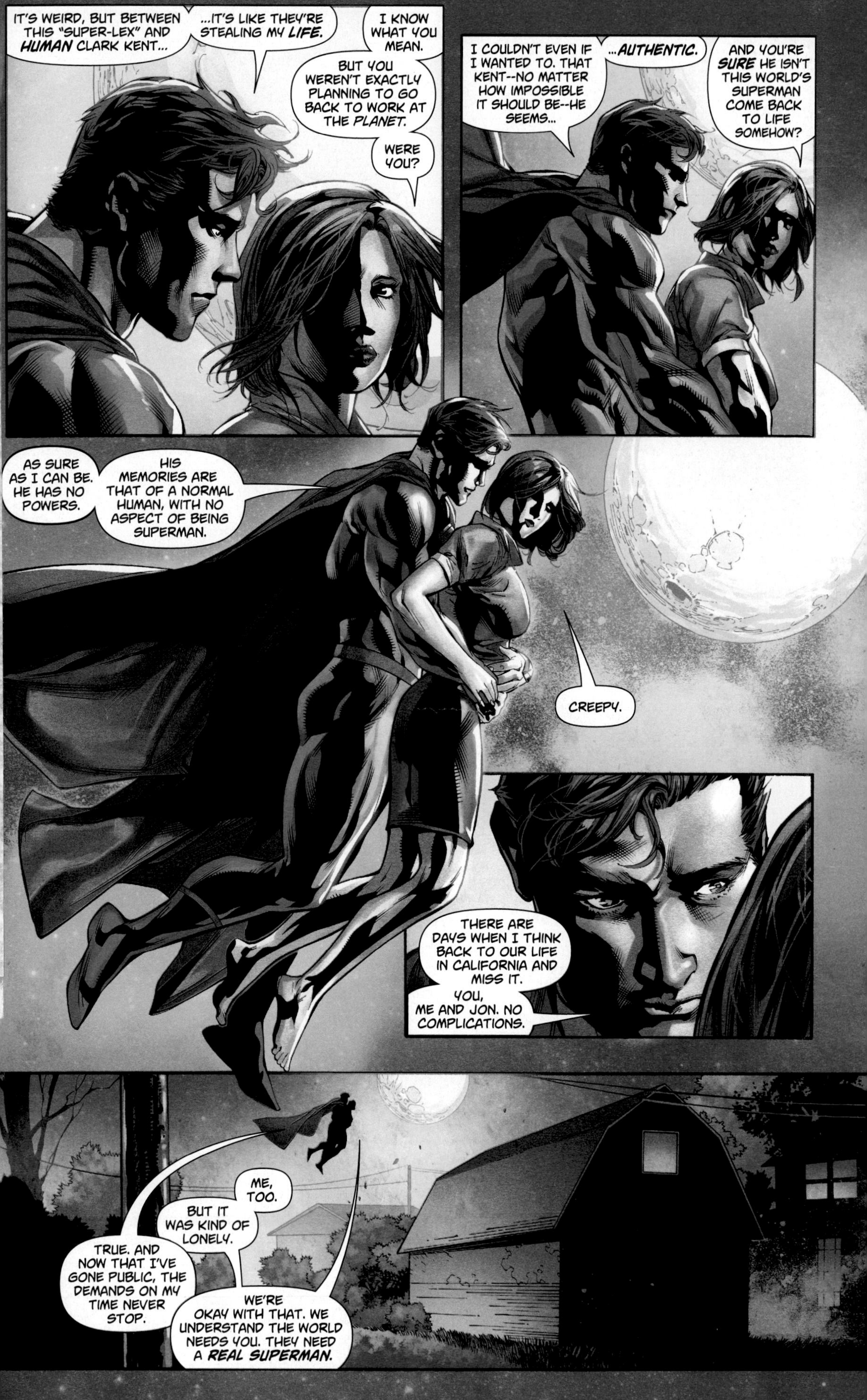

IT'S WEIRD, BUT BETWEEN THIS "SUPER-LEX" AND HUMAN CLARK KENT...
...IT'S LIKE THEY'RE STEALING MY LIFE.
I KNOW WHAT YOU MEAN.
BUT YOU WEREN'T EXACTLY PLANNING TO GO BACK TO WORK AT THE PLANET.
WERE YOU?
I COULDN'T EVEN IF I WANTED TO. THAT KENT--NO MATTER HOW IMPOSSIBLE IT SHOULD BE--HE SEEMS...
...AUTHENTIC.
AND YOU'RE SURE HE ISN'T THIS WORLD'S SUPERMAN COME BACK TO LIFE SOMEHOW?
AS SURE AS I CAN BE. HE HAS NO POWERS.
HIS MEMORIES ARE THAT OF A NORMAL HUMAN, WITH NO ASPECT OF BEING SUPERMAN.
CREEPY.
THERE ARE DAYS WHEN I THINK BACK TO OUR LIFE IN CALIFORNIA AND MISS IT.
YOU, ME AND JON. NO COMPLICATIONS.
ME, TOO.
BUT IT WAS KIND OF LONELY.
TRUE. AND NOW THAT I'VE GONE PUBLIC, THE DEMANDS ON MY TIME NEVER STOP.
WE'RE OKAY WITH THAT. WE UNDERSTAND THE WORLD NEEDS YOU. THEY NEED A REAL SUPERMAN.

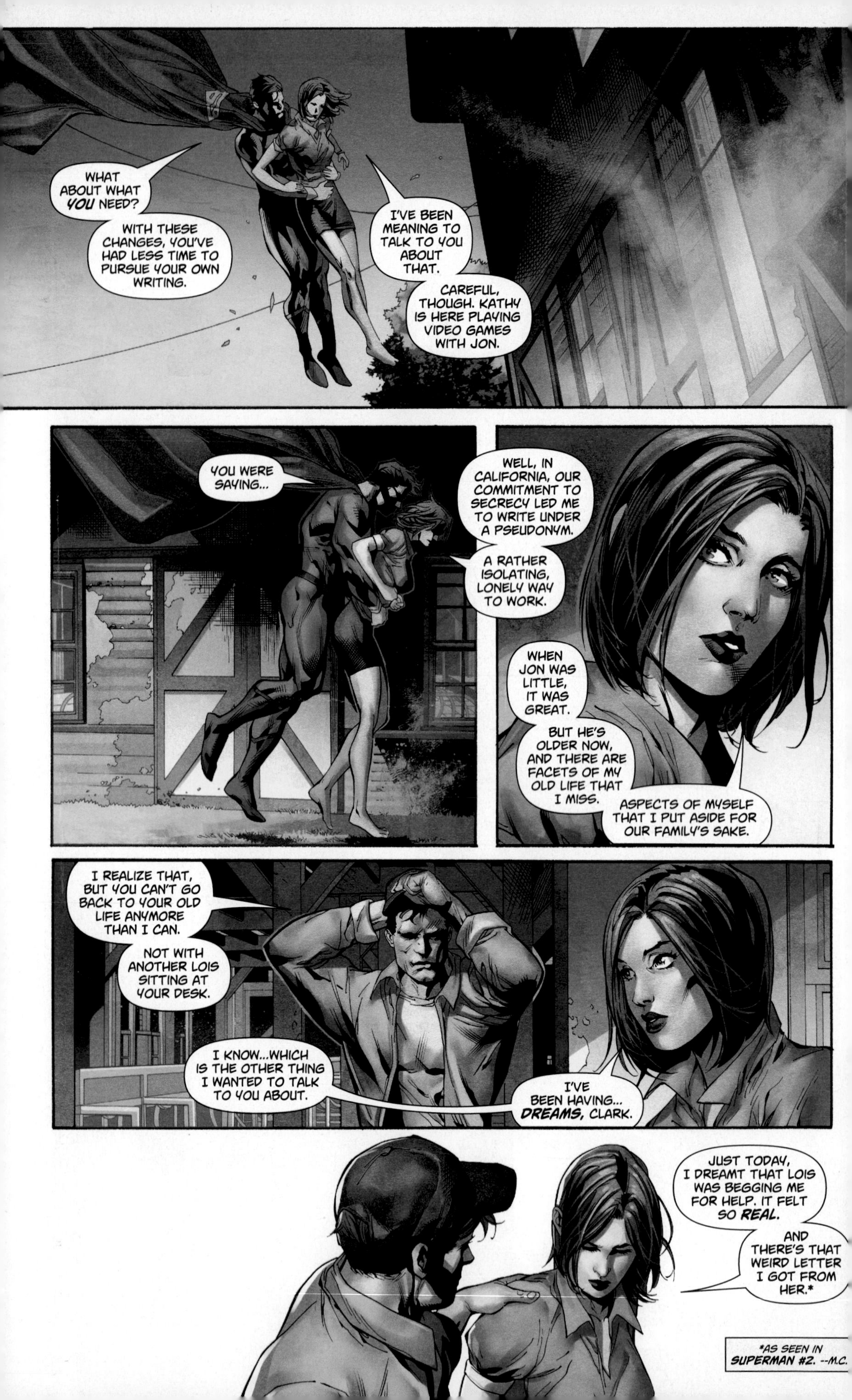
WHAT ABOUT WHAT *YOU* NEED?
WITH THESE CHANGES, YOU'VE HAD LESS TIME TO PURSUE YOUR OWN WRITING.
I'VE BEEN MEANING TO TALK TO YOU ABOUT THAT.
CAREFUL, THOUGH. KATHY IS HERE PLAYING VIDEO GAMES WITH JON.
YOU WERE SAYING...
WELL, IN CALIFORNIA, OUR COMMITMENT TO SECRECY LED ME TO WRITE UNDER A PSEUDONYM.
A RATHER ISOLATING, LONELY WAY TO WORK.
WHEN JON WAS LITTLE, IT WAS GREAT.
BUT HE'S OLDER NOW, AND THERE ARE FACETS OF MY OLD LIFE THAT I MISS.
ASPECTS OF MYSELF THAT I PUT ASIDE FOR OUR FAMILY'S SAKE.
I REALIZE THAT, BUT YOU CAN'T GO BACK TO YOUR OLD LIFE ANYMORE THAN I CAN.
NOT WITH ANOTHER LOIS SITTING AT YOUR DESK.
I KNOW...WHICH IS THE OTHER THING I WANTED TO TALK TO YOU ABOUT.
I'VE BEEN HAVING... *DREAMS,* CLARK.
JUST TODAY, I DREAMT THAT LOIS WAS BEGGING ME FOR HELP. IT FELT SO *REAL.*
AND THERE'S THAT WEIRD LETTER I GOT FROM HER.*
*AS SEEN IN *SUPERMAN #2.* --M.C.

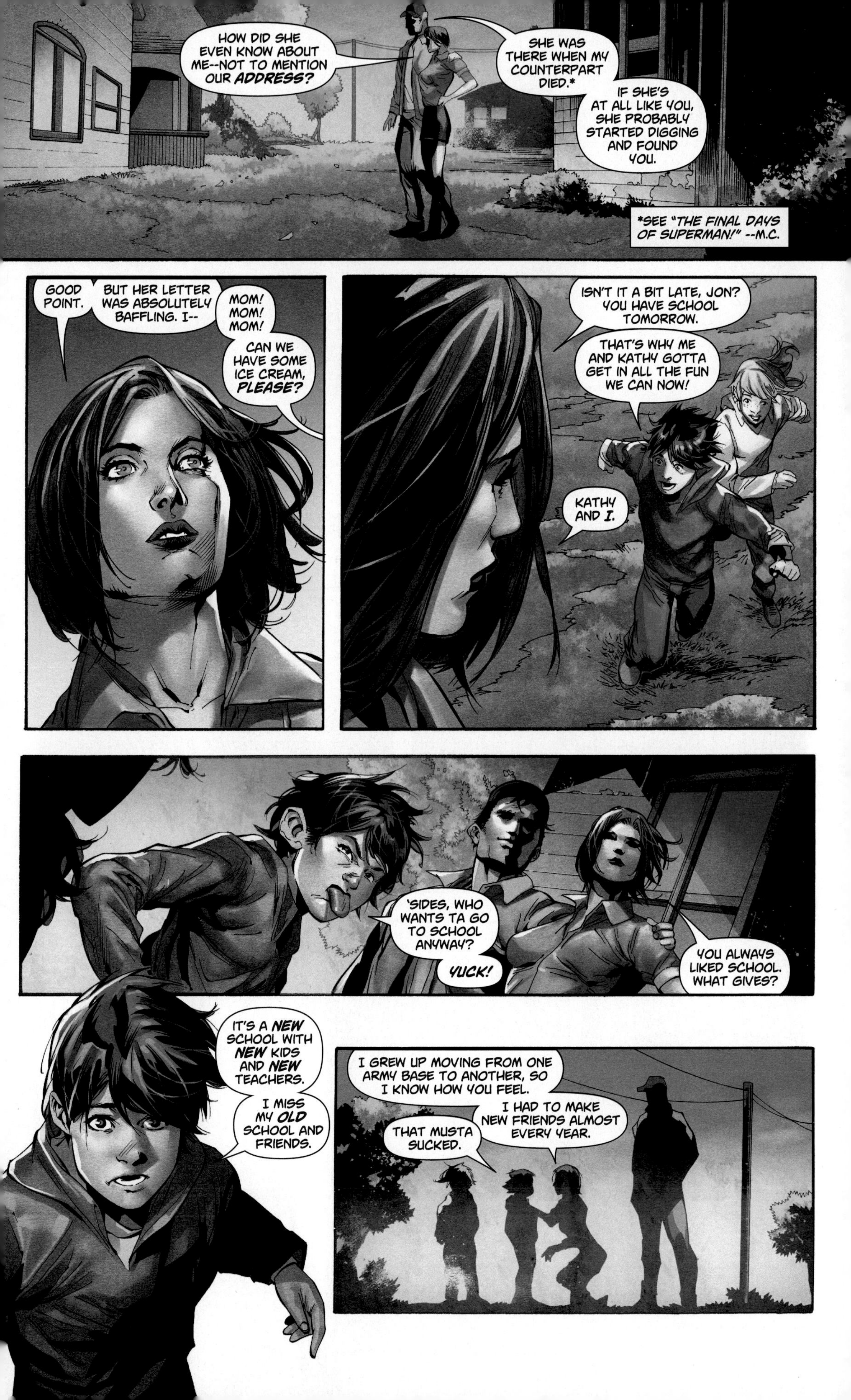
HOW DID SHE EVEN KNOW ABOUT ME--NOT TO MENTION OUR ADDRESS?
SHE WAS THERE WHEN MY COUNTERPART DIED.*
IF SHE'S AT ALL LIKE YOU, SHE PROBABLY STARTED DIGGING AND FOUND YOU.
*SEE "THE FINAL DAYS OF SUPERMAN!" --M.C.
GOOD POINT.
BUT HER LETTER WAS ABSOLUTELY BAFFLING. I--
MOM! MOM! MOM!
CAN WE HAVE SOME ICE CREAM, PLEASE?
ISN'T IT A BIT LATE, JON? YOU HAVE SCHOOL TOMORROW.
THAT'S WHY ME AND KATHY GOTTA GET IN ALL THE FUN WE CAN NOW!
KATHY AND I.
'SIDES, WHO WANTS TA GO TO SCHOOL ANYWAY?
YUCK!
YOU ALWAYS LIKED SCHOOL. WHAT GIVES?
IT'S A NEW SCHOOL WITH NEW KIDS AND NEW TEACHERS.
I MISS MY OLD SCHOOL AND FRIENDS.
I GREW UP MOVING FROM ONE ARMY BASE TO ANOTHER, SO I KNOW HOW YOU FEEL.
I HAD TO MAKE NEW FRIENDS ALMOST EVERY YEAR.
THAT MUSTA SUCKED.

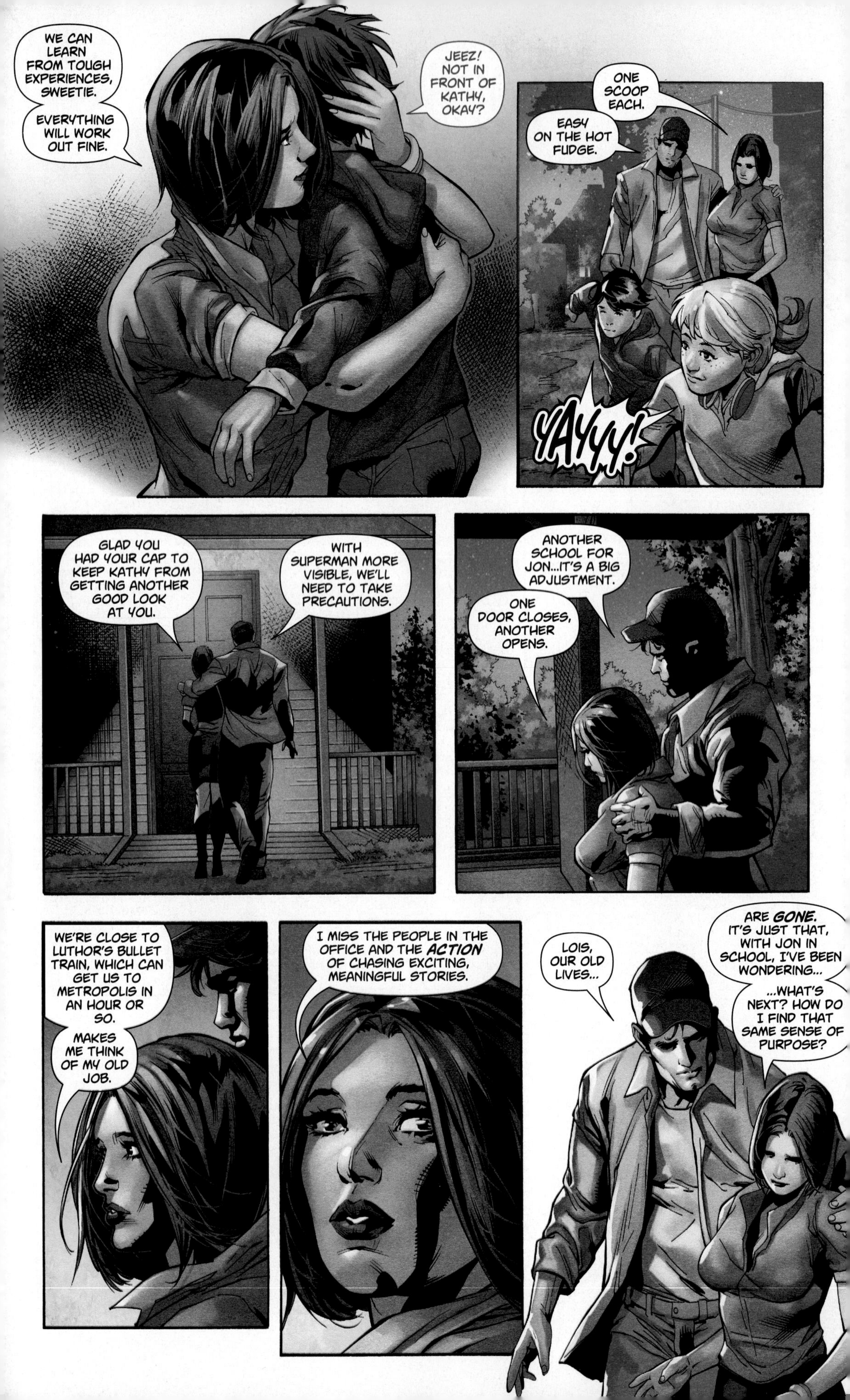
WE CAN LEARN FROM TOUGH EXPERIENCES, SWEETIE.
EVERYTHING WILL WORK OUT FINE.
JEEZ! NOT IN FRONT OF KATHY, OKAY?
ONE SCOOP EACH.
EASY ON THE HOT FUDGE.
YAYYY!
GLAD YOU HAD YOUR CAP TO KEEP KATHY FROM GETTING ANOTHER GOOD LOOK AT YOU.
WITH SUPERMAN MORE VISIBLE, WE'LL NEED TO TAKE PRECAUTIONS.
ANOTHER SCHOOL FOR JON...IT'S A BIG ADJUSTMENT.
ONE DOOR CLOSES, ANOTHER OPENS.
WE'RE CLOSE TO LUTHOR'S BULLET TRAIN, WHICH CAN GET US TO METROPOLIS IN AN HOUR OR SO.
MAKES ME THINK OF MY OLD JOB.
I MISS THE PEOPLE IN THE OFFICE AND THE ACTION OF CHASING EXCITING, MEANINGFUL STORIES.
LOIS, OUR OLD LIVES...
ARE GONE. IT'S JUST THAT, WITH JON IN SCHOOL, I'VE BEEN WONDERING...
...WHAT'S NEXT? HOW DO I FIND THAT SAME SENSE OF PURPOSE?

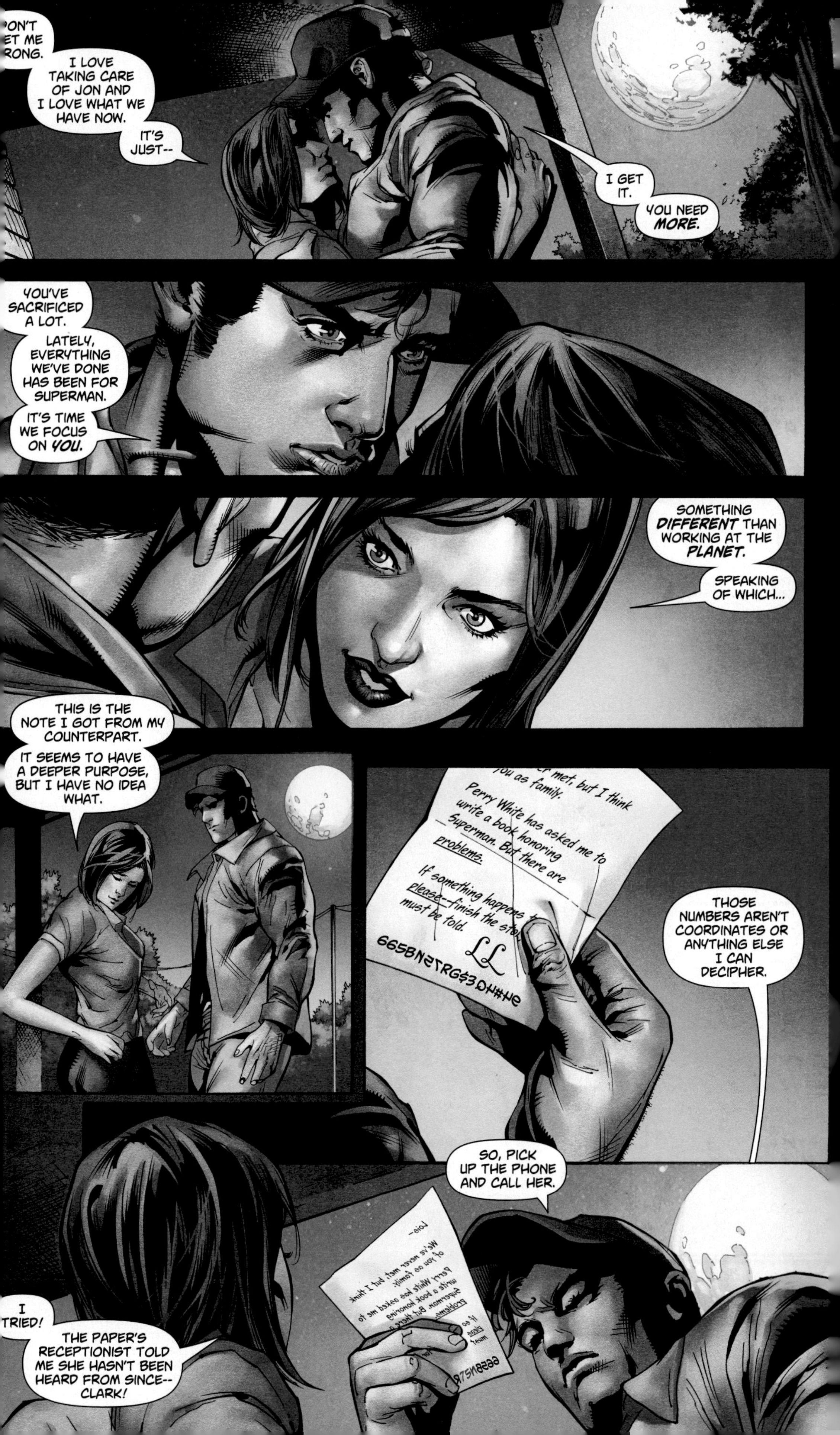

ON'T ET ME RONG.
I LOVE TAKING CARE OF JON AND I LOVE WHAT WE HAVE NOW.
IT'S JUST--
I GET IT.
YOU NEED MORE.
YOU'VE SACRIFICED A LOT.
LATELY, EVERYTHING WE'VE DONE HAS BEEN FOR SUPERMAN.
IT'S TIME WE FOCUS ON YOU.
SOMETHING DIFFERENT THAN WORKING AT THE PLANET.
SPEAKING OF WHICH...
THIS IS THE NOTE I GOT FROM MY COUNTERPART.
IT SEEMS TO HAVE A DEEPER PURPOSE, BUT I HAVE NO IDEA WHAT.
you as family.
Perry White has asked me to write a book honoring Superman. But there are problems.
If something happens to please--finish the sto must be told.
LL
THOSE NUMBERS AREN'T COORDINATES OR ANYTHING ELSE I CAN DECIPHER.
SO, PICK UP THE PHONE AND CALL HER.
I TRIED!
THE PAPER'S RECEPTIONIST TOLD ME SHE HASN'T BEEN HEARD FROM SINCE--
CLARK!

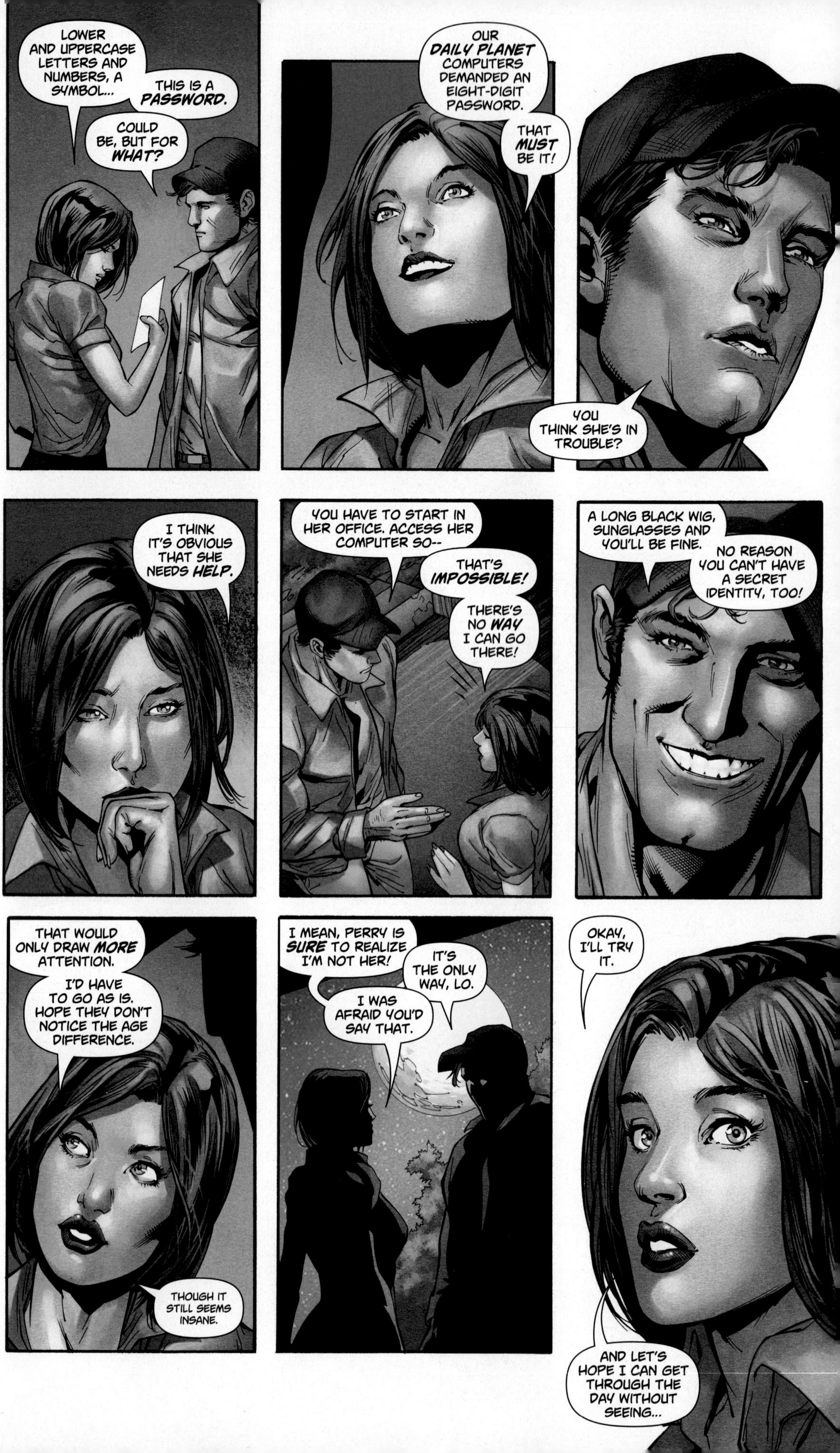
LOWER AND UPPERCASE LETTERS AND NUMBERS, A SYMBOL...
THIS IS A PASSWORD.
COULD BE, BUT FOR WHAT?
OUR DAILY PLANET COMPUTERS DEMANDED AN EIGHT-DIGIT PASSWORD.
THAT MUST BE IT!
YOU THINK SHE'S IN TROUBLE?
I THINK IT'S OBVIOUS THAT SHE NEEDS HELP.
YOU HAVE TO START IN HER OFFICE. ACCESS HER COMPUTER SO--
THAT'S IMPOSSIBLE!
THERE'S NO WAY I CAN GO THERE!
A LONG BLACK WIG, SUNGLASSES AND YOU'LL BE FINE.
NO REASON YOU CAN'T HAVE A SECRET IDENTITY, TOO!
THAT WOULD ONLY DRAW MORE ATTENTION.
I'D HAVE TO GO AS IS. HOPE THEY DON'T NOTICE THE AGE DIFFERENCE.
THOUGH IT STILL SEEMS INSANE.
I MEAN, PERRY IS SURE TO REALIZE I'M NOT HER!
IT'S THE ONLY WAY, LO.
I WAS AFRAID YOU'D SAY THAT.
OKAY, I'LL TRY IT.
AND LET'S HOPE I CAN GET THROUGH THE DAY WITHOUT SEEING...

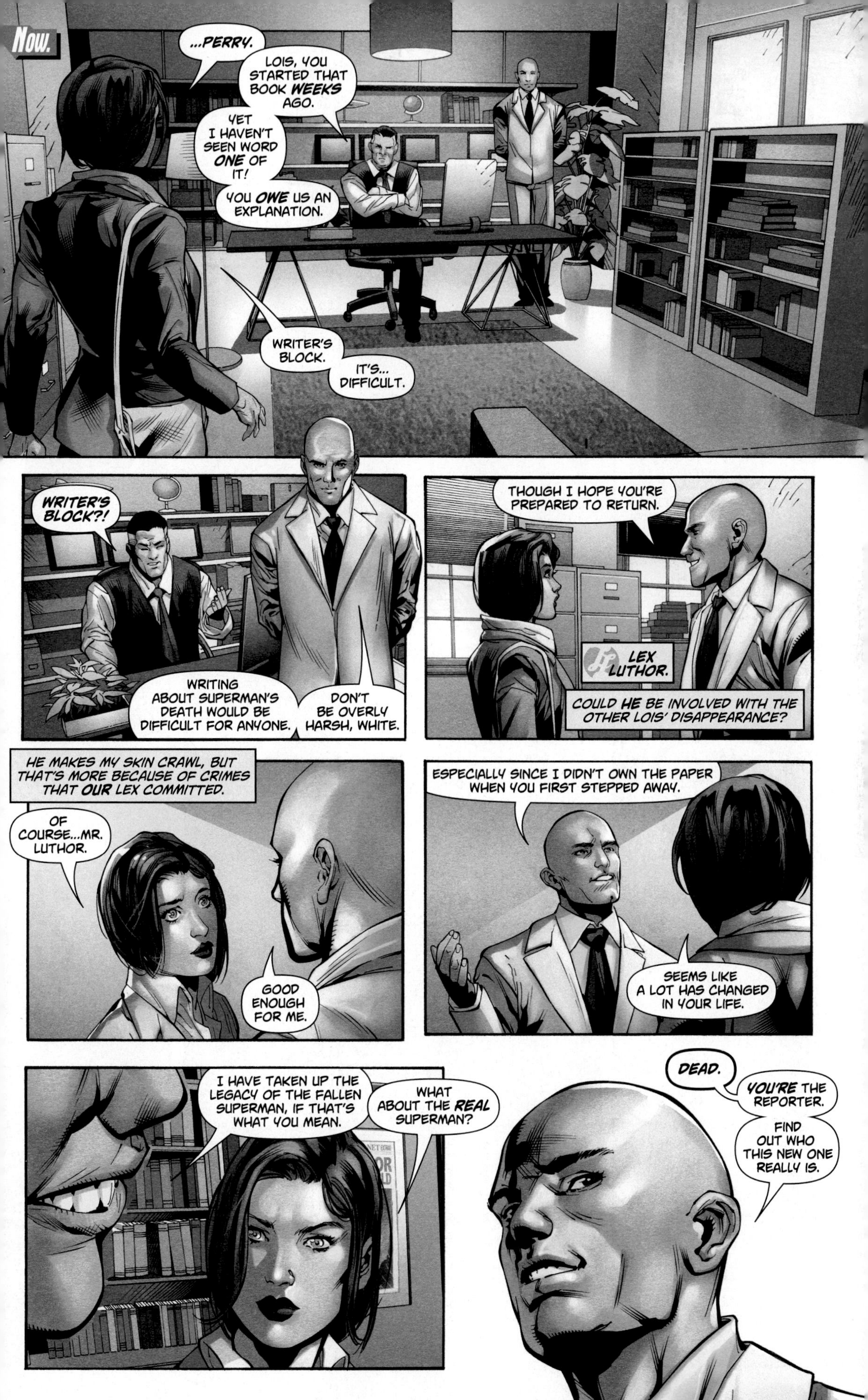
NOW.
...PERRY.
LOIS, YOU STARTED THAT BOOK WEEKS AGO.
YET I HAVEN'T SEEN WORD ONE OF IT!
YOU OWE US AN EXPLANATION.
WRITER'S BLOCK.
IT'S... DIFFICULT.
WRITER'S BLOCK?!
WRITING ABOUT SUPERMAN'S DEATH WOULD BE DIFFICULT FOR ANYONE.
DON'T BE OVERLY HARSH, WHITE.
THOUGH I HOPE YOU'RE PREPARED TO RETURN.
LEX LUTHOR.
COULD HE BE INVOLVED WITH THE OTHER LOIS' DISAPPEARANCE?
HE MAKES MY SKIN CRAWL, BUT THAT'S MORE BECAUSE OF CRIMES THAT OUR LEX COMMITTED.
OF COURSE...MR. LUTHOR.
GOOD ENOUGH FOR ME.
ESPECIALLY SINCE I DIDN'T OWN THE PAPER WHEN YOU FIRST STEPPED AWAY.
SEEMS LIKE A LOT HAS CHANGED IN YOUR LIFE.
I HAVE TAKEN UP THE LEGACY OF THE FALLEN SUPERMAN, IF THAT'S WHAT YOU MEAN.
WHAT ABOUT THE REAL SUPERMAN?
DEAD.
YOU'RE THE REPORTER.
FIND OUT WHO THIS NEW ONE REALLY IS.

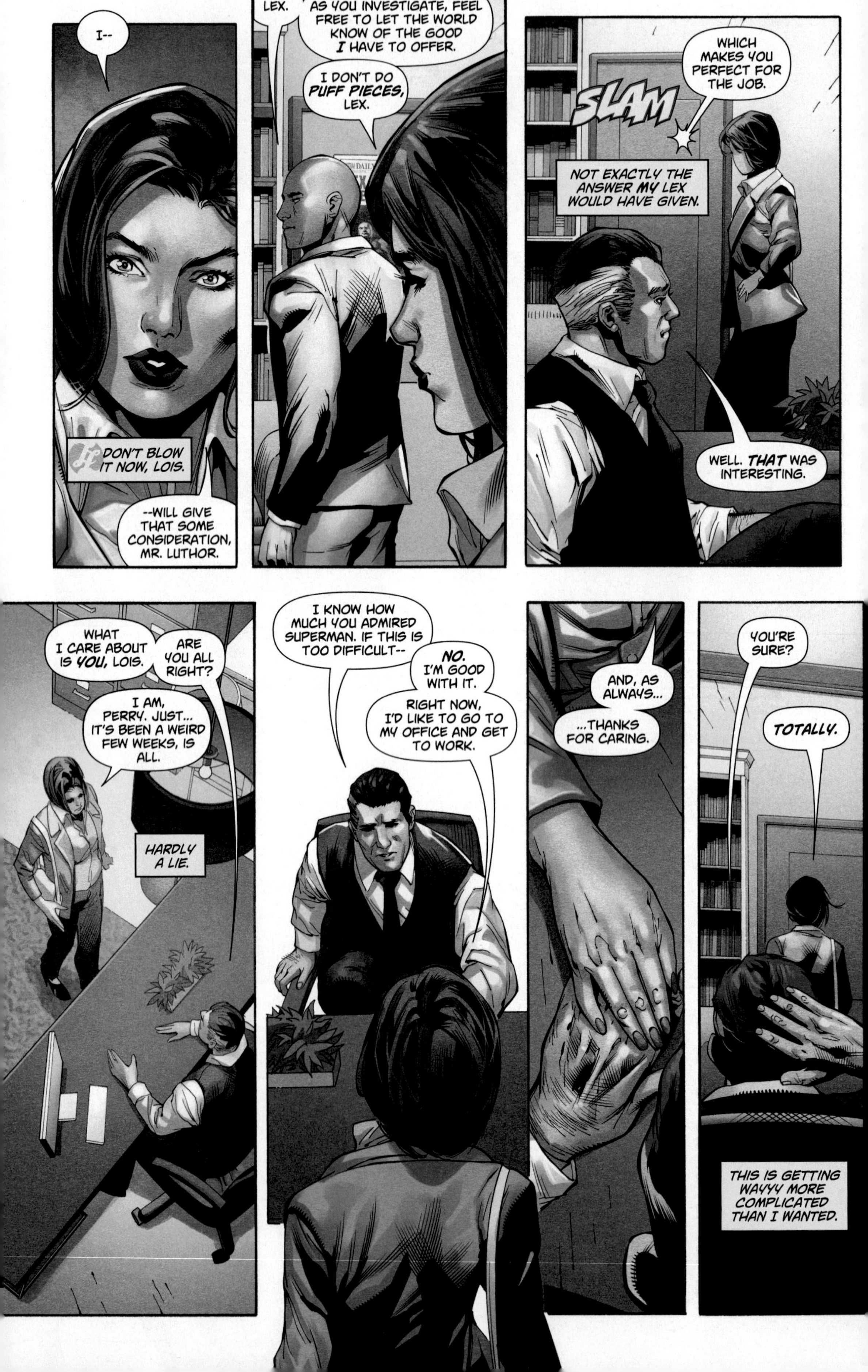
I--
DON'T BLOW IT NOW, LOIS.
--WILL GIVE THAT SOME CONSIDERATION, MR. LUTHOR.
LEX.
AS YOU INVESTIGATE, FEEL FREE TO LET THE WORLD KNOW OF THE GOOD I HAVE TO OFFER.
I DON'T DO PUFF PIECES, LEX.
WHICH MAKES YOU PERFECT FOR THE JOB.
SLAM
NOT EXACTLY THE ANSWER MY LEX WOULD HAVE GIVEN.
WELL. THAT WAS INTERESTING.
WHAT I CARE ABOUT IS YOU, LOIS.
ARE YOU ALL RIGHT?
I AM, PERRY. JUST... IT'S BEEN A WEIRD FEW WEEKS, IS ALL.
HARDLY A LIE.
I KNOW HOW MUCH YOU ADMIRED SUPERMAN. IF THIS IS TOO DIFFICULT--
NO. I'M GOOD WITH IT.
RIGHT NOW, I'D LIKE TO GO TO MY OFFICE AND GET TO WORK.
AND, AS ALWAYS...
...THANKS FOR CARING.
YOU'RE SURE?
TOTALLY.
THIS IS GETTING WAYYY MORE COMPLICATED THAN I WANTED.

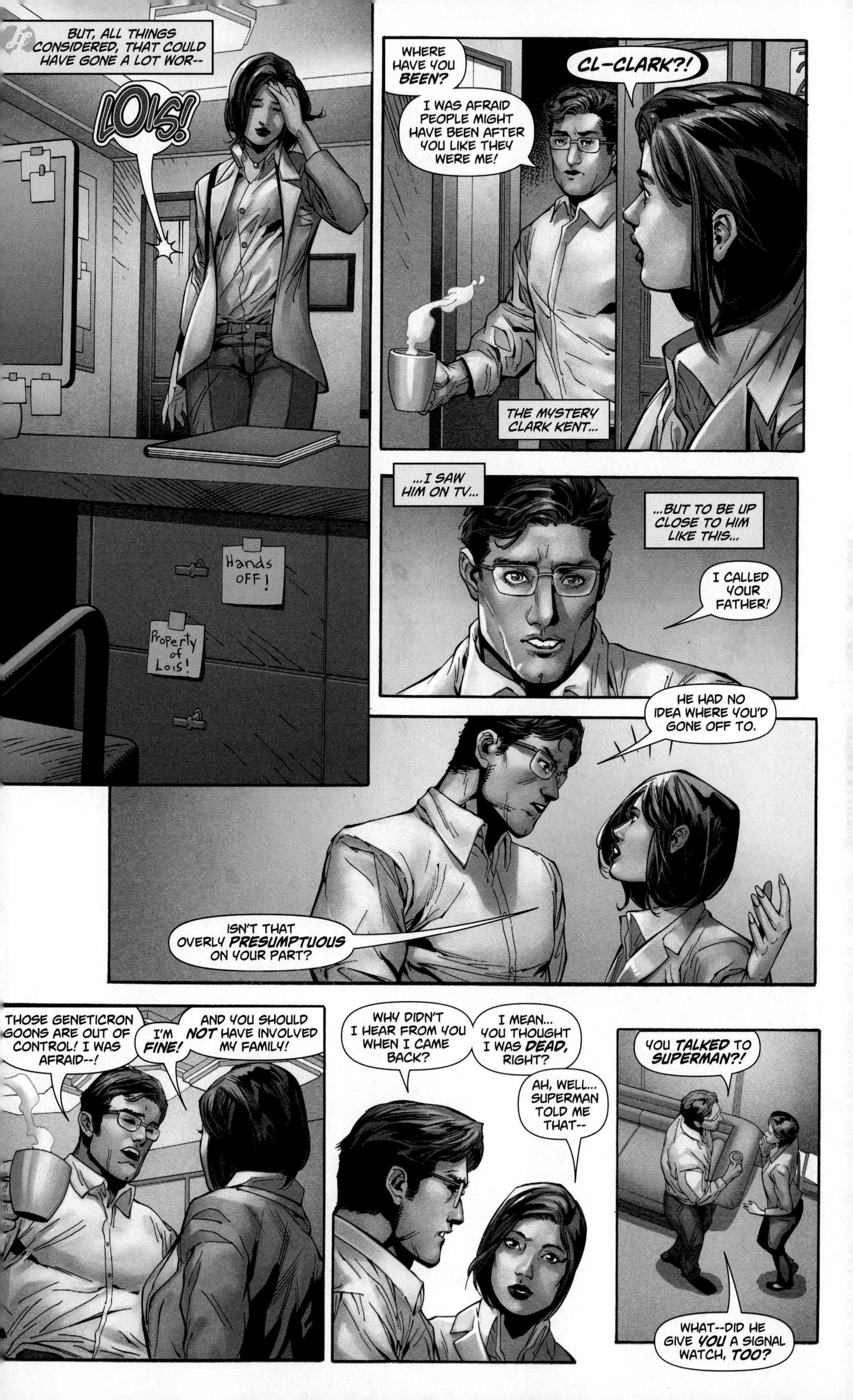
BUT, ALL THINGS CONSIDERED, THAT COULD HAVE GONE A LOT WOR--
LOIS!
Hands OFF!
Property of Lois!
WHERE HAVE YOU BEEN?
I WAS AFRAID PEOPLE MIGHT HAVE BEEN AFTER YOU LIKE THEY WERE ME!
CL--CLARK?!
THE MYSTERY CLARK KENT...
...I SAW HIM ON TV...
...BUT TO BE UP CLOSE TO HIM LIKE THIS...
I CALLED YOUR FATHER!
HE HAD NO IDEA WHERE YOU'D GONE OFF TO.
ISN'T THAT OVERLY PRESUMPTUOUS ON YOUR PART?
THOSE GENETICRON GOONS ARE OUT OF CONTROL! I WAS AFRAID--!
I'M FINE!
AND YOU SHOULD NOT HAVE INVOLVED MY FAMILY!
WHY DIDN'T I HEAR FROM YOU WHEN I CAME BACK?
I MEAN... YOU THOUGHT I WAS DEAD, RIGHT?
AH, WELL... SUPERMAN TOLD ME THAT--
YOU TALKED TO SUPERMAN?!
WHAT--DID HE GIVE YOU A SIGNAL WATCH, TOO?

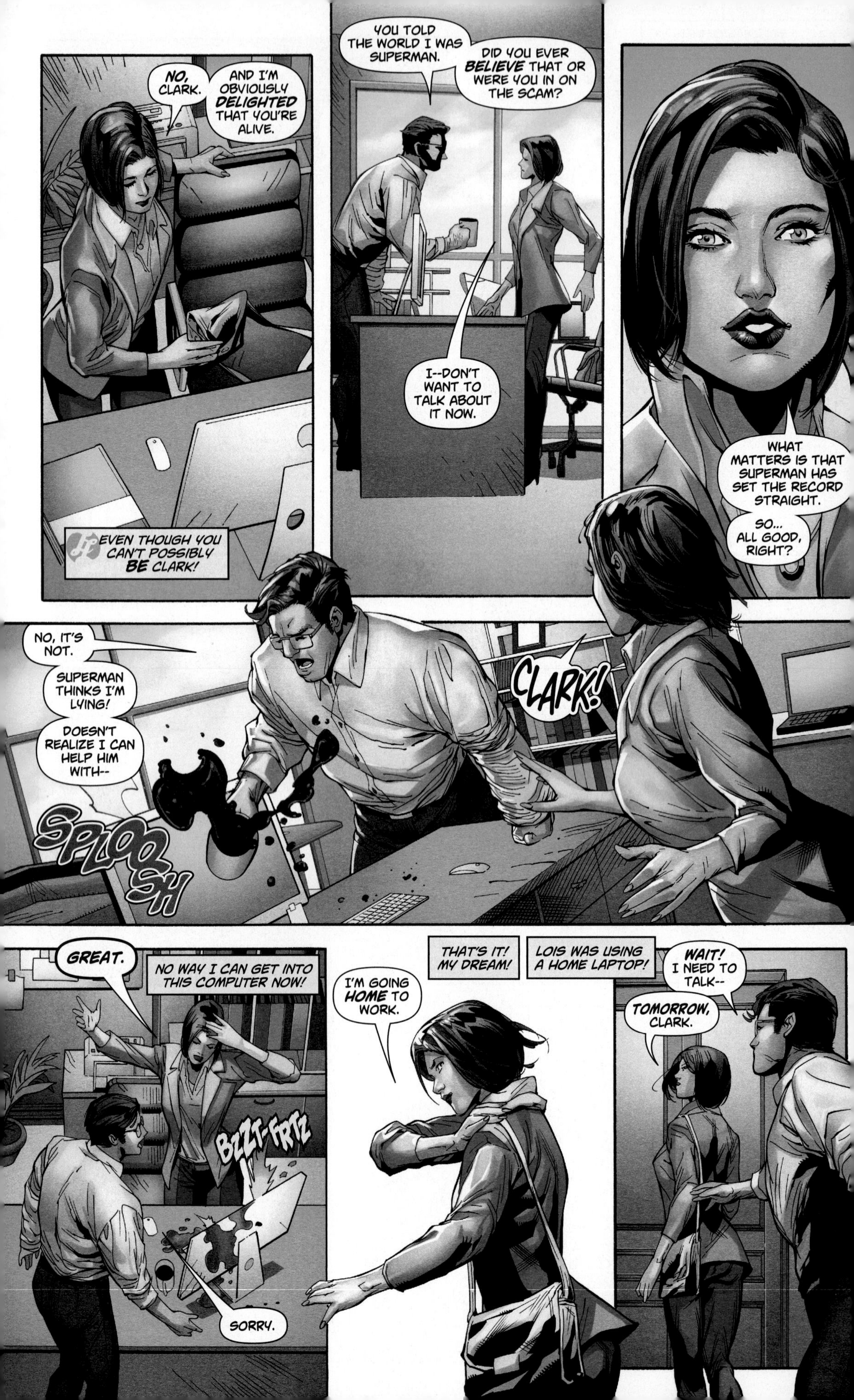
NO, CLARK.
AND I'M OBVIOUSLY DELIGHTED THAT YOU'RE ALIVE.
EVEN THOUGH YOU CAN'T POSSIBLY BE CLARK!
YOU TOLD THE WORLD I WAS SUPERMAN.
DID YOU EVER BELIEVE THAT OR WERE YOU IN ON THE SCAM?
I--DON'T WANT TO TALK ABOUT IT NOW.
WHAT MATTERS IS THAT SUPERMAN HAS SET THE RECORD STRAIGHT.
SO... ALL GOOD, RIGHT?
NO, IT'S NOT.
SUPERMAN THINKS I'M LYING!
DOESN'T REALIZE I CAN HELP HIM WITH--
SPLOOSH
CLARK!
GREAT.
NO WAY I CAN GET INTO THIS COMPUTER NOW!
BZZT-FRTZ
SORRY.
I'M GOING HOME TO WORK.
THAT'S IT! MY DREAM!
LOIS WAS USING A HOME LAPTOP!
WAIT! I NEED TO TALK--
TOMORROW, CLARK.

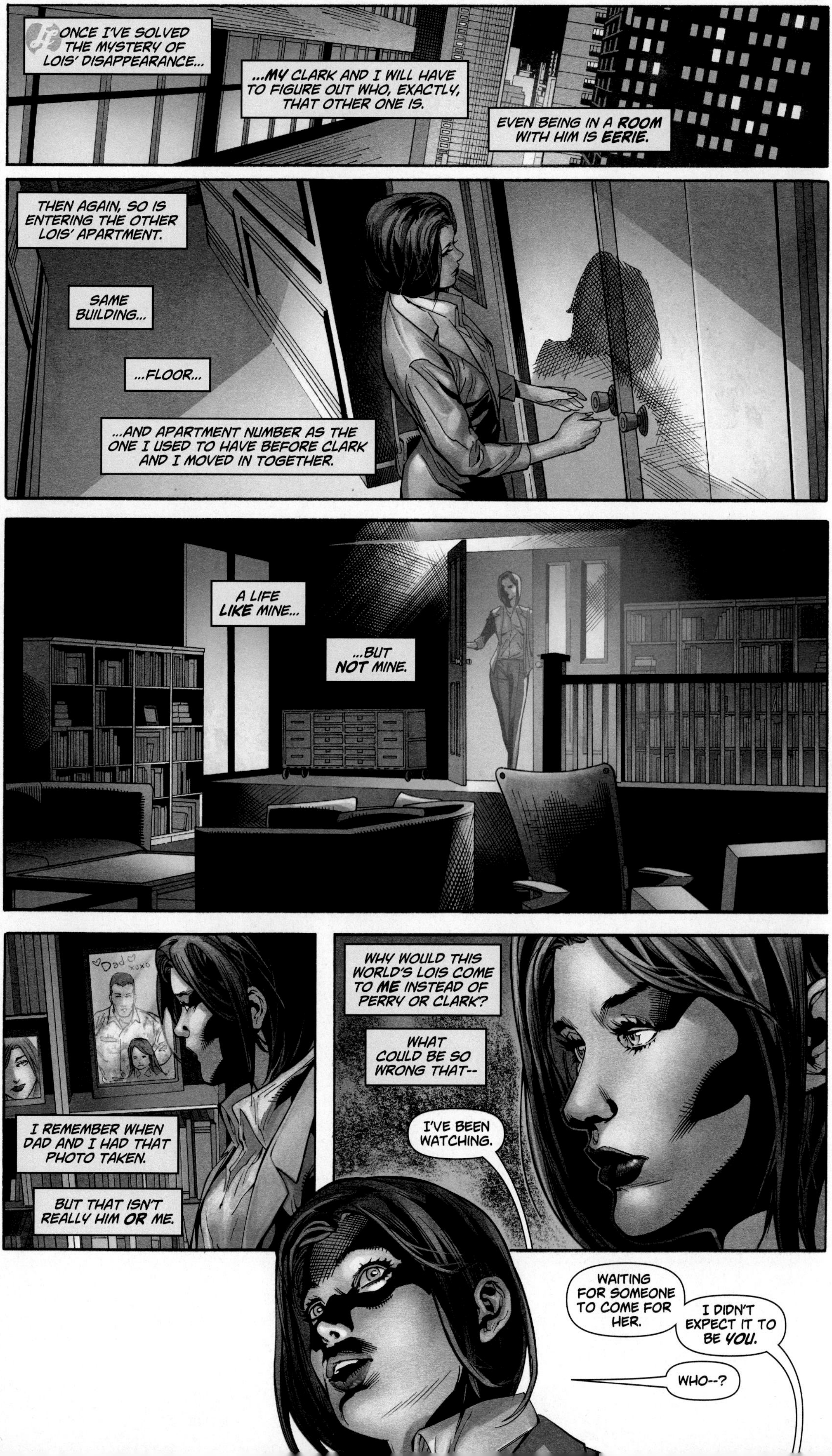

ONCE I'VE SOLVED THE MYSTERY OF LOIS' DISAPPEARANCE...
...MY CLARK AND I WILL HAVE TO FIGURE OUT WHO, EXACTLY, THAT OTHER ONE IS.
EVEN BEING IN A ROOM WITH HIM IS EERIE.
THEN AGAIN, SO IS ENTERING THE OTHER LOIS' APARTMENT.
SAME BUILDING...
...FLOOR...
...AND APARTMENT NUMBER AS THE ONE I USED TO HAVE BEFORE CLARK AND I MOVED IN TOGETHER.
A LIFE LIKE MINE...
...BUT NOT MINE.
Dad xoxo
I REMEMBER WHEN DAD AND I HAD THAT PHOTO TAKEN.
BUT THAT ISN'T REALLY HIM OR ME.
WHY WOULD THIS WORLD'S LOIS COME TO ME INSTEAD OF PERRY OR CLARK?
WHAT COULD BE SO WRONG THAT--
I'VE BEEN WATCHING.
WAITING FOR SOMEONE TO COME FOR HER.
I DIDN'T EXPECT IT TO BE YOU.
WHO--?

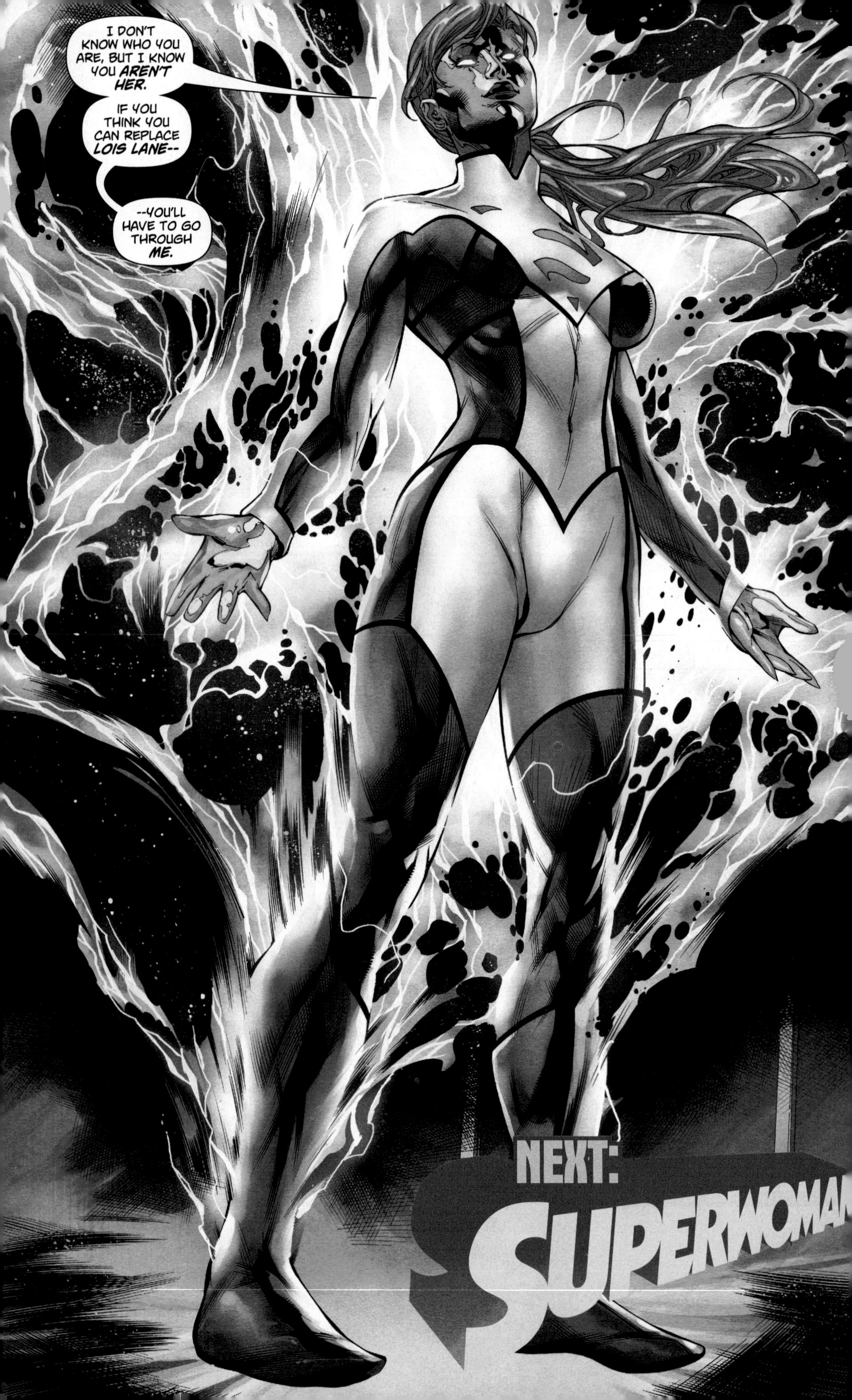
I DON'T KNOW WHO YOU ARE, BUT I KNOW YOU **AREN'T HER.**
IF YOU THINK YOU CAN REPLACE **LOIS LANE--**
--YOU'LL HAVE TO GO THROUGH **ME.**
NEXT:
SUPERWOMAN

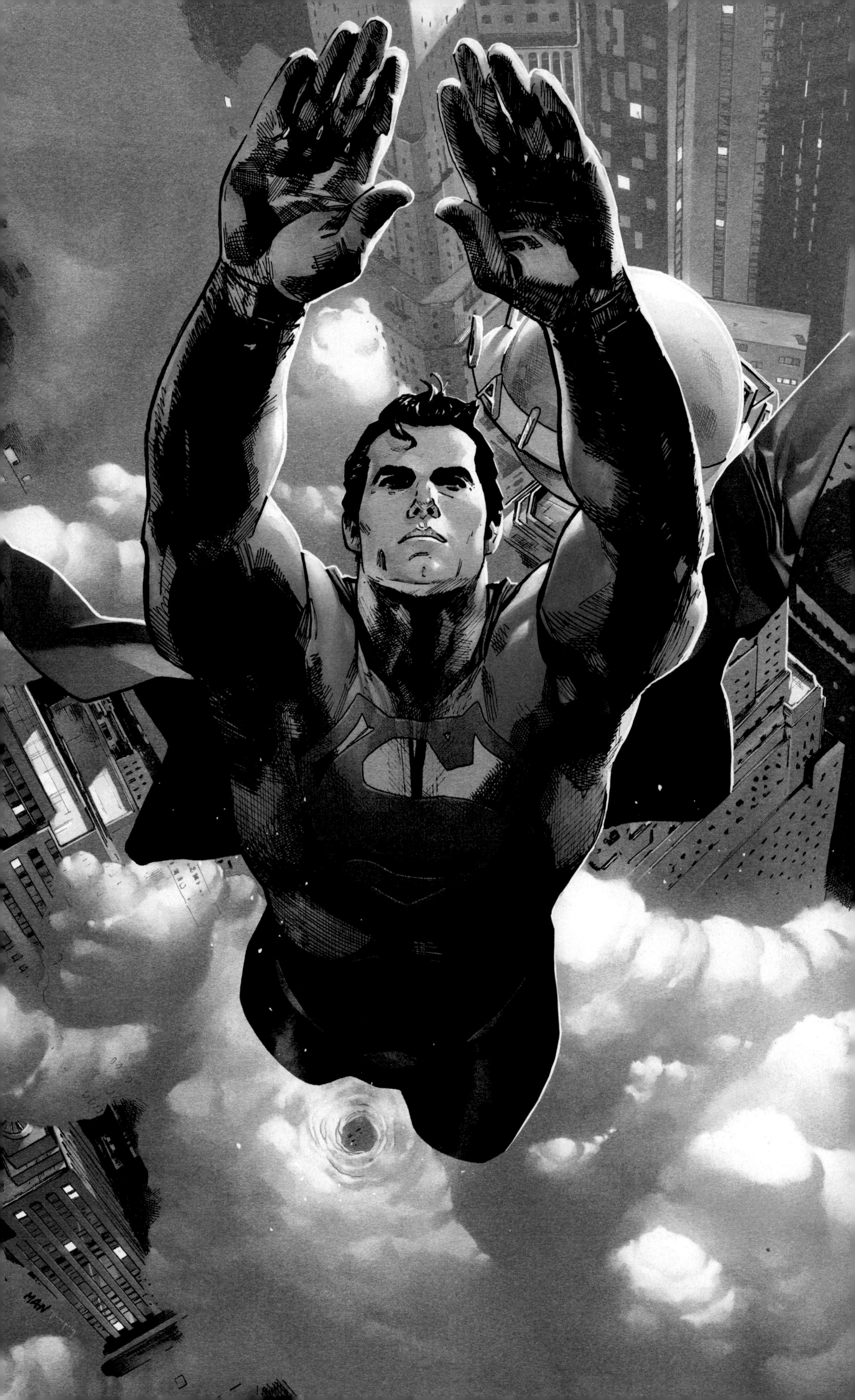
MAN

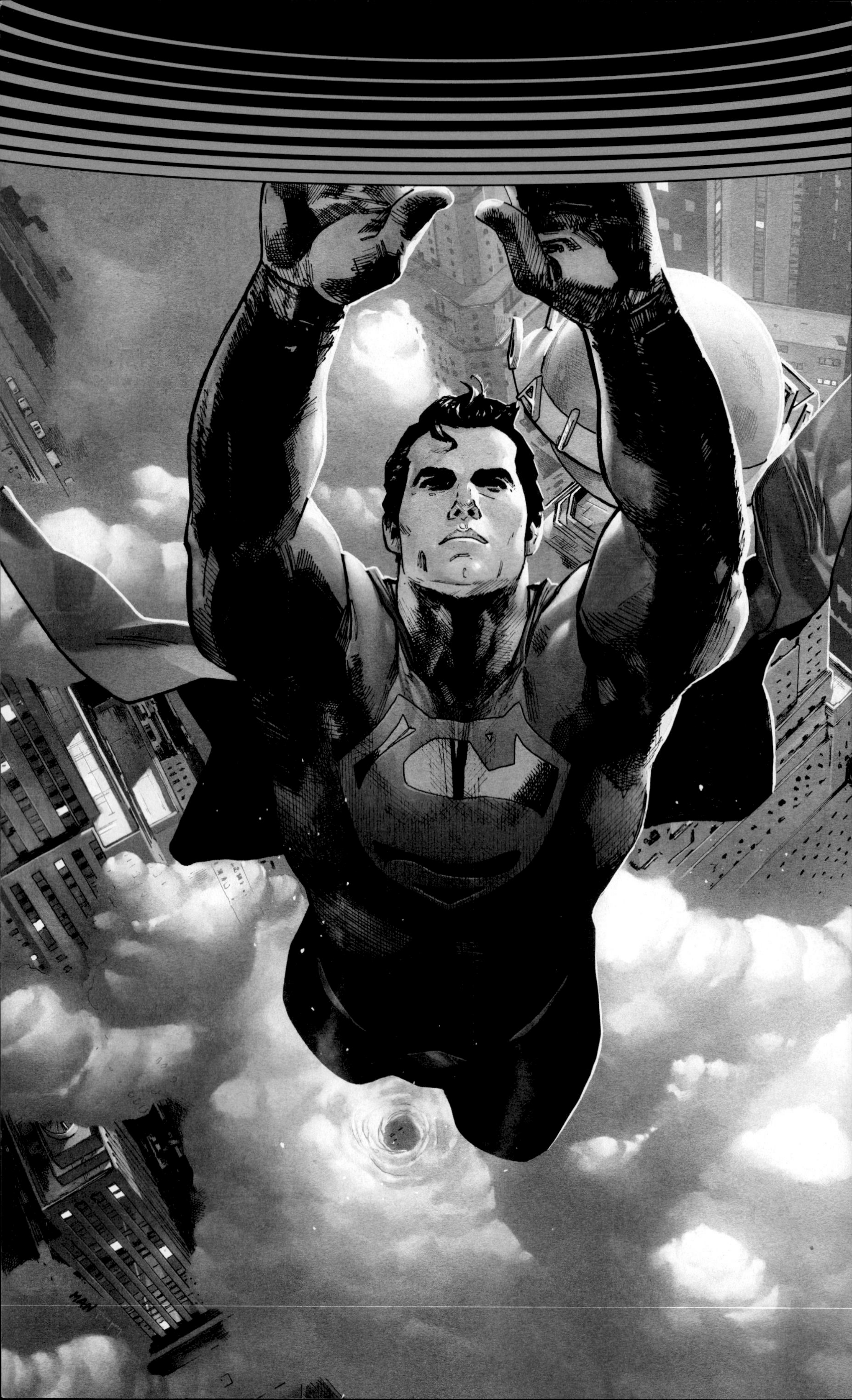

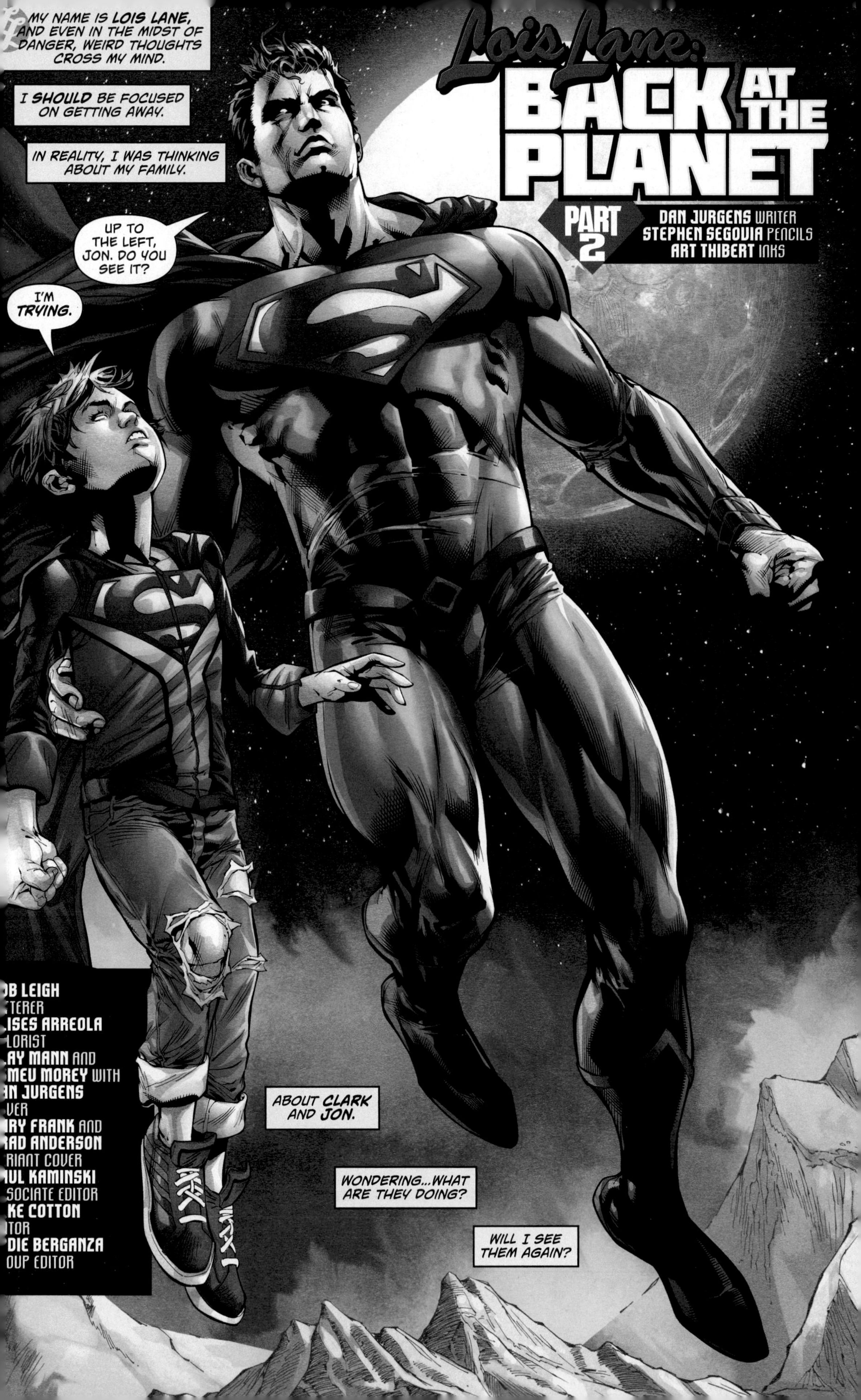

MY NAME IS LOIS LANE, AND EVEN IN THE MIDST OF DANGER, WEIRD THOUGHTS CROSS MY MIND.
I SHOULD BE FOCUSED ON GETTING AWAY.
IN REALITY, I WAS THINKING ABOUT MY FAMILY.
Lois Lane: BACK AT THE PLANET
PART 2
DAN JURGENS WRITER
STEPHEN SEGOVIA PENCILS
ART THIBERT INKS
UP TO THE LEFT, JON. DO YOU SEE IT?
I'M TRYING.
OB LEIGH
TERER
ISES ARREOLA
LORIST
AY MANN AND
MEU MOREY WITH
N JURGENS
VER
RY FRANK AND
RAD ANDERSON
RIANT COVER
UL KAMINSKI
SOCIATE EDITOR
KE COTTON
ITOR
DIE BERGANZA
OUP EDITOR
ABOUT CLARK AND JON.
WONDERING...WHAT ARE THEY DOING?
WILL I SEE THEM AGAIN?

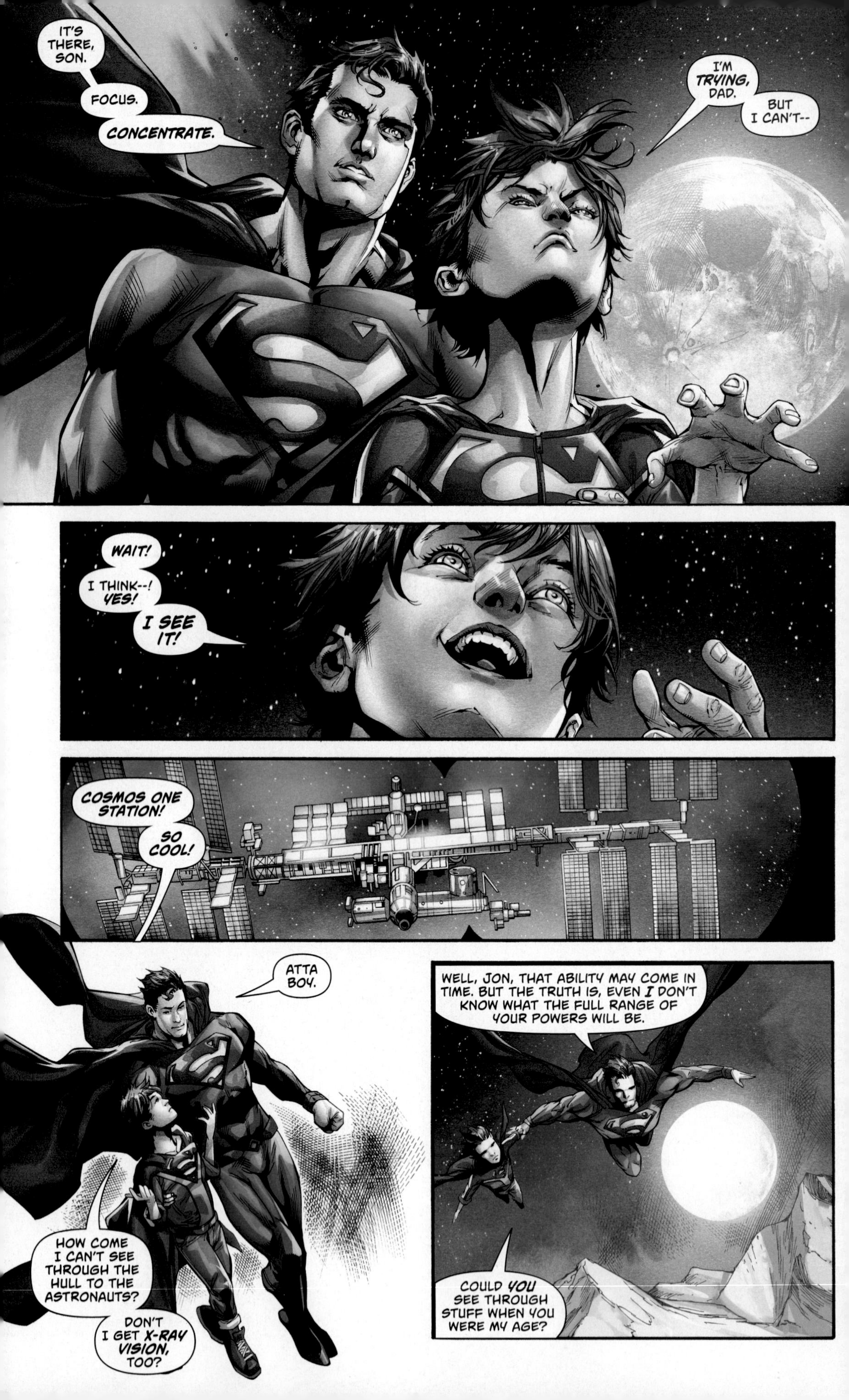
IT'S THERE, SON.
FOCUS.
CONCENTRATE.
I'M TRYING, DAD.
BUT I CAN'T--
WAIT!
I THINK--! YES!
I SEE IT!
COSMOS ONE STATION!
SO COOL!
ATTA BOY.
HOW COME I CAN'T SEE THROUGH THE HULL TO THE ASTRONAUTS?
DON'T I GET X-RAY VISION, TOO?
WELL, JON, THAT ABILITY MAY COME IN TIME. BUT THE TRUTH IS, EVEN I DON'T KNOW WHAT THE FULL RANGE OF YOUR POWERS WILL BE.
COULD YOU SEE THROUGH STUFF WHEN YOU WERE MY AGE?

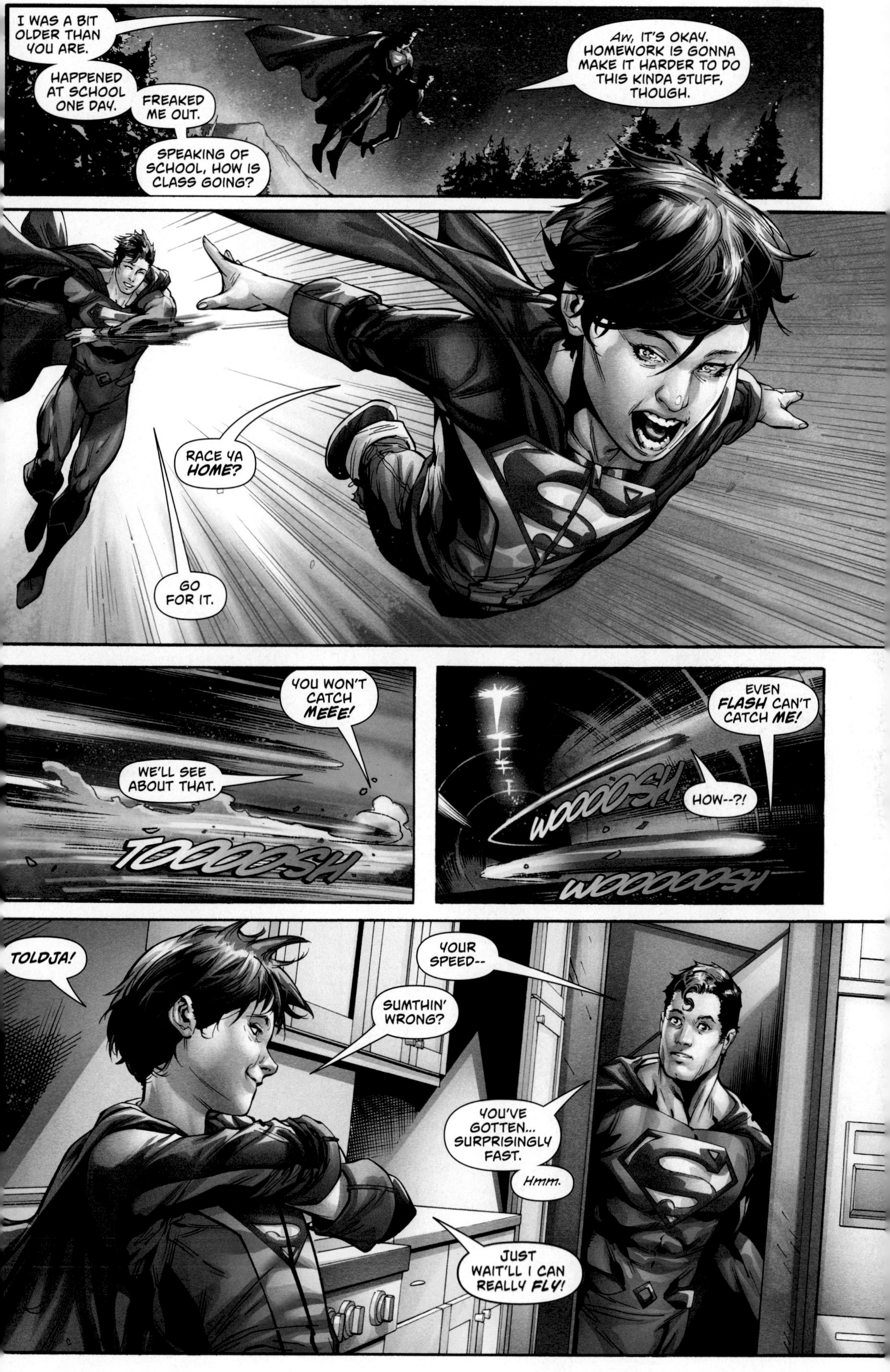
I WAS A BIT OLDER THAN YOU ARE.
HAPPENED AT SCHOOL ONE DAY.
FREAKED ME OUT.
SPEAKING OF SCHOOL, HOW IS CLASS GOING?
Aw, IT'S OKAY. HOMEWORK IS GONNA MAKE IT HARDER TO DO THIS KINDA STUFF, THOUGH.
RACE YA HOME?
GO FOR IT.
YOU WON'T CATCH MEEE!
WE'LL SEE ABOUT THAT.
TOOOOOSH
EVEN FLASH CAN'T CATCH ME!
HOW--?!
WOOOOOSH
WOOOOOOSH
TOLDJA!
YOUR SPEED--
SUMTHIN' WRONG?
YOU'VE GOTTEN... SURPRISINGLY FAST.
Hmm.
JUST WAIT'LL I CAN REALLY FLY!

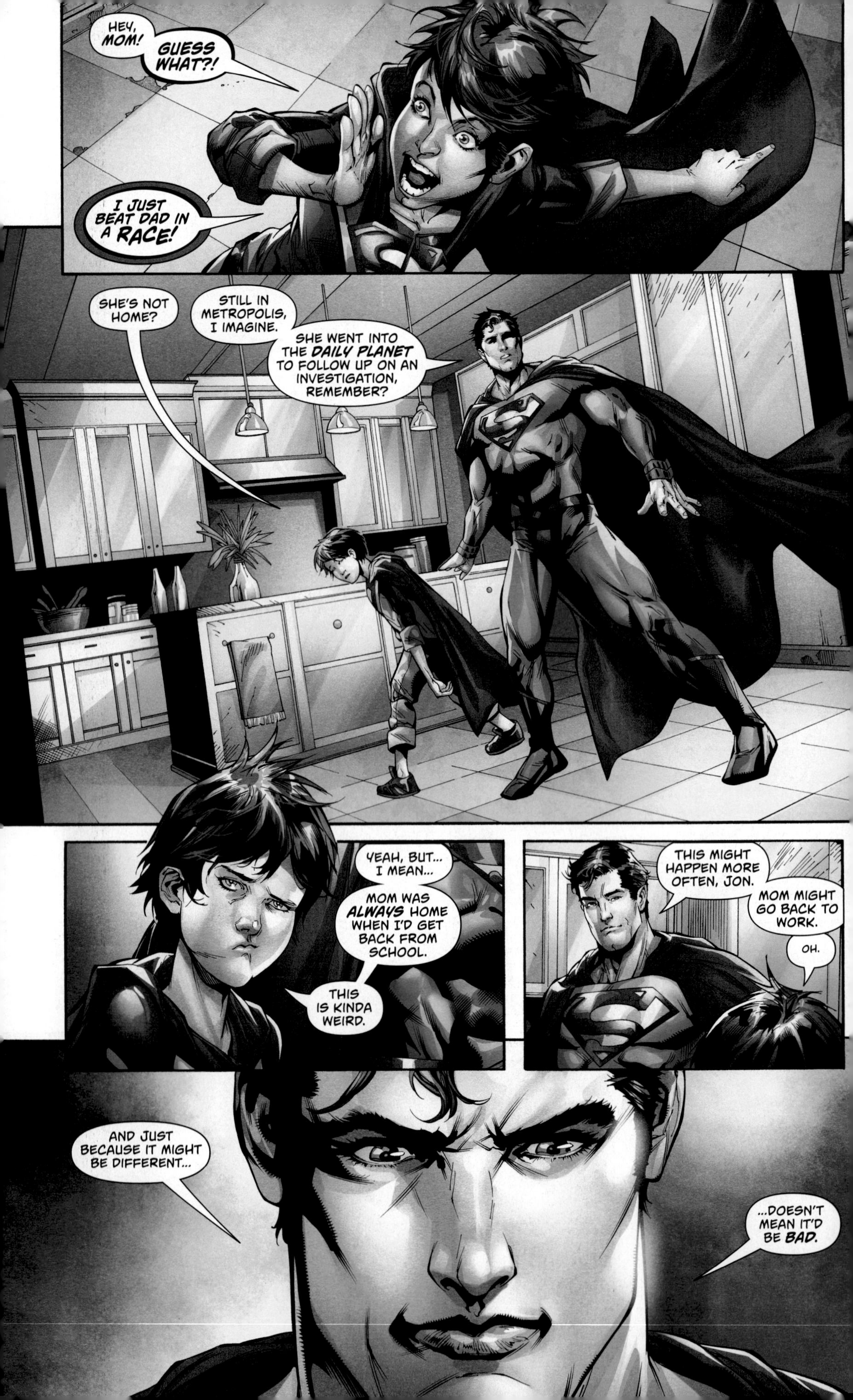
HEY, MOM! GUESS WHAT?!
I JUST BEAT DAD IN A RACE!
SHE'S NOT HOME?
STILL IN METROPOLIS, I IMAGINE.
SHE WENT INTO THE DAILY PLANET TO FOLLOW UP ON AN INVESTIGATION, REMEMBER?
YEAH, BUT... I MEAN...
MOM WAS ALWAYS HOME WHEN I'D GET BACK FROM SCHOOL.
THIS IS KINDA WEIRD.
THIS MIGHT HAPPEN MORE OFTEN, JON.
MOM MIGHT GO BACK TO WORK.
OH.
AND JUST BECAUSE IT MIGHT BE DIFFERENT...
...DOESN'T MEAN IT'D BE BAD.

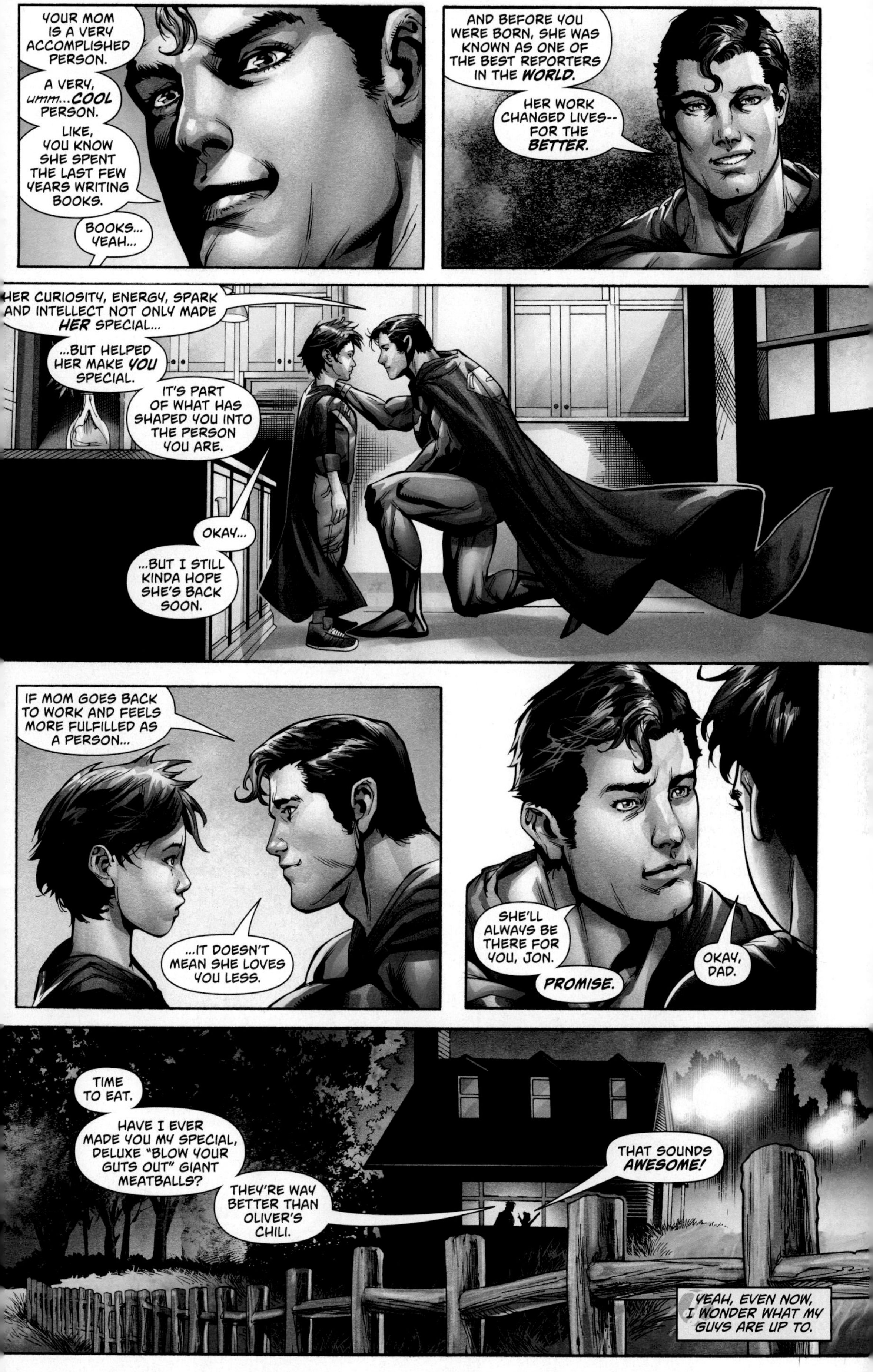
YOUR MOM IS A VERY ACCOMPLISHED PERSON.
A VERY, umm... COOL PERSON.
LIKE, YOU KNOW SHE SPENT THE LAST FEW YEARS WRITING BOOKS.
BOOKS... YEAH...
AND BEFORE YOU WERE BORN, SHE WAS KNOWN AS ONE OF THE BEST REPORTERS IN THE WORLD.
HER WORK CHANGED LIVES-- FOR THE BETTER.
HER CURIOSITY, ENERGY, SPARK AND INTELLECT NOT ONLY MADE HER SPECIAL...
...BUT HELPED HER MAKE YOU SPECIAL.
IT'S PART OF WHAT HAS SHAPED YOU INTO THE PERSON YOU ARE.
OKAY...
...BUT I STILL KINDA HOPE SHE'S BACK SOON.
IF MOM GOES BACK TO WORK AND FEELS MORE FULFILLED AS A PERSON...
...IT DOESN'T MEAN SHE LOVES YOU LESS.
SHE'LL ALWAYS BE THERE FOR YOU, JON.
PROMISE.
OKAY, DAD.
TIME TO EAT.
HAVE I EVER MADE YOU MY SPECIAL, DELUXE "BLOW YOUR GUTS OUT" GIANT MEATBALLS?
THEY'RE WAY BETTER THAN OLIVER'S CHILI.
THAT SOUNDS AWESOME!
YEAH, EVEN NOW, I WONDER WHAT MY GUYS ARE UP TO.

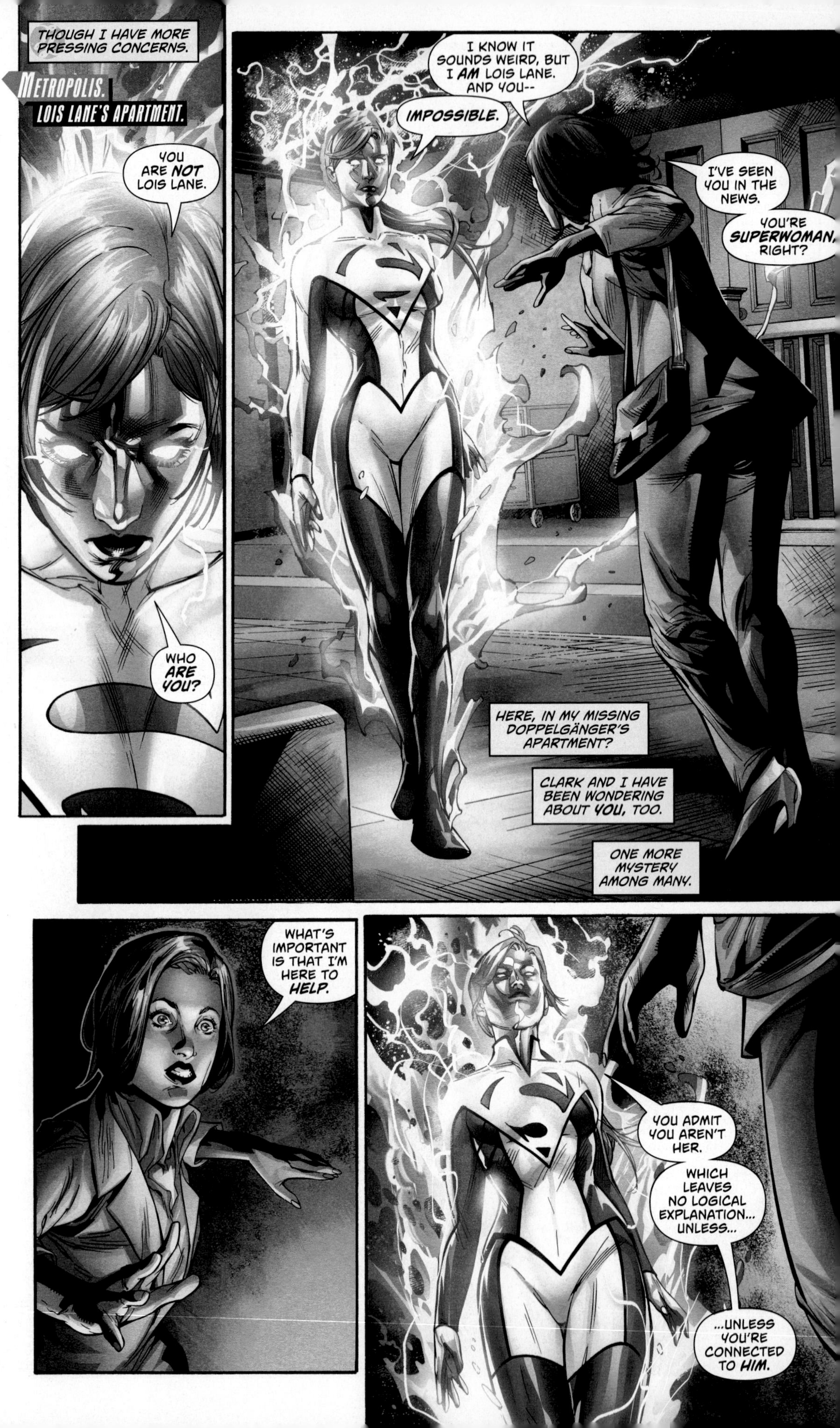
THOUGH I HAVE MORE PRESSING CONCERNS.
METROPOLIS.
LOIS LANE'S APARTMENT.
YOU ARE NOT LOIS LANE.
WHO ARE YOU?
I KNOW IT SOUNDS WEIRD, BUT I AM LOIS LANE. AND YOU--
IMPOSSIBLE.
I'VE SEEN YOU IN THE NEWS.
YOU'RE SUPERWOMAN, RIGHT?
HERE, IN MY MISSING DOPPELGÄNGER'S APARTMENT?
CLARK AND I HAVE BEEN WONDERING ABOUT YOU, TOO.
ONE MORE MYSTERY AMONG MANY.
WHAT'S IMPORTANT IS THAT I'M HERE TO HELP.
YOU ADMIT YOU AREN'T HER.
WHICH LEAVES NO LOGICAL EXPLANATION... UNLESS...
...UNLESS YOU'RE CONNECTED TO HIM.

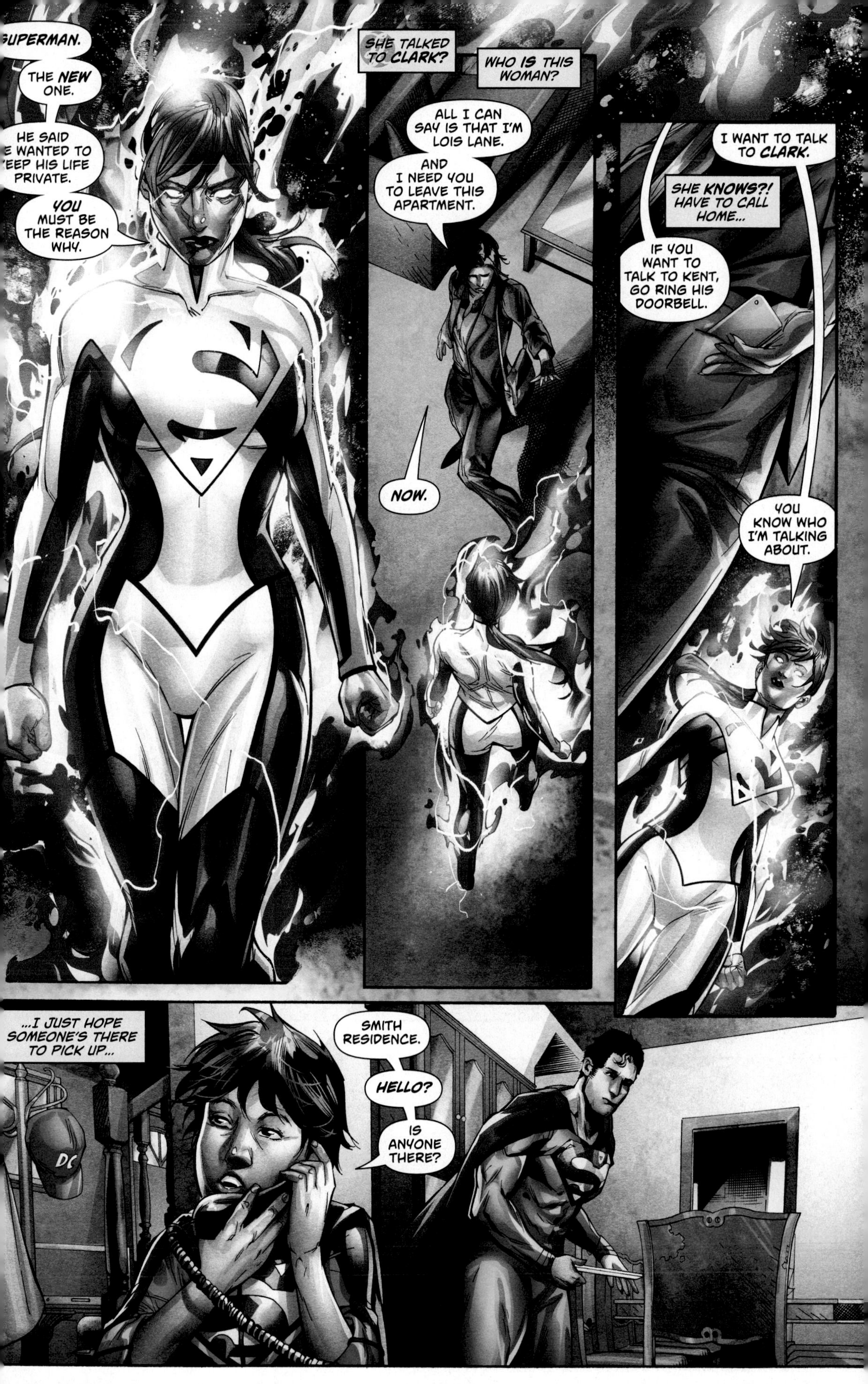
SUPERMAN.
THE NEW ONE.
HE SAID E WANTED TO EEP HIS LIFE PRIVATE.
YOU MUST BE THE REASON WHY.
SHE TALKED TO CLARK?
WHO IS THIS WOMAN?
ALL I CAN SAY IS THAT I'M LOIS LANE.
AND I NEED YOU TO LEAVE THIS APARTMENT.
NOW.
I WANT TO TALK TO CLARK.
SHE KNOWS?! HAVE TO CALL HOME...
IF YOU WANT TO TALK TO KENT, GO RING HIS DOORBELL.
YOU KNOW WHO I'M TALKING ABOUT.
...I JUST HOPE SOMEONE'S THERE TO PICK UP...
SMITH RESIDENCE.
HELLO?
IS ANYONE THERE?
DC

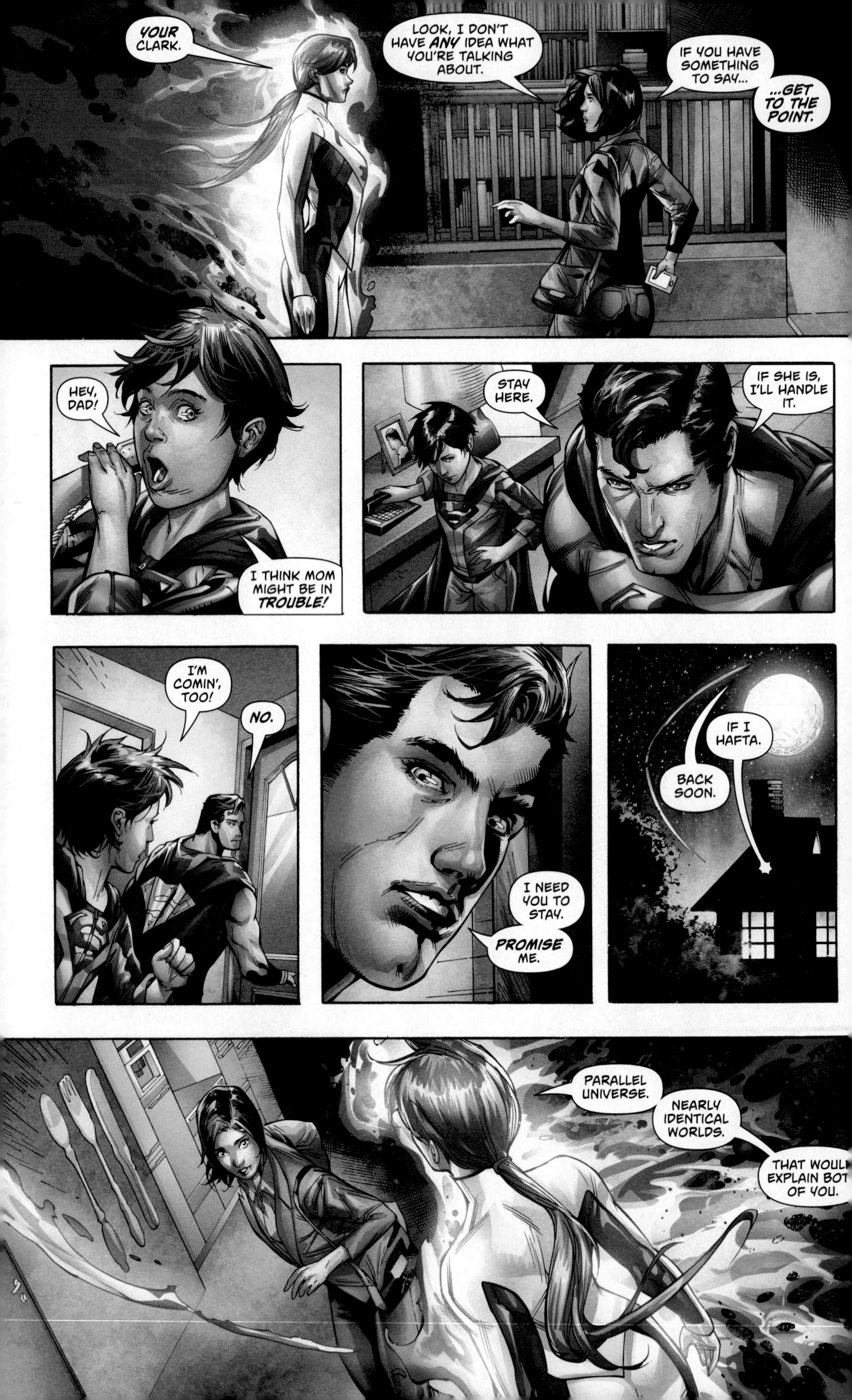
YOUR CLARK.
LOOK, I DON'T HAVE ANY IDEA WHAT YOU'RE TALKING ABOUT.
IF YOU HAVE SOMETHING TO SAY...
...GET TO THE POINT.
HEY, DAD!
I THINK MOM MIGHT BE IN TROUBLE!
STAY HERE.
IF SHE IS, I'LL HANDLE IT.
I'M COMIN', TOO!
NO.
I NEED YOU TO STAY.
PROMISE ME.
IF I HAFTA.
BACK SOON.
PARALLEL UNIVERSE.
NEARLY IDENTICAL WORLDS.
THAT WOUL
EXPLAIN BOT
OF YOU.

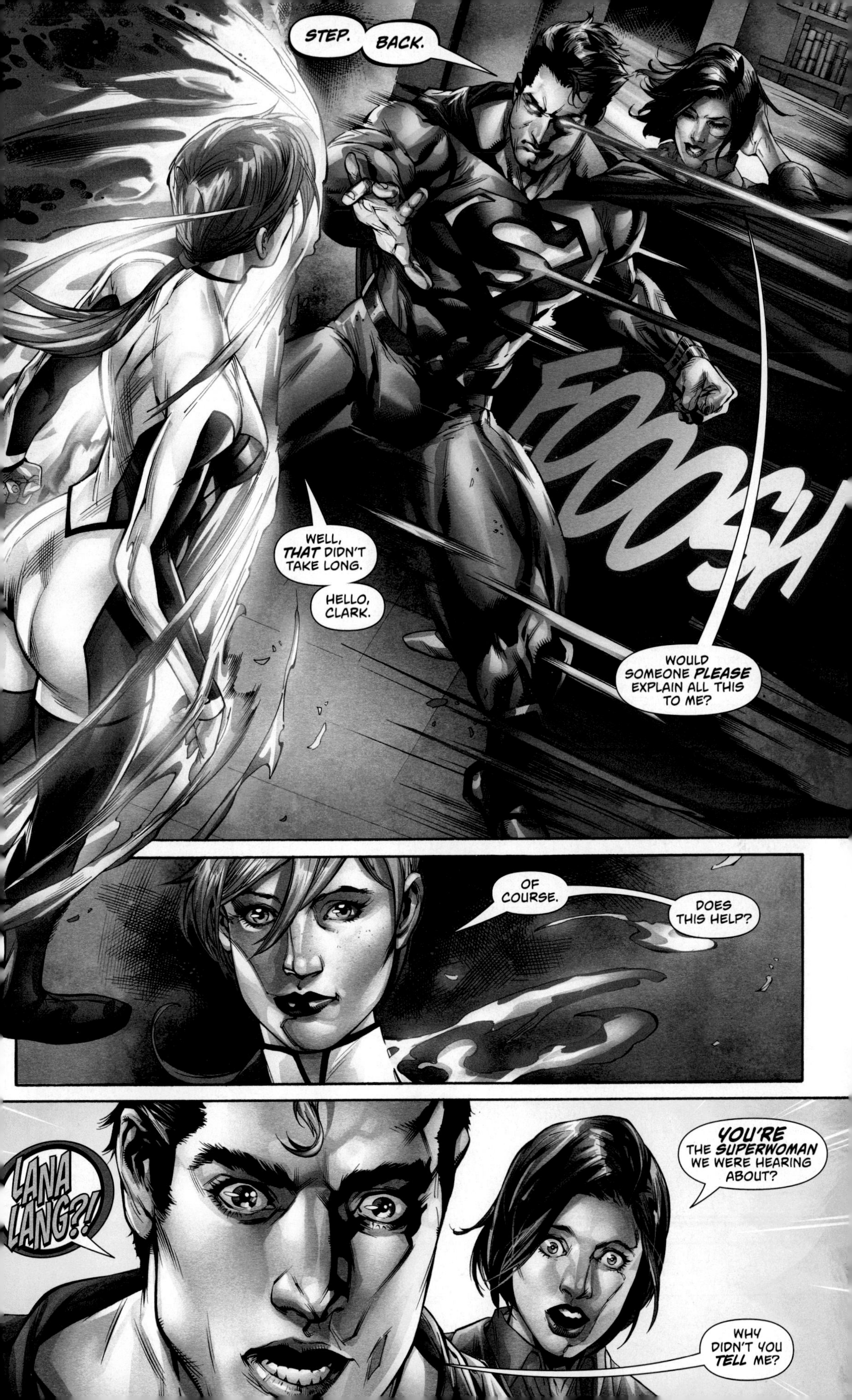
STEP.
BACK.
FOOOSH
WELL, THAT DIDN'T TAKE LONG.
HELLO, CLARK.
WOULD SOMEONE PLEASE EXPLAIN ALL THIS TO ME?
OF COURSE.
DOES THIS HELP?
LANA LANG?!
YOU'RE THE SUPERWOMAN WE WERE HEARING ABOUT?
WHY DIDN'T YOU TELL ME?

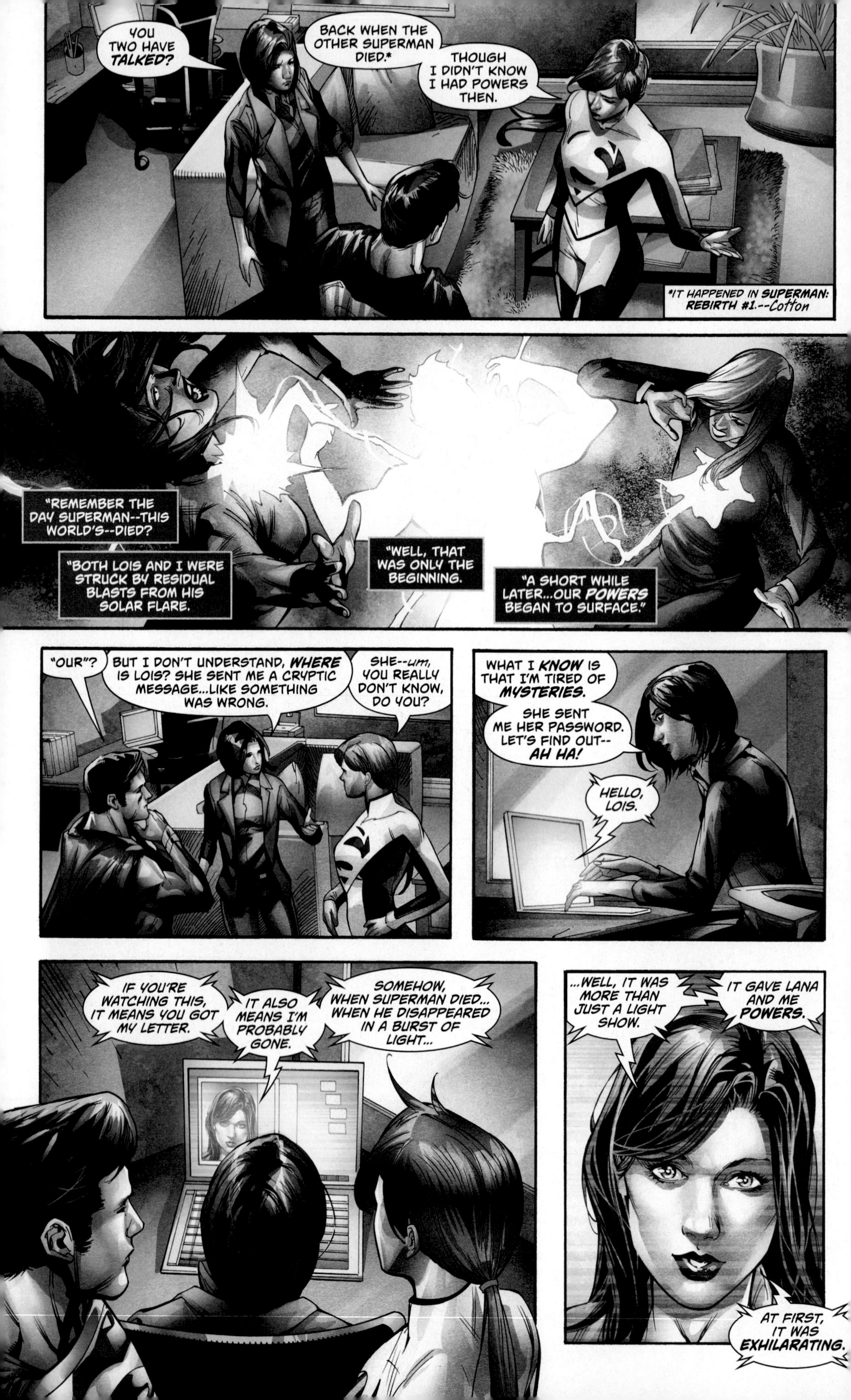
YOU TWO HAVE TALKED?
BACK WHEN THE OTHER SUPERMAN DIED.*
THOUGH I DIDN'T KNOW I HAD POWERS THEN.
*IT HAPPENED IN SUPERMAN: REBIRTH #1.--Cotton
"REMEMBER THE DAY SUPERMAN--THIS WORLD'S--DIED?
"BOTH LOIS AND I WERE STRUCK BY RESIDUAL BLASTS FROM HIS SOLAR FLARE.
"WELL, THAT WAS ONLY THE BEGINNING.
"A SHORT WHILE LATER...OUR POWERS BEGAN TO SURFACE."
"OUR"?
BUT I DON'T UNDERSTAND, WHERE IS LOIS? SHE SENT ME A CRYPTIC MESSAGE...LIKE SOMETHING WAS WRONG.
SHE--UM, YOU REALLY DON'T KNOW, DO YOU?
WHAT I KNOW IS THAT I'M TIRED OF MYSTERIES.
SHE SENT ME HER PASSWORD. LET'S FIND OUT-- AH HA!
HELLO, LOIS.
IF YOU'RE WATCHING THIS, IT MEANS YOU GOT MY LETTER.
IT ALSO MEANS I'M PROBABLY GONE.
SOMEHOW, WHEN SUPERMAN DIED... WHEN HE DISAPPEARED IN A BURST OF LIGHT...
...WELL, IT WAS MORE THAN JUST A LIGHT SHOW.
IT GAVE LANA AND ME POWERS.
AT FIRST, IT WAS EXHILARATING.

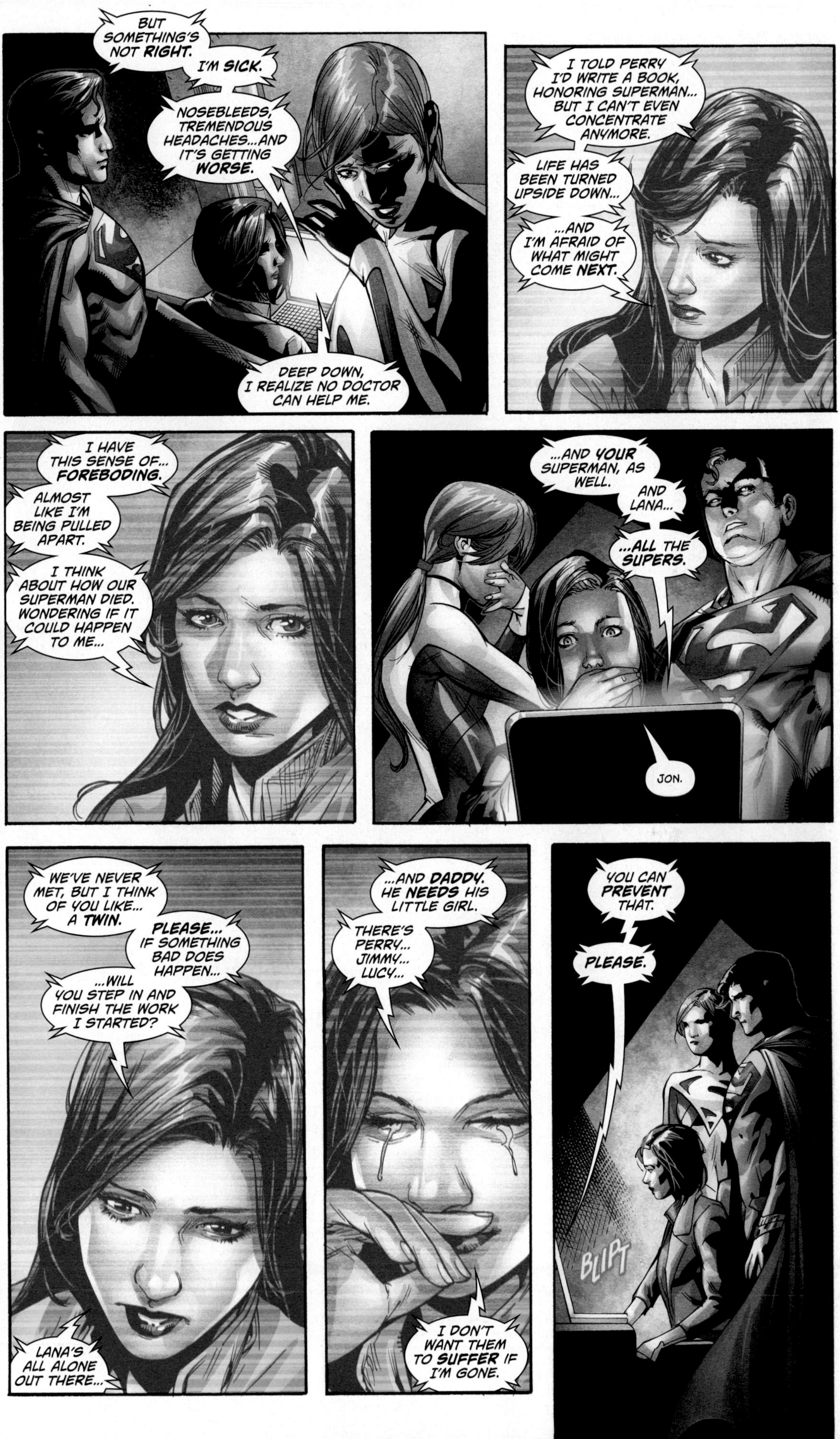
BUT SOMETHING'S NOT RIGHT.
I'M SICK.
NOSEBLEEDS, TREMENDOUS HEADACHES...AND IT'S GETTING WORSE.
DEEP DOWN, I REALIZE NO DOCTOR CAN HELP ME.
I TOLD PERRY I'D WRITE A BOOK, HONORING SUPERMAN... BUT I CAN'T EVEN CONCENTRATE ANYMORE.
LIFE HAS BEEN TURNED UPSIDE DOWN...
...AND I'M AFRAID OF WHAT MIGHT COME NEXT.
I HAVE THIS SENSE OF... FOREBODING.
ALMOST LIKE I'M BEING PULLED APART.
I THINK ABOUT HOW OUR SUPERMAN DIED. WONDERING IF IT COULD HAPPEN TO ME...
...AND YOUR SUPERMAN, AS WELL.
AND LANA...
...ALL THE SUPERS.
JON.
WE'VE NEVER MET, BUT I THINK OF YOU LIKE... A TWIN.
PLEASE... IF SOMETHING BAD DOES HAPPEN...
...WILL YOU STEP IN AND FINISH THE WORK I STARTED?
LANA'S ALL ALONE OUT THERE...
...AND DADDY. HE NEEDS HIS LITTLE GIRL.
THERE'S PERRY... JIMMY... LUCY...
I DON'T WANT THEM TO SUFFER IF I'M GONE.
YOU CAN PREVENT THAT.
PLEASE.
BLIPT

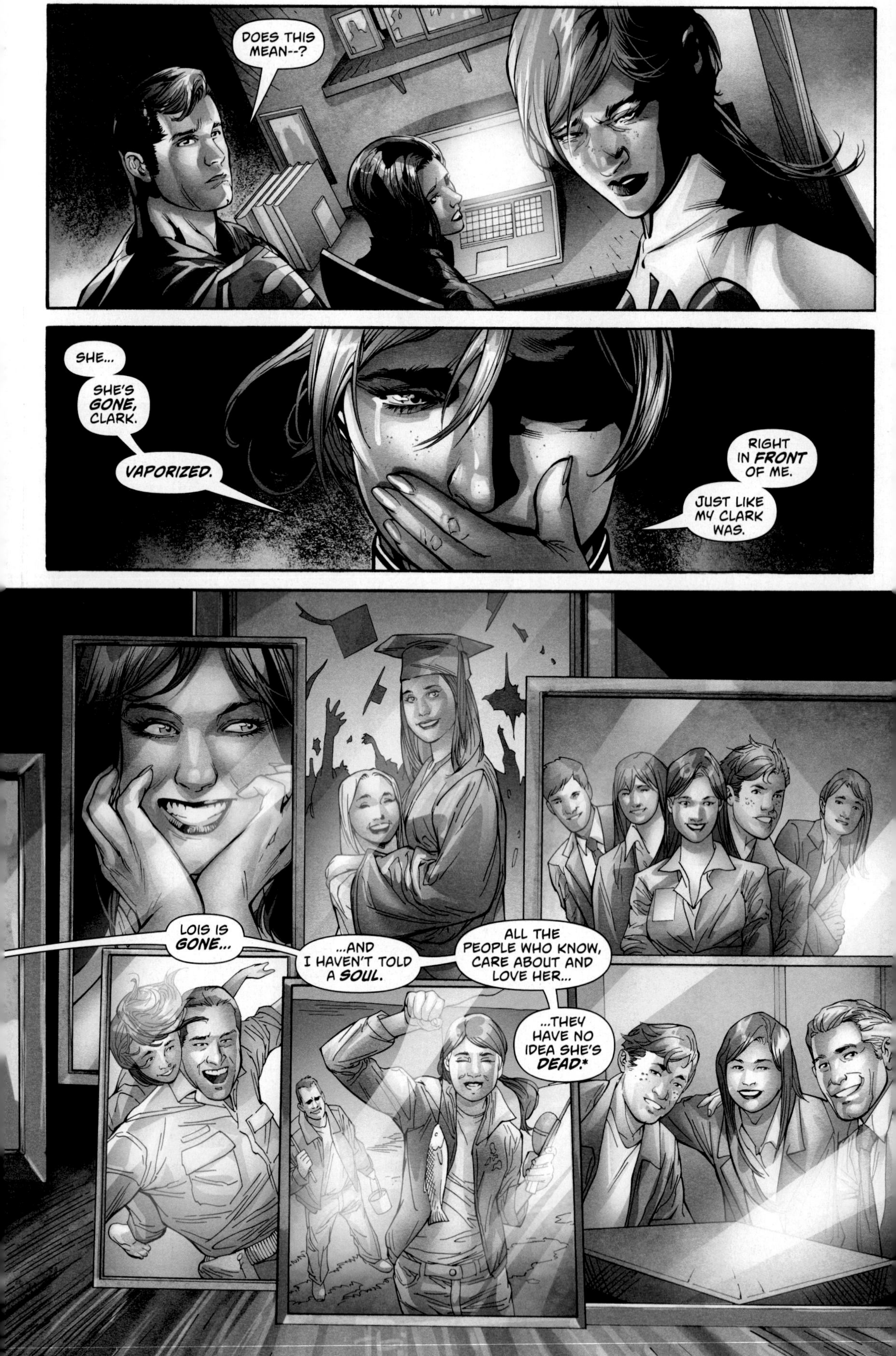
DOES THIS MEAN--?
SHE...
SHE'S GONE, CLARK.
VAPORIZED.
RIGHT IN FRONT OF ME.
JUST LIKE MY CLARK WAS.
LOIS IS GONE...
...AND I HAVEN'T TOLD A SOUL.
ALL THE PEOPLE WHO KNOW, CARE ABOUT AND LOVE HER...
...THEY HAVE NO IDEA SHE'S DEAD.*
*SEE RECENT ISSUES OF SUPERWOMAN FOR THE FULL STORY. --Cotton

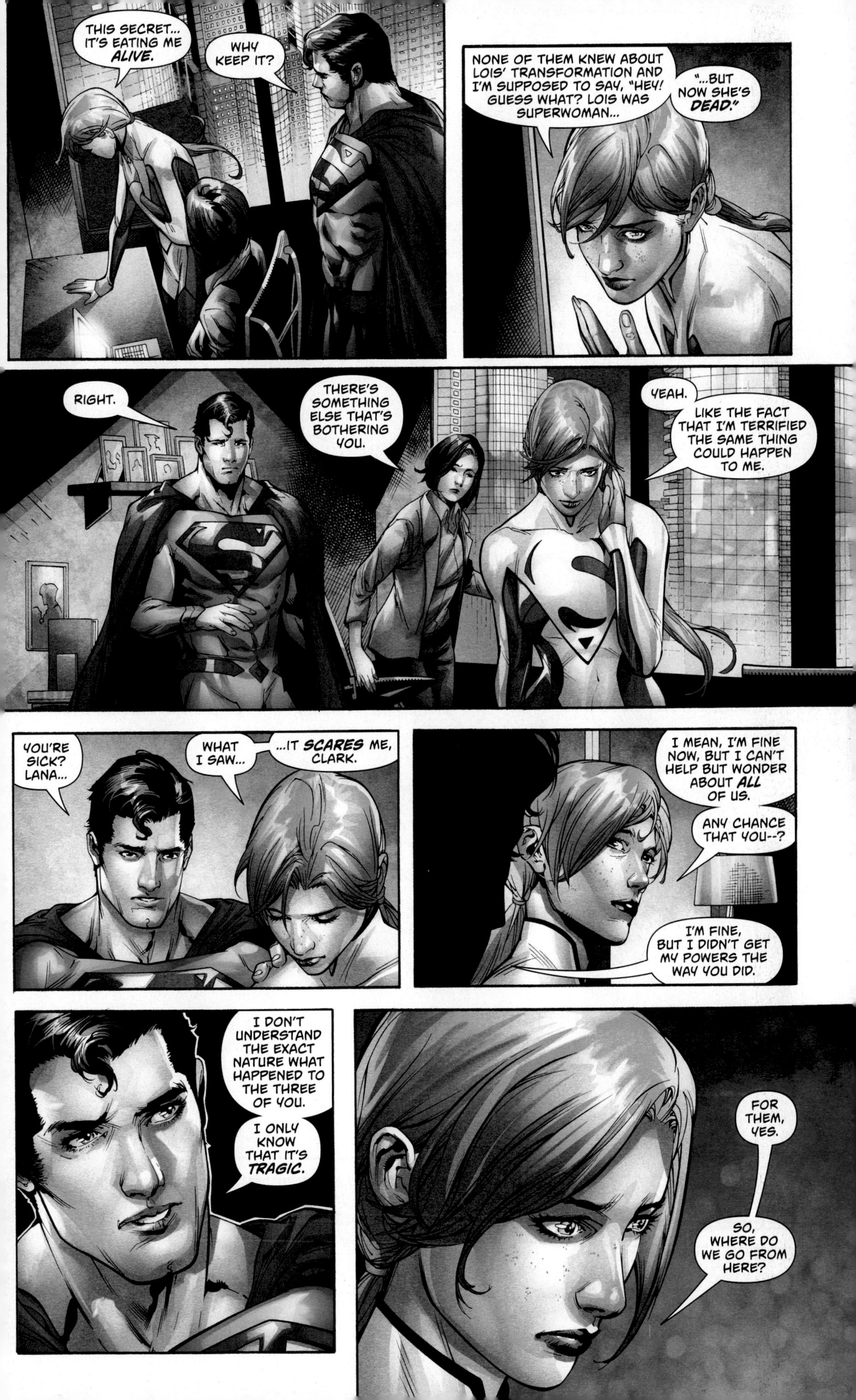
THIS SECRET... IT'S EATING ME ALIVE.
WHY KEEP IT?
NONE OF THEM KNEW ABOUT LOIS' TRANSFORMATION AND I'M SUPPOSED TO SAY, "HEY! GUESS WHAT? LOIS WAS SUPERWOMAN...
"...BUT NOW SHE'S DEAD."
RIGHT.
THERE'S SOMETHING ELSE THAT'S BOTHERING YOU.
YEAH.
LIKE THE FACT THAT I'M TERRIFIED THE SAME THING COULD HAPPEN TO ME.
YOU'RE SICK? LANA...
WHAT I SAW...
...IT SCARES ME, CLARK.
I MEAN, I'M FINE NOW, BUT I CAN'T HELP BUT WONDER ABOUT ALL OF US.
ANY CHANCE THAT YOU--?
I'M FINE, BUT I DIDN'T GET MY POWERS THE WAY YOU DID.
I DON'T UNDERSTAND THE EXACT NATURE WHAT HAPPENED TO THE THREE OF YOU.
I ONLY KNOW THAT IT'S TRAGIC.
FOR THEM, YES.
SO, WHERE DO WE GO FROM HERE?

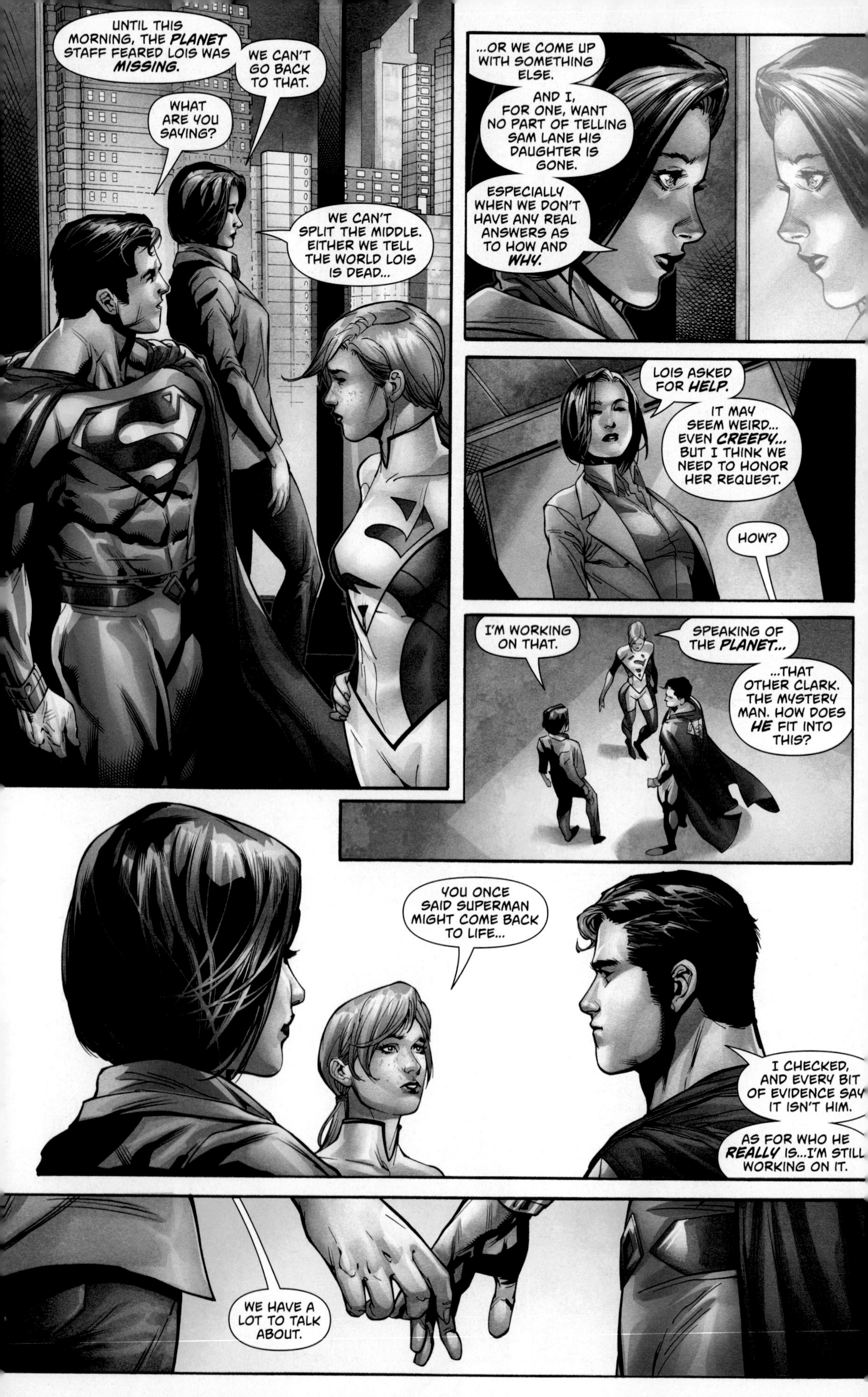
UNTIL THIS MORNING, THE PLANET STAFF FEARED LOIS WAS MISSING.
WE CAN'T GO BACK TO THAT.
WHAT ARE YOU SAYING?
WE CAN'T SPLIT THE MIDDLE. EITHER WE TELL THE WORLD LOIS IS DEAD...
...OR WE COME UP WITH SOMETHING ELSE.
AND I, FOR ONE, WANT NO PART OF TELLING SAM LANE HIS DAUGHTER IS GONE.
ESPECIALLY WHEN WE DON'T HAVE ANY REAL ANSWERS AS TO HOW AND WHY.
LOIS ASKED FOR HELP.
IT MAY SEEM WEIRD... EVEN CREEPY... BUT I THINK WE NEED TO HONOR HER REQUEST.
HOW?
I'M WORKING ON THAT.
SPEAKING OF THE PLANET...
...THAT OTHER CLARK. THE MYSTERY MAN. HOW DOES HE FIT INTO THIS?
YOU ONCE SAID SUPERMAN MIGHT COME BACK TO LIFE...
I CHECKED, AND EVERY BIT OF EVIDENCE SAY IT ISN'T HIM.
AS FOR WHO HE REALLY IS...I'M STILL WORKING ON IT.
WE HAVE A LOT TO TALK ABOUT.

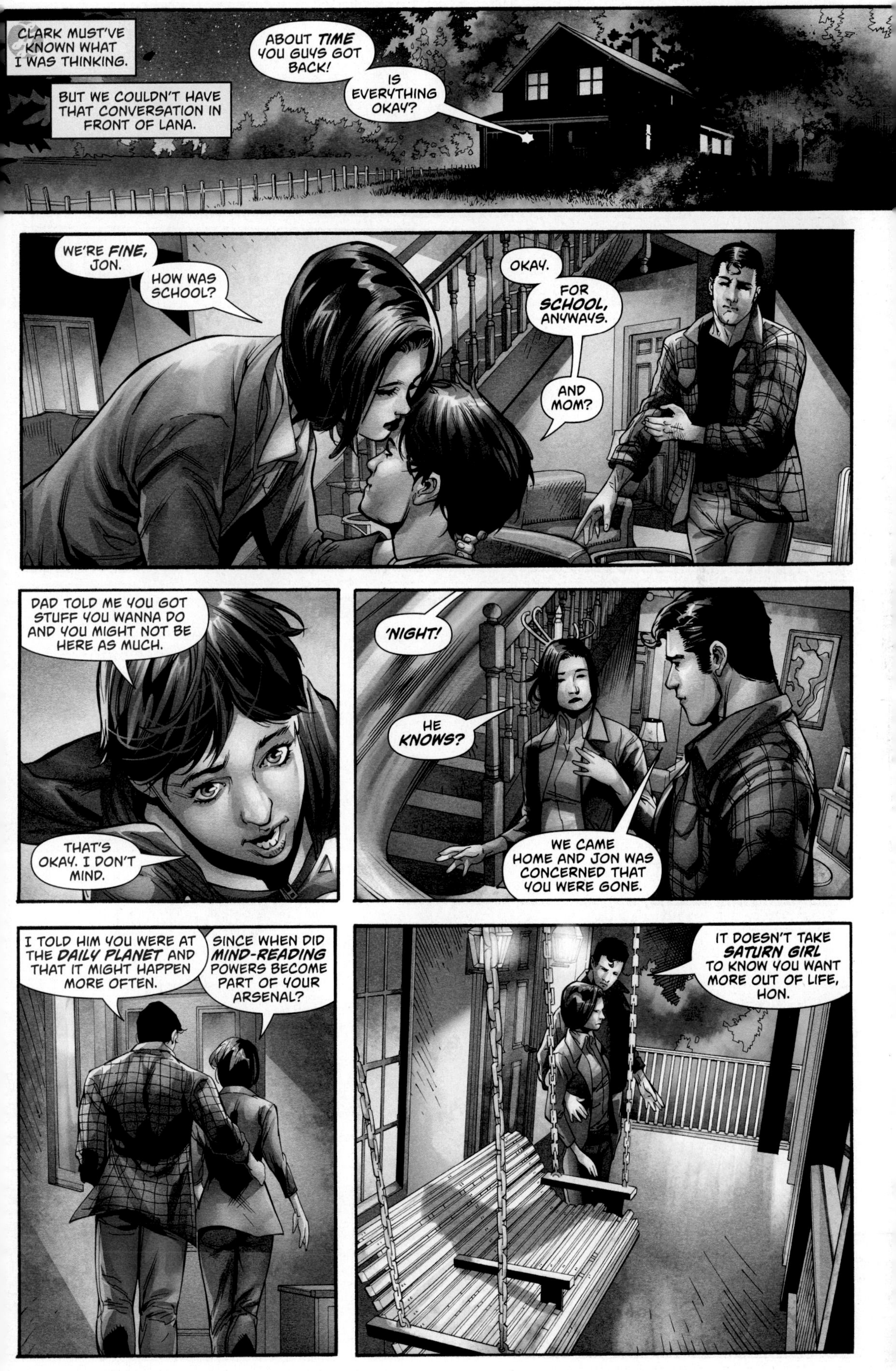
CLARK MUST'VE KNOWN WHAT I WAS THINKING.
BUT WE COULDN'T HAVE THAT CONVERSATION IN FRONT OF LANA.
ABOUT TIME YOU GUYS GOT BACK!
IS EVERYTHING OKAY?
WE'RE FINE, JON.
HOW WAS SCHOOL?
OKAY.
FOR SCHOOL, ANYWAYS.
AND MOM?
DAD TOLD ME YOU GOT STUFF YOU WANNA DO AND YOU MIGHT NOT BE HERE AS MUCH.
THAT'S OKAY. I DON'T MIND.
'NIGHT!
HE KNOWS?
WE CAME HOME AND JON WAS CONCERNED THAT YOU WERE GONE.
I TOLD HIM YOU WERE AT THE DAILY PLANET AND THAT IT MIGHT HAPPEN MORE OFTEN.
SINCE WHEN DID MIND-READING POWERS BECOME PART OF YOUR ARSENAL?
IT DOESN'T TAKE SATURN GIRL TO KNOW YOU WANT MORE OUT OF LIFE, HON.

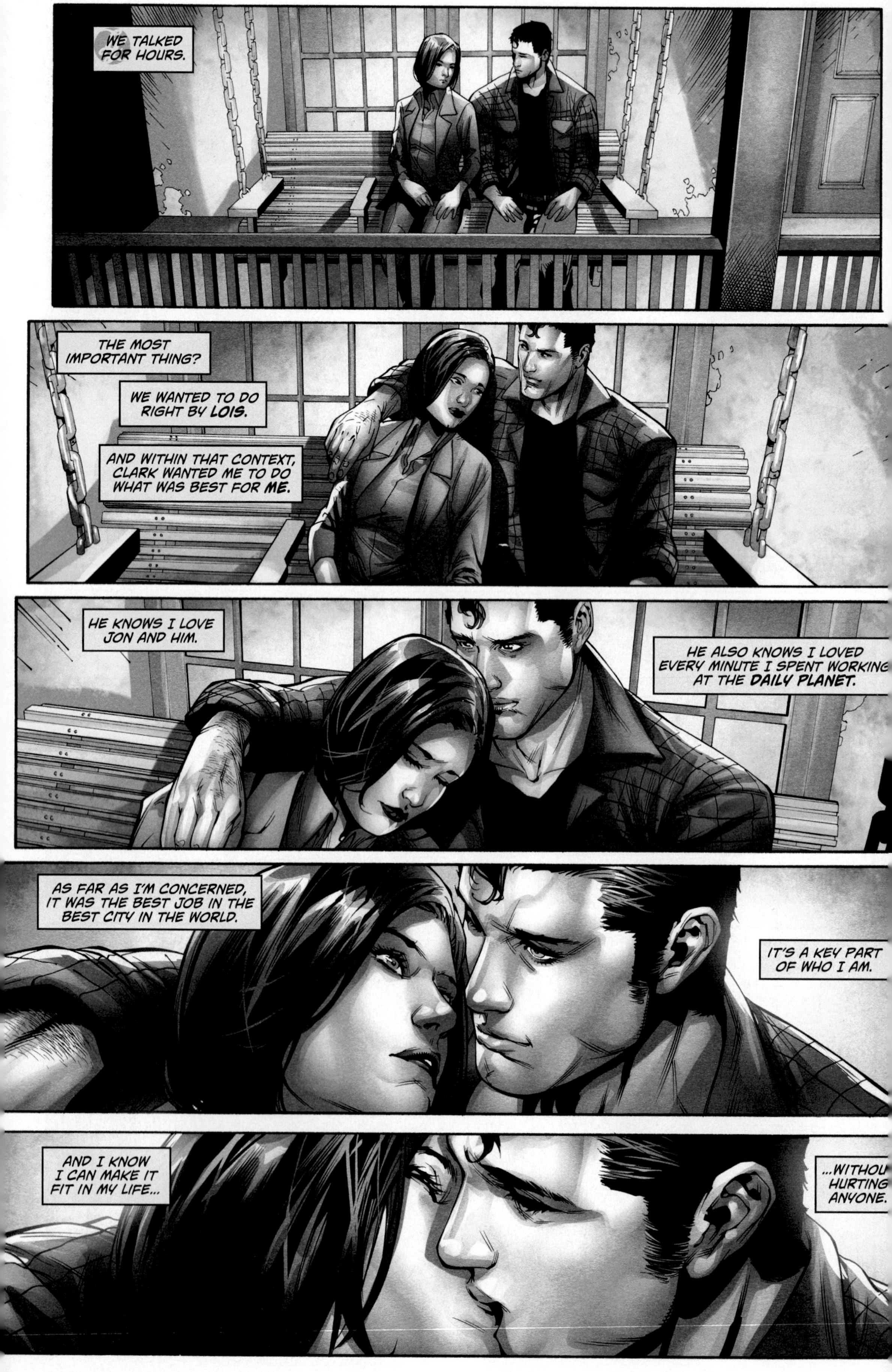

WE TALKED FOR HOURS.
THE MOST IMPORTANT THING?
WE WANTED TO DO RIGHT BY LOIS.
AND WITHIN THAT CONTEXT, CLARK WANTED ME TO DO WHAT WAS BEST FOR ME.
HE KNOWS I LOVE JON AND HIM.
HE ALSO KNOWS I LOVED EVERY MINUTE I SPENT WORKING AT THE DAILY PLANET.
AS FAR AS I'M CONCERNED, IT WAS THE BEST JOB IN THE BEST CITY IN THE WORLD.
IT'S A KEY PART OF WHO I AM.
AND I KNOW I CAN MAKE IT FIT IN MY LIFE...
...WITHOU HURTING ANYONE.

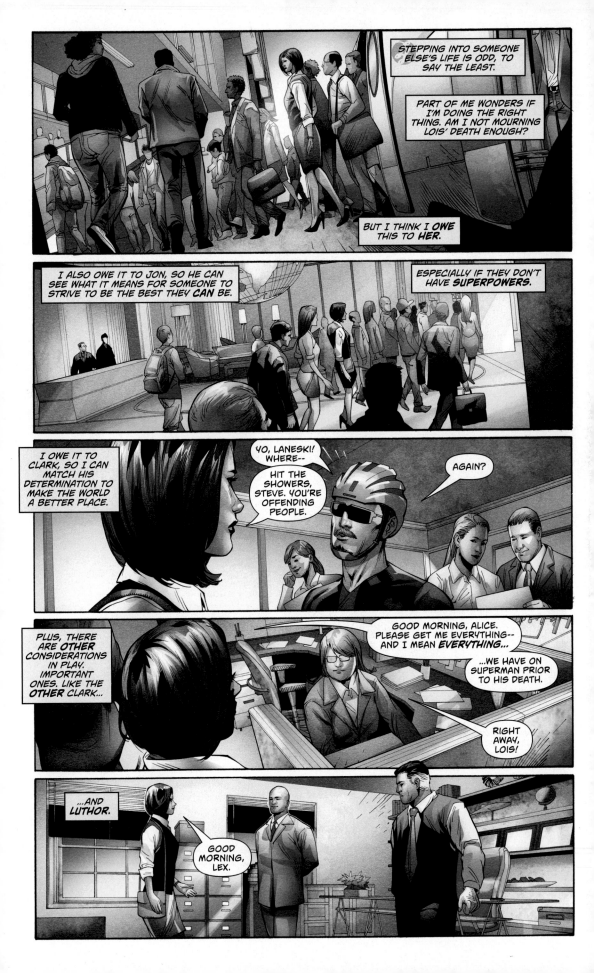

STEPPING INTO SOMEONE ELSE'S LIFE IS ODD, TO SAY THE LEAST.

PART OF ME WONDERS IF I'M DOING THE RIGHT THING. AM I NOT MOURNING LOIS' DEATH ENOUGH?

BUT I THINK I *OWE* THIS TO *HER.*

I ALSO OWE IT TO JON, SO HE CAN SEE WHAT IT MEANS FOR SOMEONE TO STRIVE TO BE THE BEST THEY *CAN* BE.

ESPECIALLY IF THEY DON'T HAVE *SUPERPOWERS.*

I OWE IT TO CLARK, SO I CAN MATCH HIS DETERMINATION TO MAKE THE WORLD A BETTER PLACE.

YO, LANESKI! WHERE--

HIT THE SHOWERS, STEVE. YOU'RE OFFENDING PEOPLE.

AGAIN?

PLUS, THERE ARE *OTHER* CONSIDERATIONS IN PLAY. IMPORTANT ONES. LIKE THE *OTHER* CLARK...

GOOD MORNING, ALICE. PLEASE GET ME EVERYTHING-- AND I MEAN *EVERYTHING*...

...WE HAVE ON SUPERMAN PRIOR TO HIS DEATH.

RIGHT AWAY, LOIS!

...AND *LUTHOR.*

GOOD MORNING, LEX.

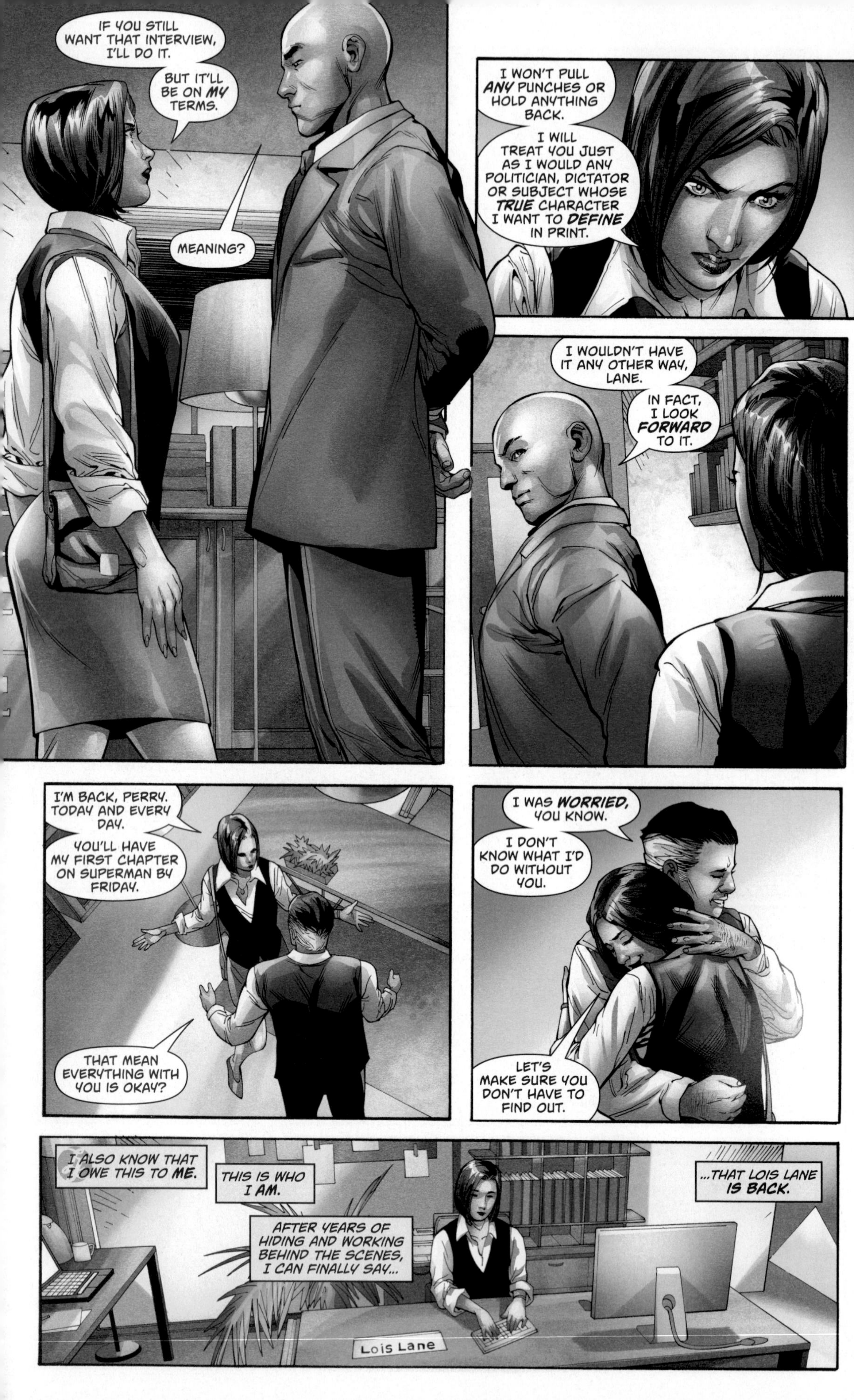
IF YOU STILL WANT THAT INTERVIEW, I'LL DO IT.
BUT IT'LL BE ON MY TERMS.
MEANING?
I WON'T PULL ANY PUNCHES OR HOLD ANYTHING BACK.
I WILL TREAT YOU JUST AS I WOULD ANY POLITICIAN, DICTATOR OR SUBJECT WHOSE TRUE CHARACTER I WANT TO DEFINE IN PRINT.
I WOULDN'T HAVE IT ANY OTHER WAY, LANE.
IN FACT, I LOOK FORWARD TO IT.
I'M BACK, PERRY. TODAY AND EVERY DAY.
YOU'LL HAVE MY FIRST CHAPTER ON SUPERMAN BY FRIDAY.
THAT MEAN EVERYTHING WITH YOU IS OKAY?
I WAS WORRIED, YOU KNOW.
I DON'T KNOW WHAT I'D DO WITHOUT YOU.
LET'S MAKE SURE YOU DON'T HAVE TO FIND OUT.
I ALSO KNOW THAT I OWE THIS TO ME.
THIS IS WHO I AM.
AFTER YEARS OF HIDING AND WORKING BEHIND THE SCENES, I CAN FINALLY SAY...
...THAT LOIS LANE IS BACK.
Lois Lane

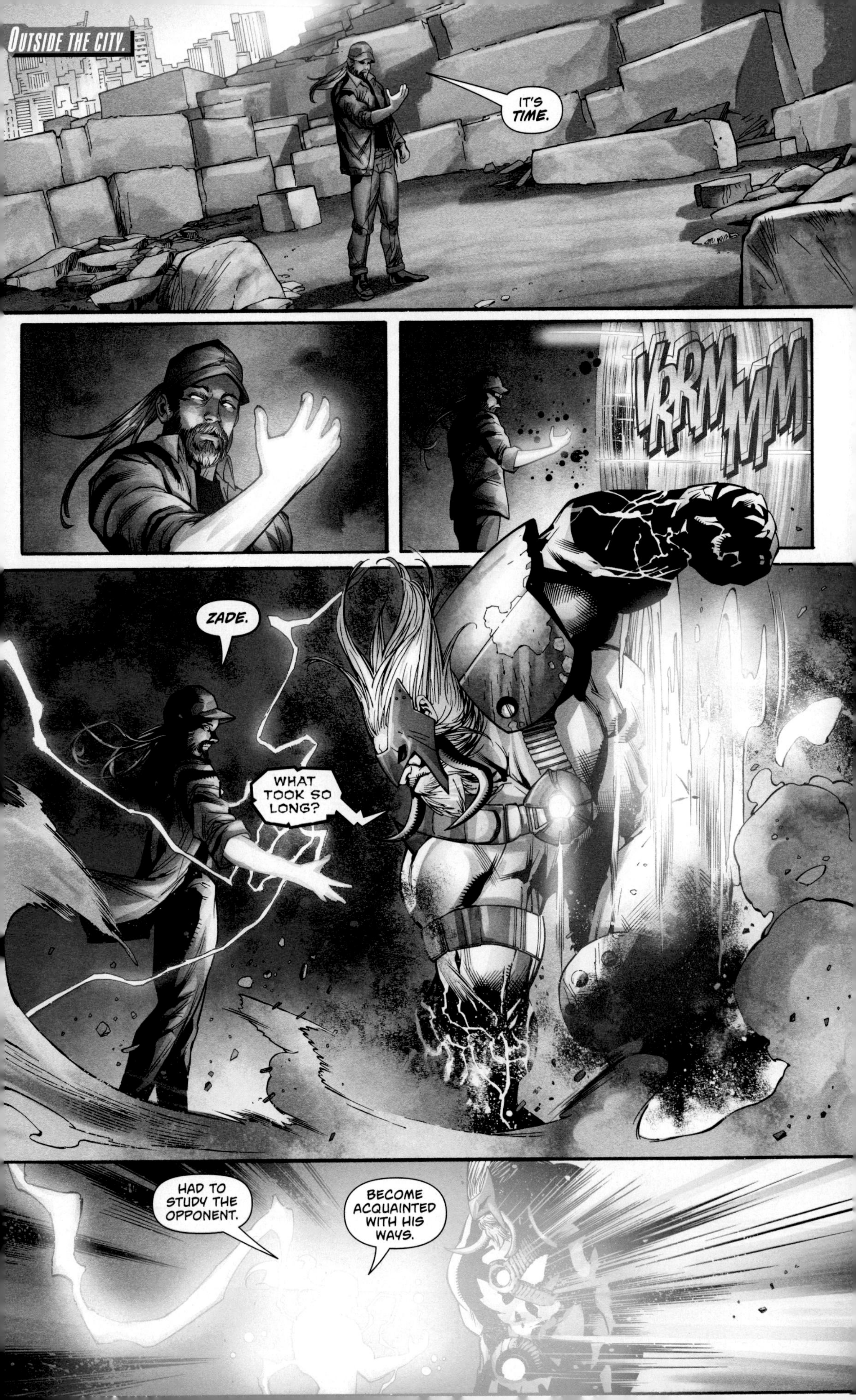
OUTSIDE THE CITY.
IT'S TIME.
VRRMMM
ZADE.
WHAT TOOK SO LONG?
HAD TO STUDY THE OPPONENT.
BECOME ACQUAINTED WITH HIS WAYS.

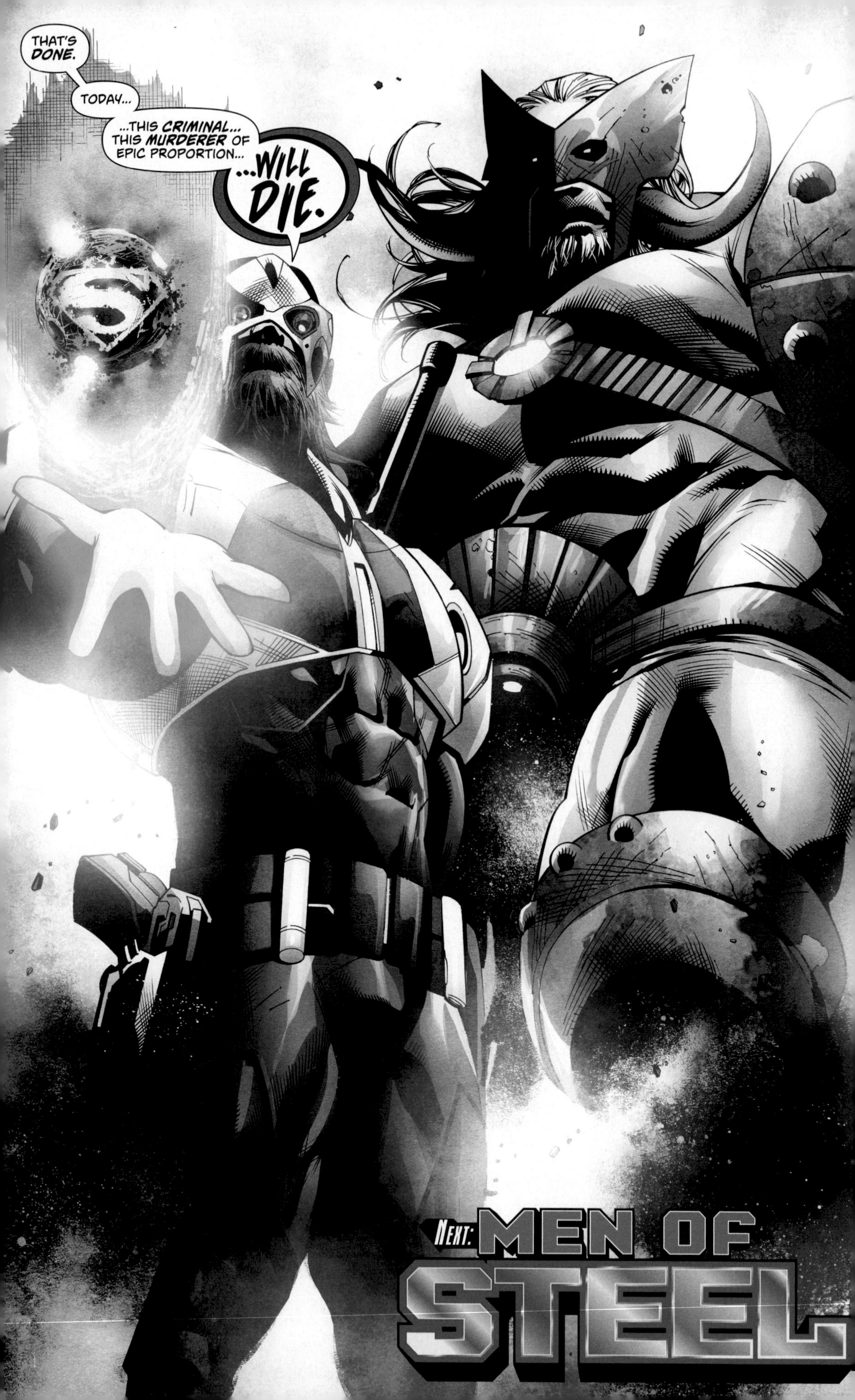
THAT'S DONE.
TODAY...
...THIS CRIMINAL... THIS MURDERER OF EPIC PROPORTION...
...WILL DIE.
NEXT: MEN OF STEEL

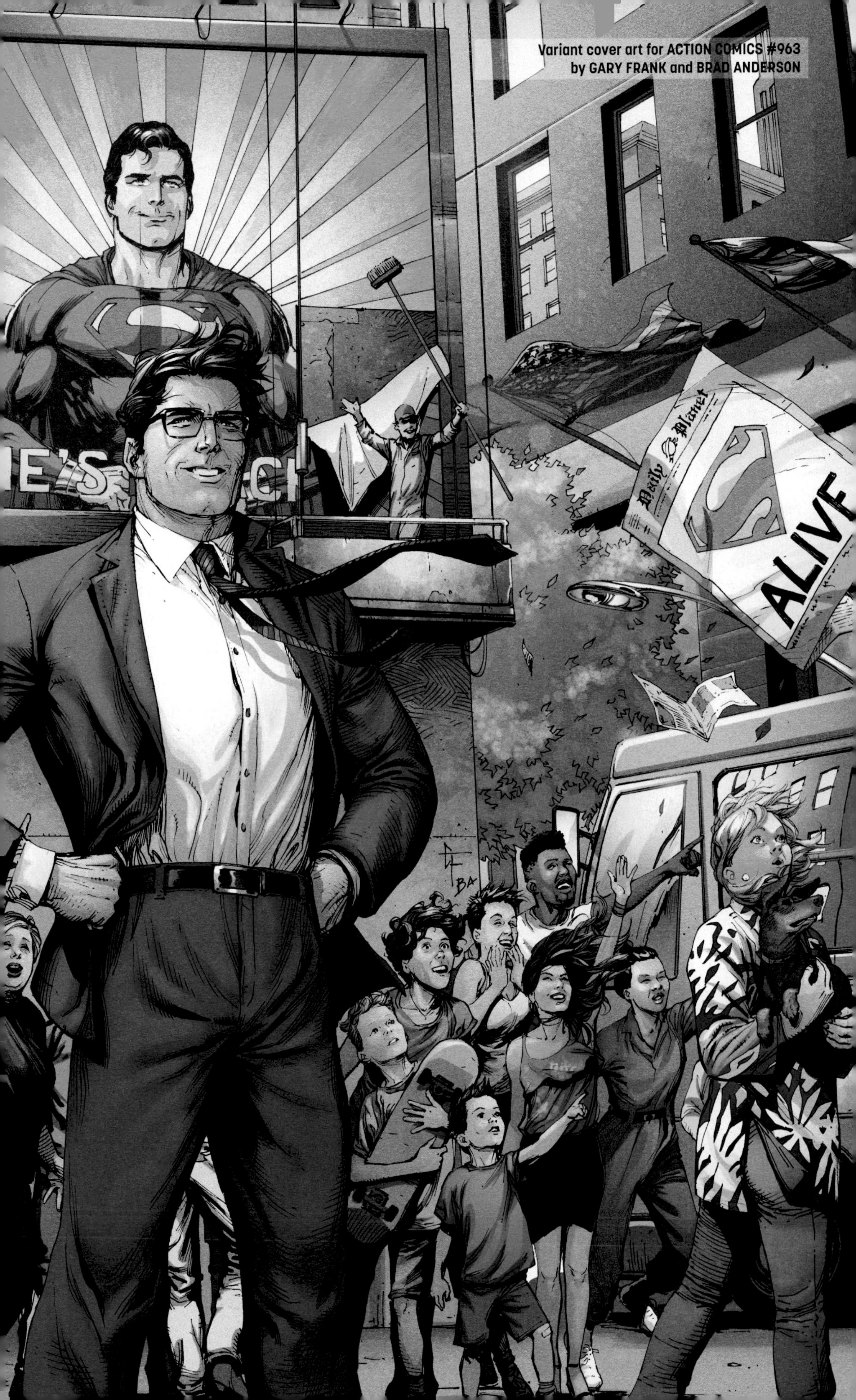
Daily Planet
ALIVE

Variant cover art for ACTION COMICS #963
by GARY FRANK and BRAD ANDERSON

Variant cover art for ACTION COMICS #964
by GARY FRANK and BRAD ANDERSON

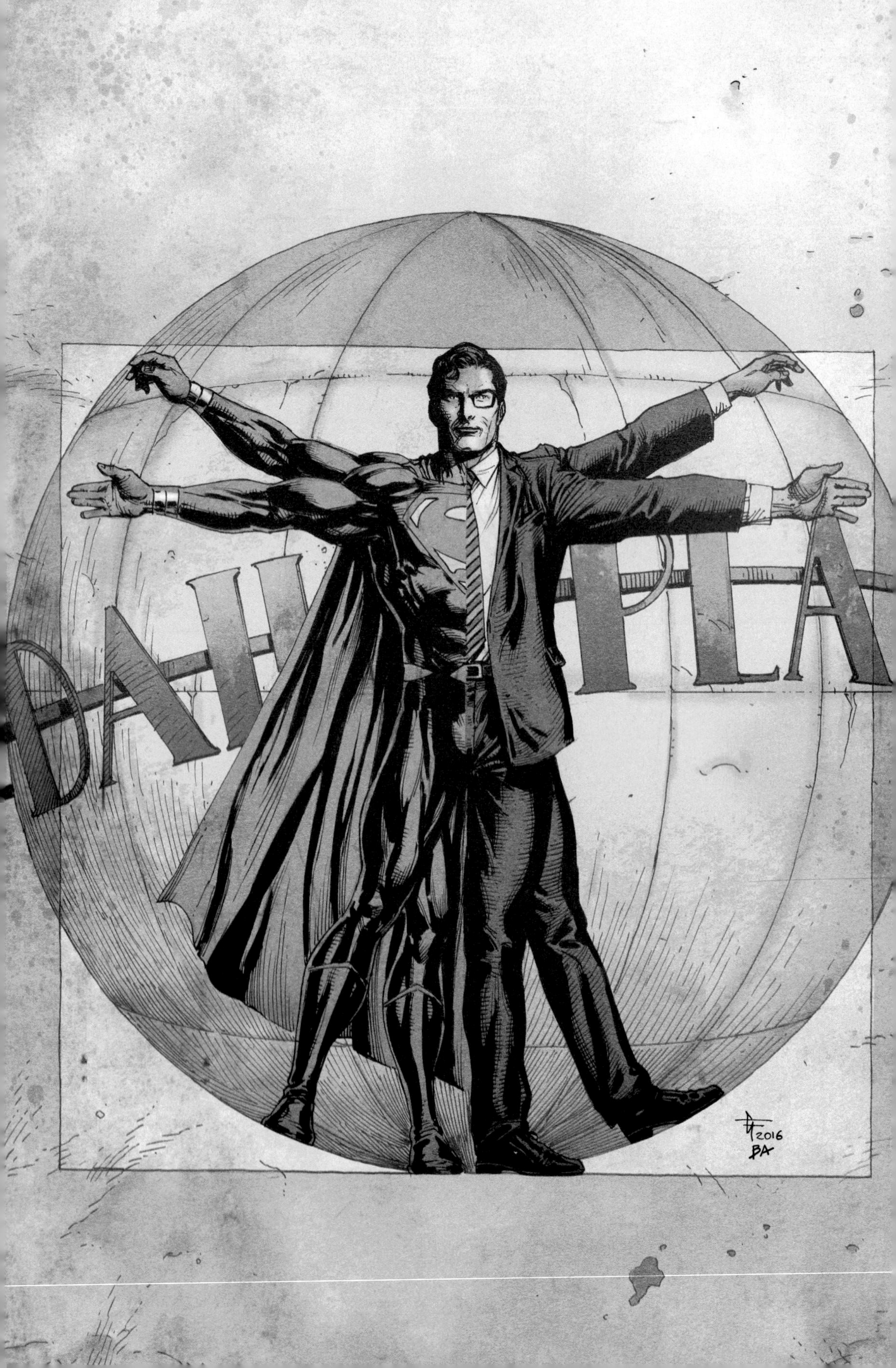

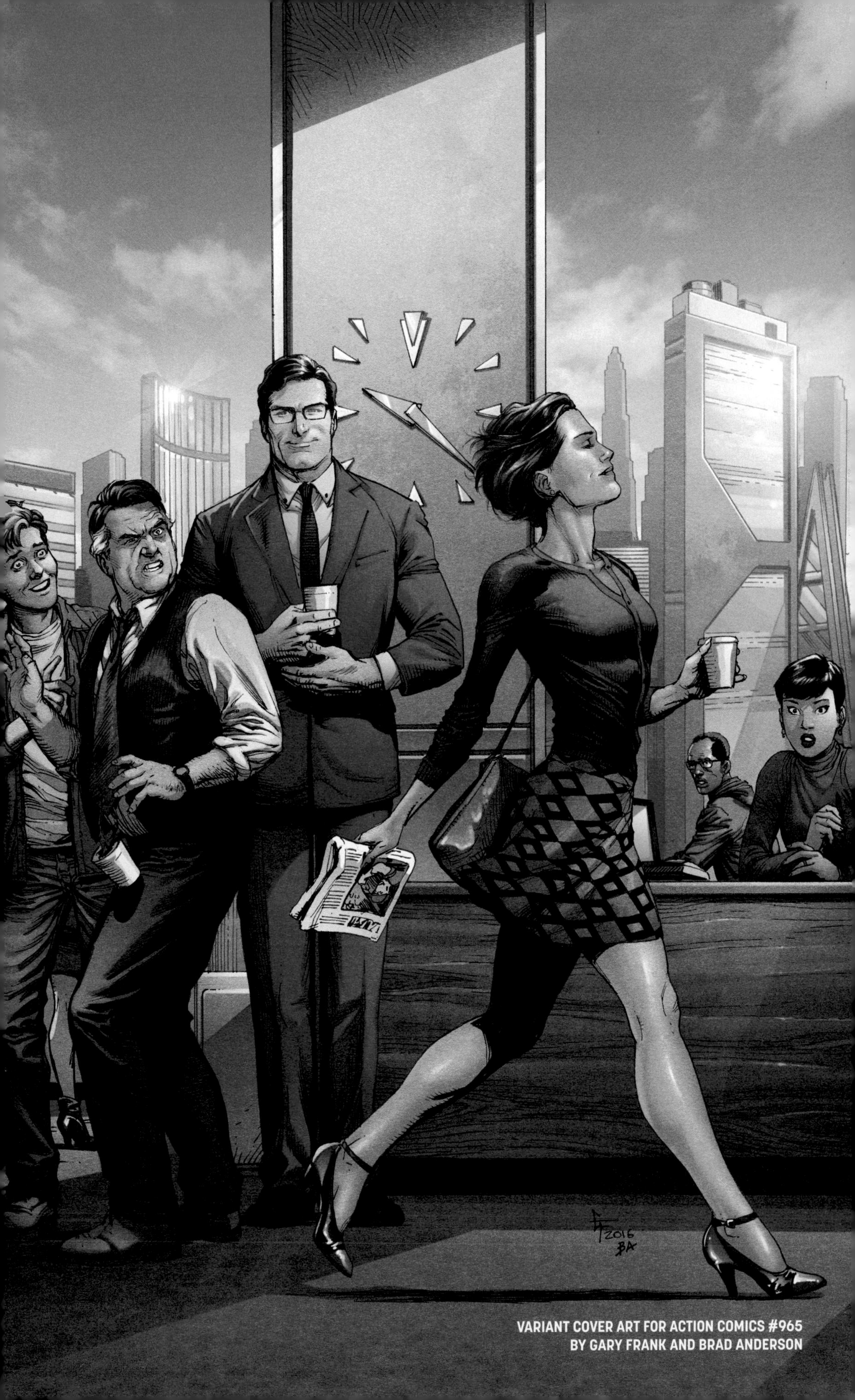
GF 2016
BA

VARIANT COVER ART FOR ACTION COMICS #965
BY GARY FRANK AND BRAD ANDERSON

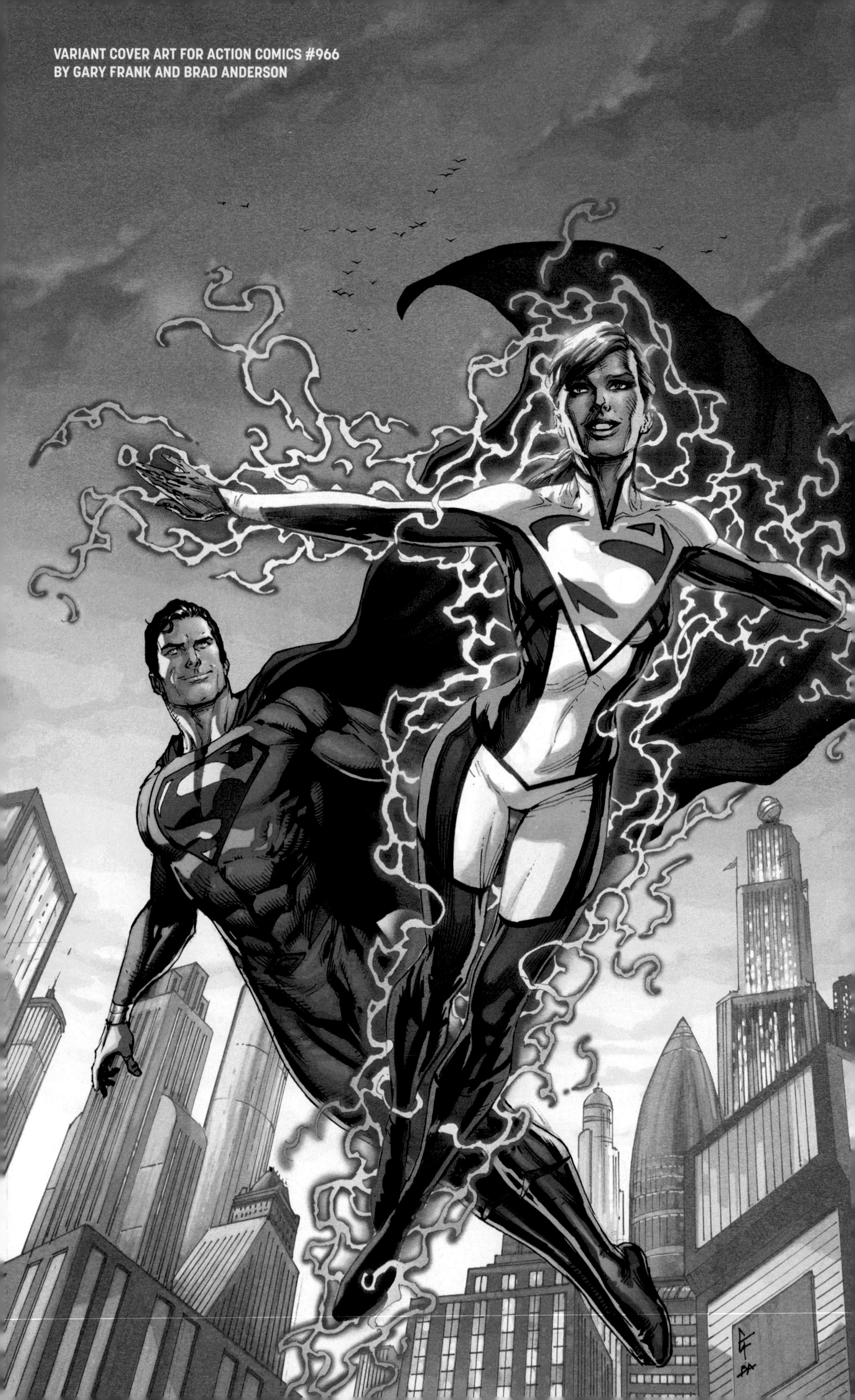

VARIANT COVER ART FOR ACTION COMICS #966
BY GARY FRANK AND BRAD ANDERSON

SECRET IDENTITIES

Cover Sketches by **Dan Jurgens**
Layouts and Finished Art by **Stephen Segovia**

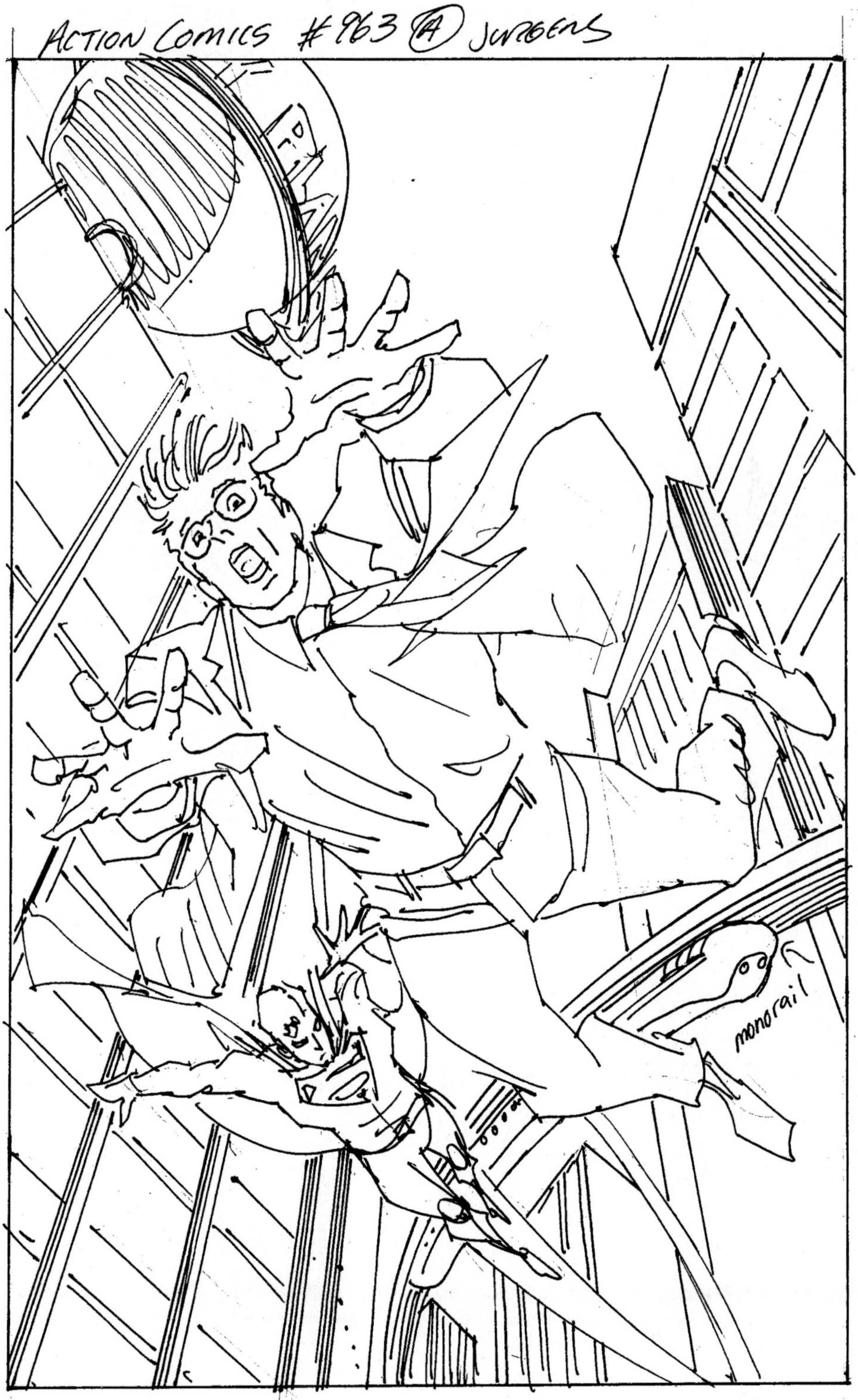
ACTION COMICS #963 (A) JURGENS
monorail

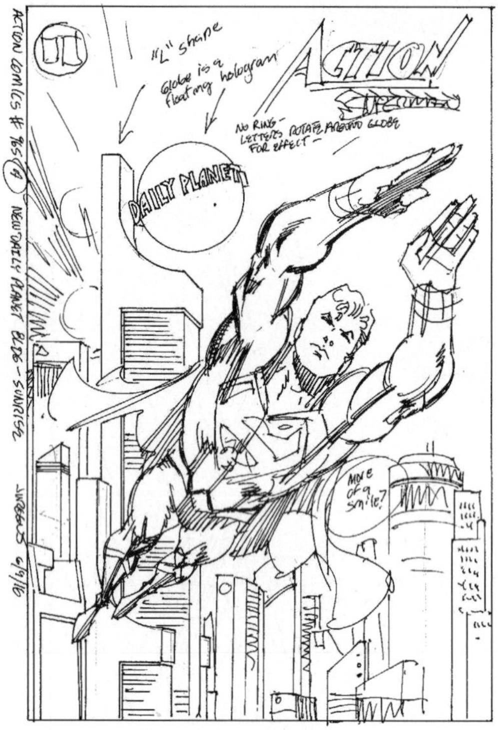
ACTION COMICS #965 (A) NEW DAILY PLANET BLDG - SUNRISE JURGENS 6/9/16
ACTION
"L" shape
Globe is a floating hologram
NO RING - LETTERS ROTATE AROUND GLOBE FOR EFFECT -
DAILY PLANET
More of a smile?

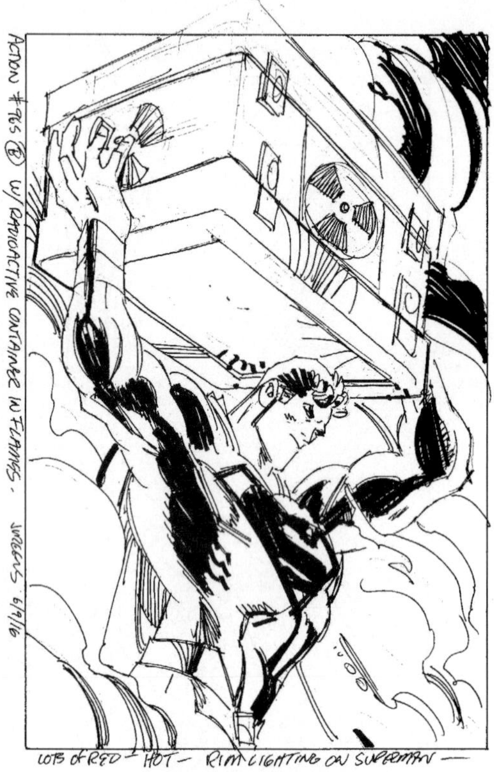
ACTION #965 (B) W/ RADIOACTIVE CONTAINER IN FLAMES. JURGENS 6/9/16
LOTS OF RED - HOT - RIM LIGHTING ON SUPERMAN -

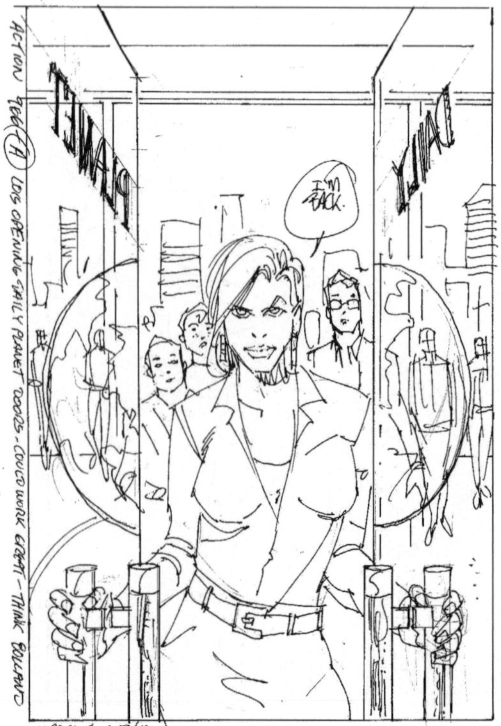
ACTION 966 (A) LOIS OPENING DAILY PLANET DOORS - COULD WORK GREAT - THINK BOLLAND
I'M BACK.
JURGENS 6/9/16

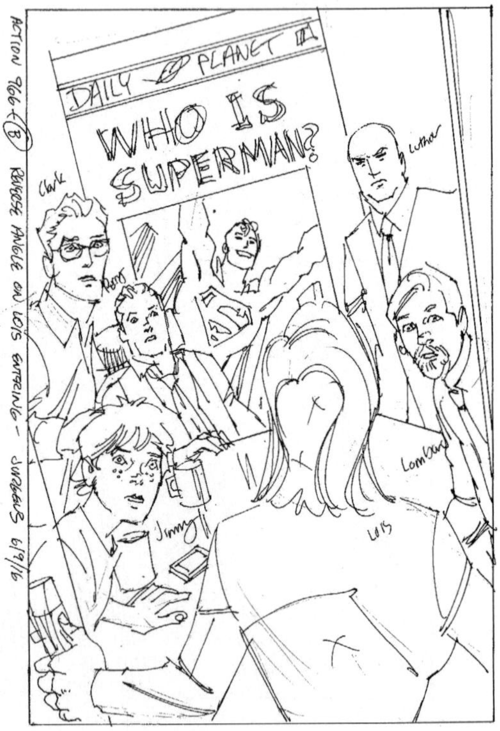
ACTION 966 (B) REVERSE ANGLE ON LOIS ENTERING - JURGENS 6/9/16
DAILY PLANET
WHO IS SUPERMAN?
Clark
Perry
Luthor
Lombard
Jimmy
Lois

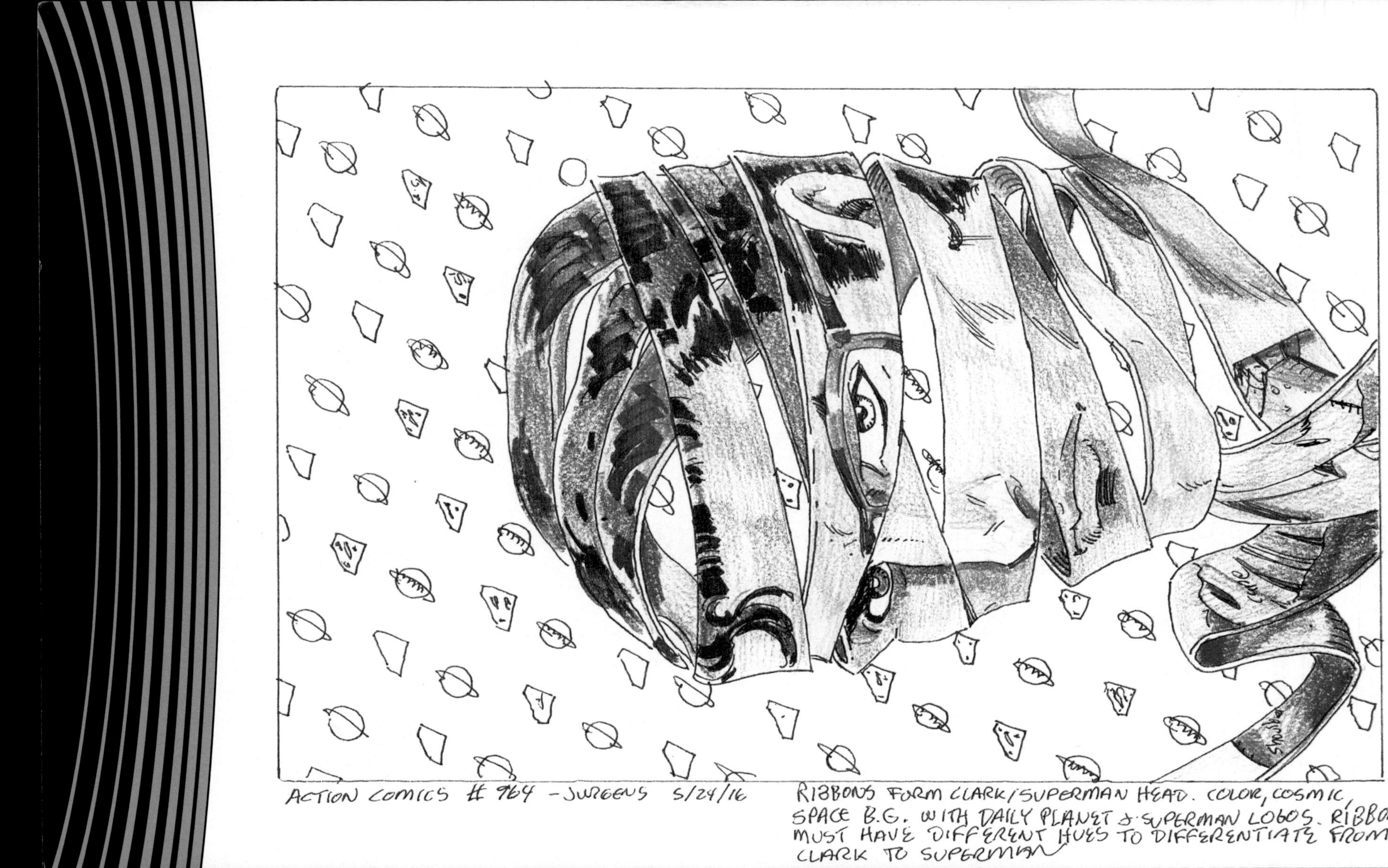

ACTION COMICS # 964 - JURGENS 5/24/16

RIBBONS FORM CLARK/SUPERMAN HEAD. COLOR, COSMIC, SPACE B.G. WITH DAILY PLANET & SUPERMAN LOGOS. RIBBONS MUST HAVE DIFFERENT HUES TO DIFFERENTIATE FROM CLARK TO SUPERMAN

ACTION COMICS #966

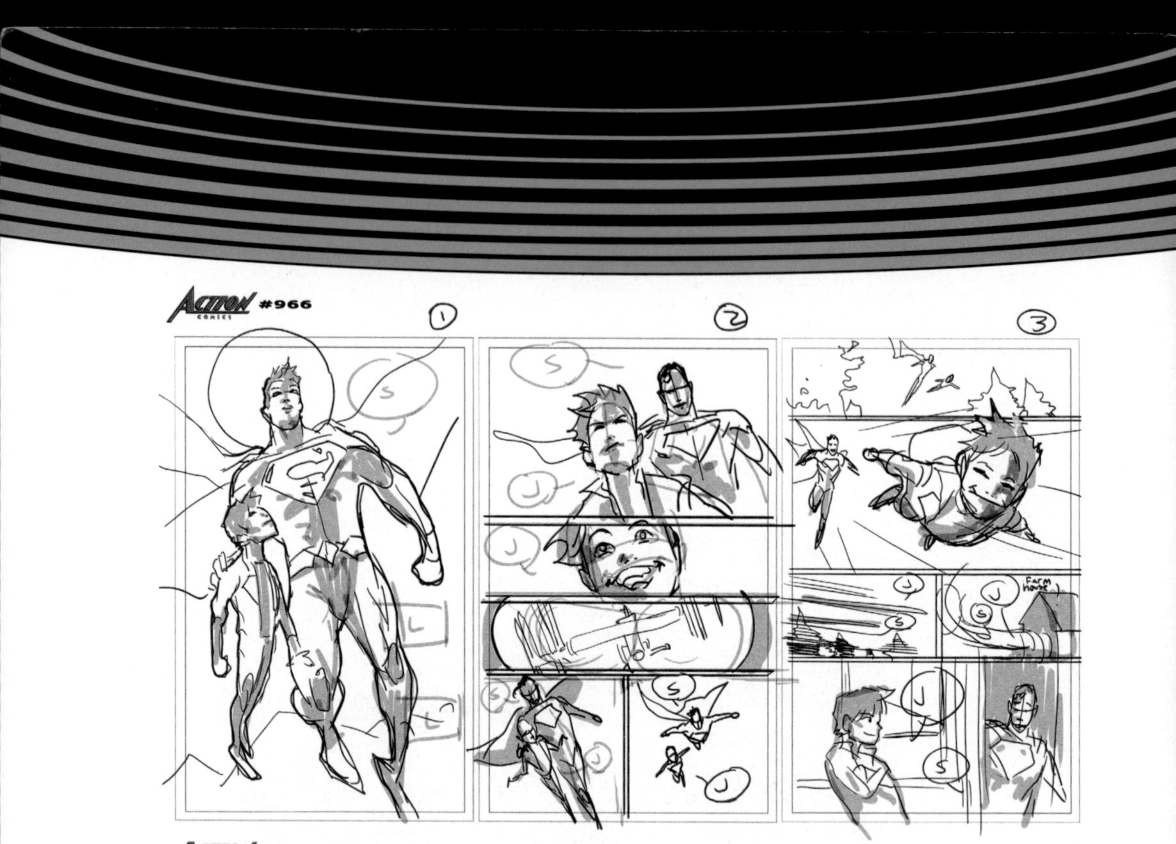
1
2
3
S
L
J
Farm house

ACTION COMICS #966

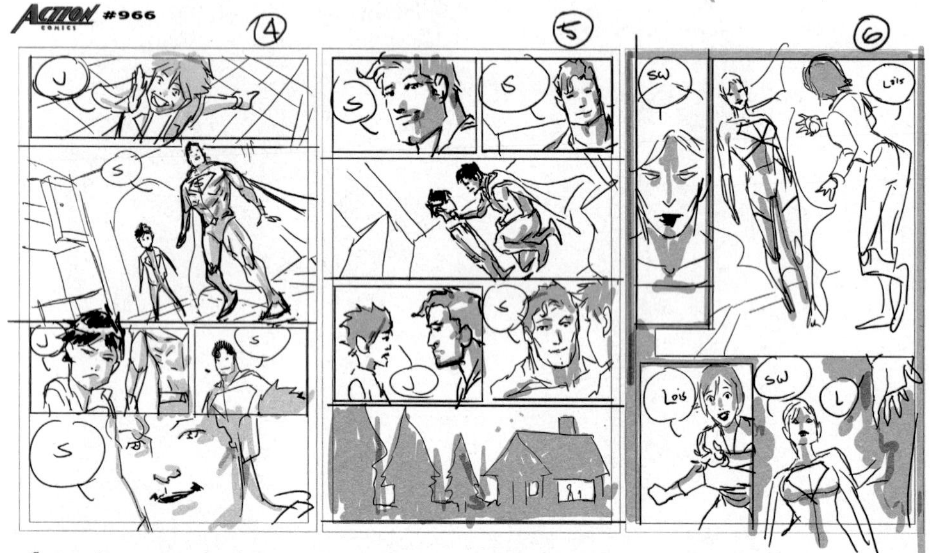
4
5
6
SW
Lois

ACTION COMICS #966

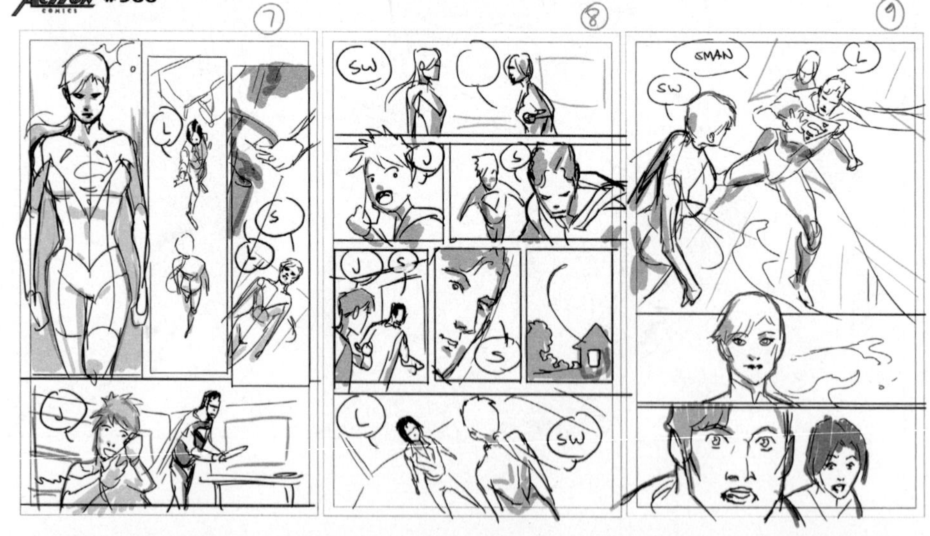
7
8
9
SW
SMAN

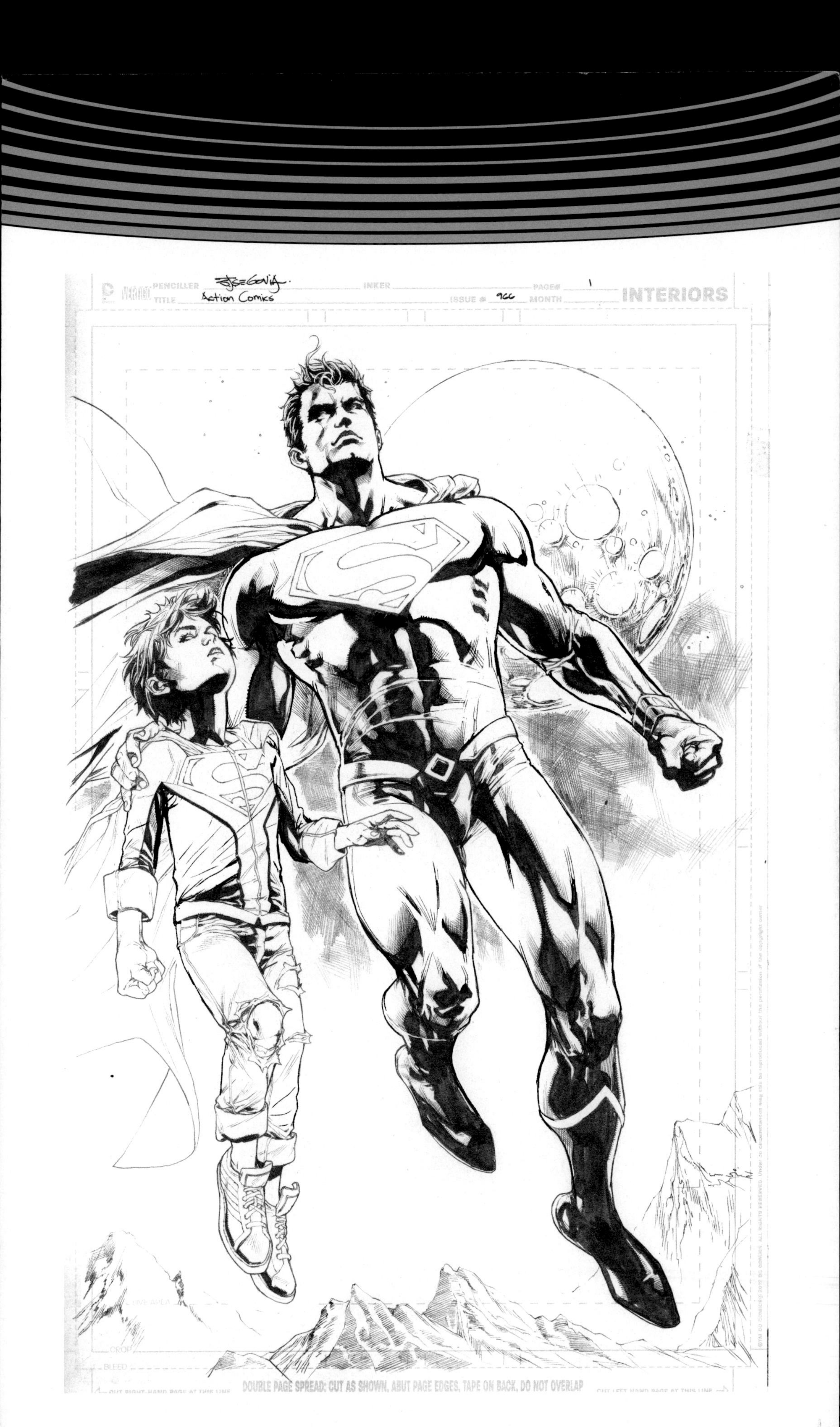
PENCILLER
INKER
PAGE# 1
INTERIORS
TITLE Action Comics
ISSUE # 966
MONTH
CROP
BLEED
DOUBLE PAGE SPREAD: CUT AS SHOWN, ABUT PAGE EDGES, TAPE ON BACK, DO NOT OVERLAP

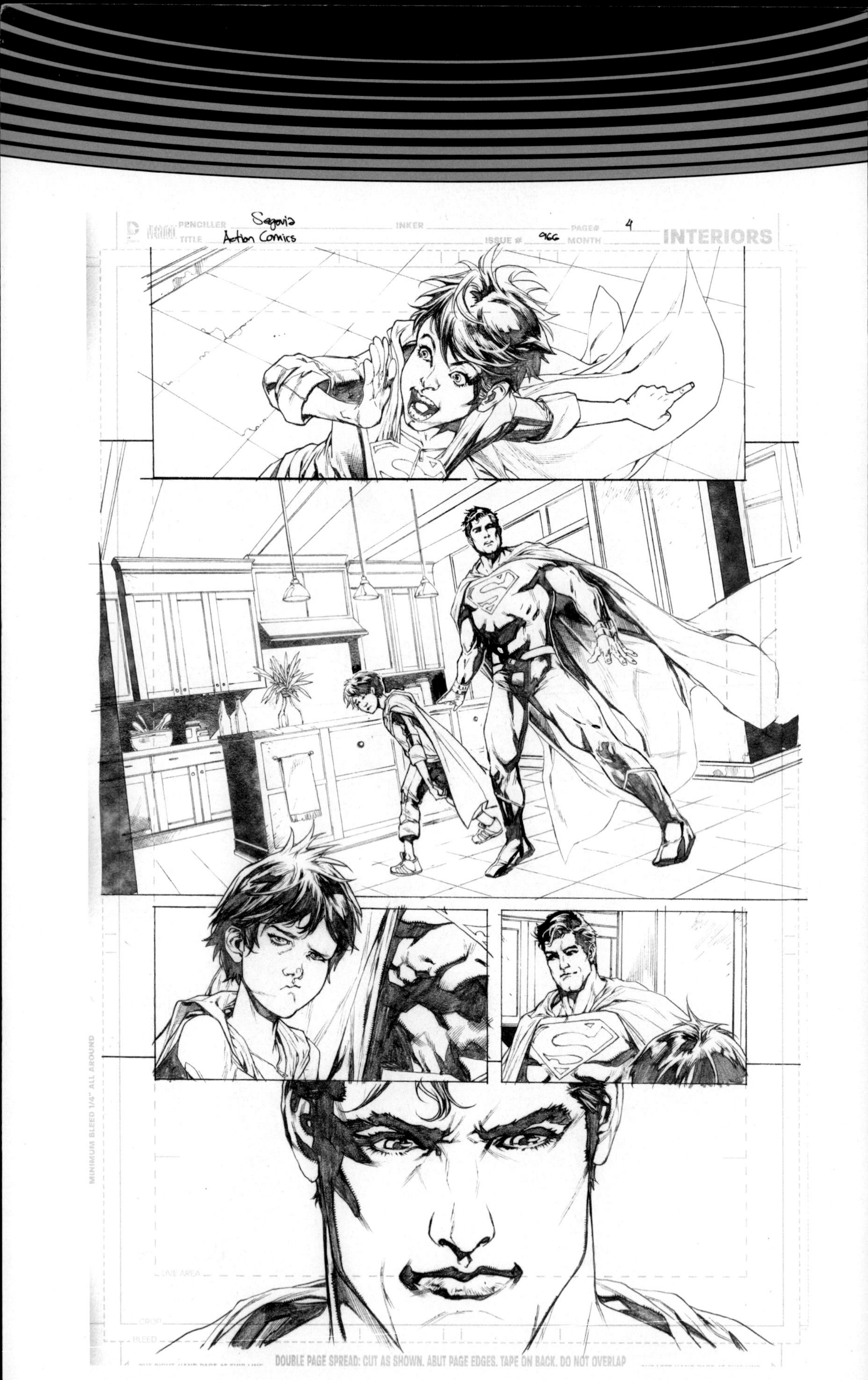
PENCILLER Segovia
INKER
PAGE# 4
TITLE Action Comics
ISSUE # 966
MONTH
INTERIORS
MINIMUM BLEED 1/4" ALL AROUND
LIVE AREA
CROP
BLEED
DOUBLE PAGE SPREAD: CUT AS SHOWN. ABUT PAGE EDGES. TAPE ON BACK. DO NOT OVERLAP

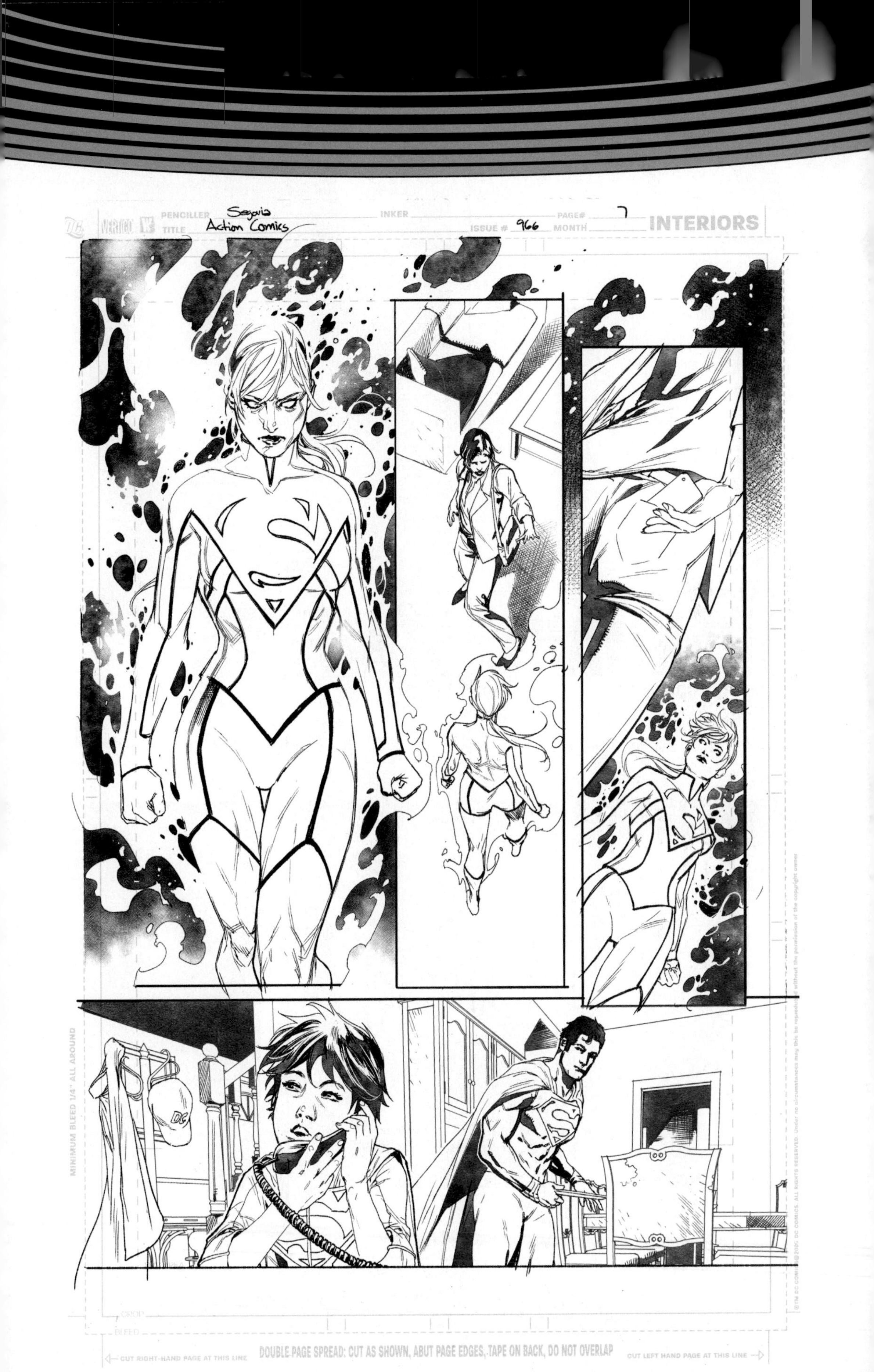
PENCILLER Segovia
TITLE Action Comics
INKER
PAGE# 7
ISSUE # 966
MONTH
INTERIORS
MINIMUM BLEED 1/4" ALL AROUND
CROP
BLEED
CUT RIGHT-HAND PAGE AT THIS LINE
DOUBLE PAGE SPREAD: CUT AS SHOWN, ABUT PAGE EDGES, TAPE ON BACK, DO NOT OVERLAP
CUT LEFT HAND PAGE AT THIS LINE

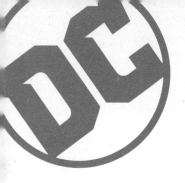

"That gorgeous spectacle is an undeniable part of Superman's appeal, but the family dynamics are what make it such an engaging read."
– A.V. CLUB

"Head and shoulders above the rest."
– NEWSARAMA

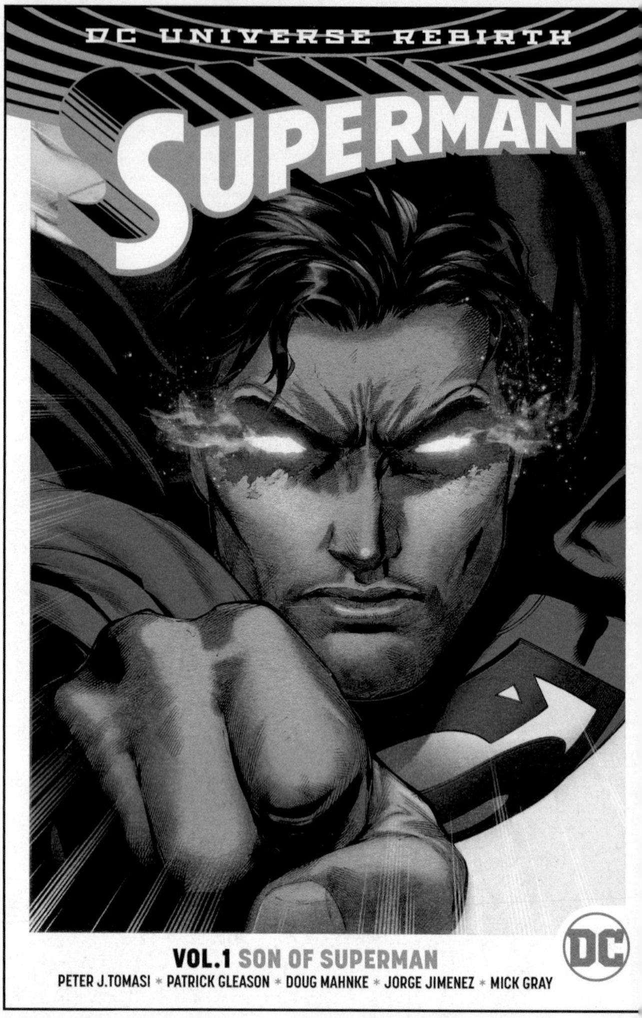
DC UNIVERSE REBIRTH
SUPERMAN
VOL.1 SON OF SUPERMAN
PETER J.TOMASI * PATRICK GLEASON * DOUG MAHNKE * JORGE JIMENEZ * MICK GRAY

DC UNIVERSE REBIRTH

SUPERMAN

VOL. 1: SON OF SUPERMAN

PETER J. TOMASI with PATRICK GLEASON, DOUG MAHNKE & JORGE JIMENEZ

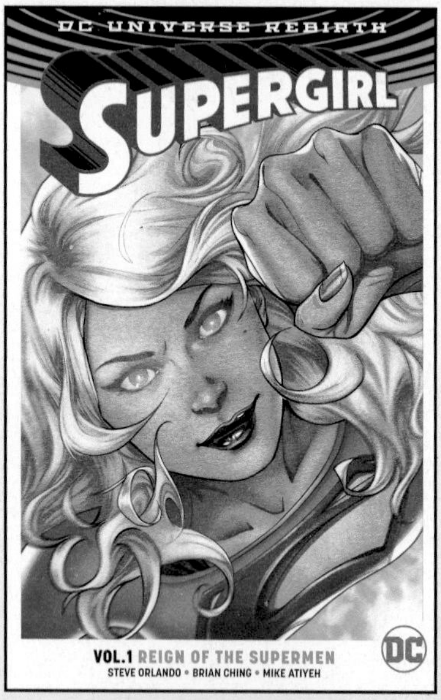
DC UNIVERSE REBIRTH
SUPERGIRL
VOL.1 REIGN OF THE SUPERMEN
STEVE ORLANDO * BRIAN CHING * MIKE ATIYEH

SUPERGIRL VOL. 1: REIGN OF THE SUPERMEN

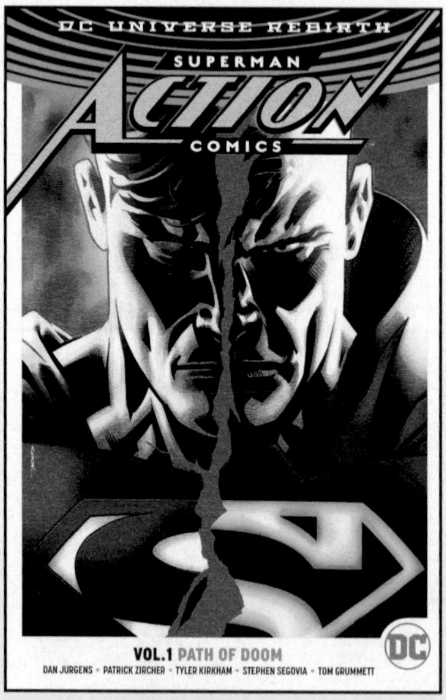
DC UNIVERSE REBIRTH
SUPERMAN
ACTION COMICS
VOL.1 PATH OF DOOM
DAN JURGENS * PATRICK ZIRCHER * TYLER KIRKHAM * STEPHEN SEGOVIA * TOM GRUMMETT

ACTION COMICS VOL. 1: PATH OF DOOM

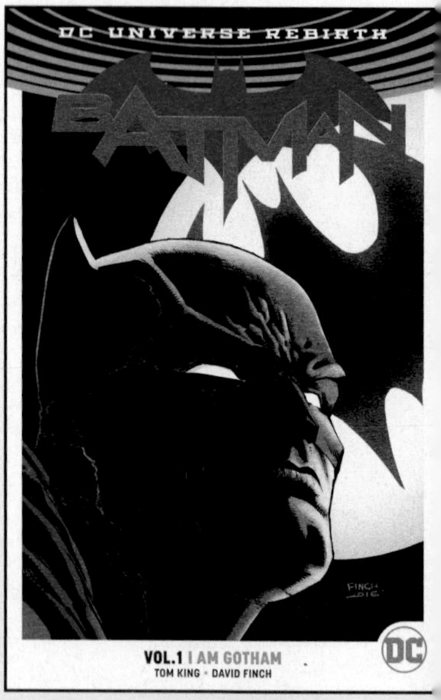
DC UNIVERSE REBIRTH
BATMAN
VOL.1 I AM GOTHAM
TOM KING * DAVID FINCH

BATMAN VOL. 1: I AM GOTHAM

Get more DC graphic novels wherever comics and books are sold!